HUMAN RIGHTS

HUMAN
RIGHTS

Comments and Interpretations

A Symposium edited by

UNESCO

with an Introduction by

JACQUES MARITAIN

GREENWOOD PRESS, PUBLISHERS
WESTPORT, CONNECTICUT

The Library of Congress has catalogued this publication as follows:

Library of Congress Cataloging in Publication Data

United Nations Educational, Scientific and Cultural
    Organization.
    Human rights.

    Reprint of the 1949 ed.
    1. Civil rights--Addresses, essays, lectures.
I. Title.
JC571.U45 1973   323.4   72-9595
ISBN 0-8371-6589-X

Originally published in 1949
by Columbia University Press, New York

Reprinted with the permission
of the United Nations Educational,
Scientific and Cultural Organization

First Greenwood Reprinting 1973

Library of Congress Catalogue Card Number 72-9595

ISBN 0-8371-6589-X

Printed in the United States of America

Contents

CONTENTS

Note

IN the year 1947, the Human Rights Commission of the
United Nations was already engaged in the preparation
of the Universal Declaration of Human Rights which the
General Assembly was to issue in December 1948 in Paris.
To contribute to its work, the United Nations Educational,
Scientific and Cultural Organisation (UNESCO) carried out,
during 1947, an enquiry into the theoretical problems raised
by such a Universal Declaration. A questionnaire was
circulated to various thinkers and writers of Member-
States of UNESCO, who were asked, as individual experts,
to give their views. This questionnaire will be found in
Appendix I.

The texts which constitute the body of the volume have
been chosen among the replies which UNESCO received. They
are an expression of the personal opinions of their authors,
and should not be taken as necessarily conforming to the
official position of the Governments of the countries to which
the authors belong.

The first group of these essays deals with the general
problems of human rights. The others deal in greater detail
with such subjects as the respect for cultural diversity,
the social implications of science, the value of objective
information, the right to education and the special position
of primitive peoples, dependent peoples, law-breakers, etc.

In selecting the texts of the replies which are included in
the volume, an attempt has been made to offer a representative sample of the whole range of opinions expressed. In
addition, it was thought desirable to give publicity to the
opinions of certain thinkers which differed from the final
conclusions of UNESCO, but which were, nevertheless,
stimulating in their originality of thought.

The conclusions of UNESCO will be found in Appendix II.
They were elaborated by a Committee of Experts which
brought together, in July 1947, Professor Edward H. Carr,
Chairman, Professor Richard McKeon, Rapporteur, and
Professors Pierre Auger, Georges Friedmann, Harold Laski,
Chung-Shu Lo and Luc Somerhausen. Unfortunately, Pro-
fessor Etienne Gilson, who had been invited, was unable to

attend the meeting of the Committee. UNESCO's conclusions were forwarded to the Human Rights Commission of the United Nations, in the hope that they would help to clarify its discussion and to explore the ground for a constructive agreement. The same Committee, which met for the second time in July 1948, edited this symposium.

Finally, the official text of the Universal Declaration of Human Rights, which the United Nations issued on December 10th, 1948, in Paris, will be found in Appendix III. It must be emphasised that the UNESCO enquiry was a theoretical investigation, carried out with expert advice from thinkers and philosophers, which was completed during 1947 and could not take into account the Declaration of the United Nations, voted by the General Assembly at a later date.

Introduction

Jacques Maritain

OF the tasks assigned to the United Nations Organisation, one of those which could and should most nearly affect the conscience of the peoples is the drawing up of an *International Declaration of Human Rights*. The task was committed to the Economic and Social Council of the United Nations. UNESCO's part was to consult philosophers and assemble their replies. This volume is a collection of the most significant texts thus gathered in the course of UNESCO's enquiry into the philosophic bases of human rights.

This book then is devoted to the rational interpretation and justification of those rights of the individual which society must respect and which it is desirable for our age to strive to enumerate more fully. Many schools of thought are represented, each of which brings to the whole its particular view and justification of individual rights, leaning in various degrees towards the classical, or the revolutionary, interpretation: it is not the first time that expert witnesses have quarrelled among themselves. The paradox is that such rational justifications are at once indispensable, and yet powerless to bring about agreement between minds. They are indispensable because each one of us believes instinctively in the truth, and will only assent to what he himself has recognised as true and based on reason. They are powerless to bring about a harmony of minds because they are fundamentally different, even antagonistic; and why should this surprise us? The questions they raise are difficult and the philosophic traditions to which they are related have long been divergent.

It is related that at one of the meetings of a UNESCO National Commission where human rights were being discussed, someone expressed astonishment that certain champions of violently opposed ideologies had agreed on a list of those rights. 'Yes,' they said, 'we agree about the rights *but on condition that no one asks us why.*' That 'why' is where the argument begins.

9

The question of human rights offers us an outstanding example of the situation I attempted to outline in an address at the Second General Conference of UNESCO, from which I venture to reproduce certain passages.

'How', I asked, 'can we imagine an agreement of minds between men who are gathered together precisely in order to accomplish a common intellectual task, men who come from the four corners of the globe and who not only belong to different cultures and civilisations, but are of antagonistic spiritual associations and schools of thought. . . ? Because, as I said at the beginning of my speech, the goal of UNESCO is a practical goal, agreement between minds can be reached spontaneously, not on the basis of common speculative ideas, but on common practical ideas, not on the affirmation of one and the same conception óf the world, of man and of knowledge, but upon the affirmation of a single body of beliefs for guidance in action. No doubt, this is little enough, but it is the last resort to intellectual agreement. It is, nevertheless, enough to enable a great task to be undertaken, and it would do much to crystallise this body of common practical convictions.

'I should like to note here that the word "ideology" and the word "principles" can be interpreted in two very different senses. I have shown that the present state of division among minds does not permit of agreement on a common *speculative ideology*, nor on common explicit principles. But, on the other hand, when we are concerned with a basic *practical* ideology and basic principles of *action* implicitly recognised today, in a live, even if not formulated state, by the consciousness of free people, we find that they constitute *grosso modo* a sort of common denominator, a sort of unwritten common law, at the point where in practice the most widely separated theoretical ideologies and mental traditions converge. To understand this, it is only necessary to make the appropriate distinction between the rational justifications involved in the spiritual dynamism of a philosophic doctrine or religious faith, and the practical conclusions which, although justified in different ways by different persons, are principles of action with a common ground of similarity for everyone. I am quite certain that my way of justifying belief in the rights of man and the ideal of liberty, equality and fraternity is the only way with a firm foundation in truth. This does not prevent me from being in agreement on these practical convictions with people who are certain that their way of justifying them, entirely different from mine or opposed to mine, in its theoretical dynamism, is equally the only way founded upon truth. If both believed in the democratic charter, a Christian and a rationalist would still give mutually incompatible justifications for their belief, if their hearts and minds and blood were involved, and they would fight each other for them. And God forbid that I should say it does not matter to know which of the two is right ! It matters essentially. The fact remains that, on the practical expression of this charter, they are in agreement and can formulate together common principles of action.

'Where it is a question of rational interpretation and justifications of speculation or theory, the problem of human rights involves the whole structure of moral and metaphysical (or anti-metaphysical) convictions held by each of us. So long as minds are not united in faith or philosophy, there will be mutual conflicts between interpretations and justifications.

'In the field of practical conclusions, on the other hand, agreement on a joint declaration is possible, given an approach pragmatic rather than theoretical, and co-operation in the comparison, recasting and fixing of formulæ, to make them acceptable to both parties as points of convergence in practice, however opposed the theoretic viewpoints. There is nothing to prevent the achievement, in this way, of a new and wider declaration of human rights, marking a notable stage in the unification of the world, and wherein more especially the concept exclusive to classical individualism of man as a being inherently entitled to rights and liberties for the working out of his personal destiny, and the concept exclusive to Marxism of man as a being with rights and liberties deriving from his rôle in the historic evolution of the community of which he is a part, would supplement and integrate each other—I mean purely pragmatically and only for the promulgation of a number of principles for action and rules of behaviour. It is not reasonably possible to hope for more than this convergence in practice in the enumeration of articles jointly agreed. The reconciling of theories and a philosophic synthesis in the true sense are only conceivable after an immense amount of investigation and elucidation of fundamentals, requiring a high degree of insight, a new systematisation and authoritative correction of a number of errors and confusions of thought. For that very reason, and even if it succeeded in influencing culture to any important degree, this synthesis would remain one doctrine among many, accepted by some and rejected by others, with no pretention in fact to universal dominion over the minds of men.'

The very diversity of the interpretations and justifications put forward in the essays in this book is in itself an important object lesson for the reader, wherein he will find, I trust, confirmation of the considerations set out above. Is there anything surprising in systems antagonistic in theory converging in their practical conclusions? It is the usual picture which the history of moral philosophy presents to us. The phenomenon proves simply that systems of moral philosophy are the products of reflection by the intellect on ethical concepts which precede and govern them, and which of themselves display, as it were, a highly complex geology of the mind where the natural operation of spontaneous reason, pre-scientific and pre-philosophic, is at every stage conditioned by the acquisitions, the constraints, the structure and the evolution of the social group. Thus, if I may be allowed the metaphor, there is a kind of plant-like formation and growth of moral knowledge and moral feeling, in itself independent of philosophic systems and the rational justifications they propound, even though there is a secondary interaction between them and itself. Is it surprising, that, while all these systems quarrel over the why and wherefore, yet in their practical conclusions they prescribe rules of behaviour which are in the main and for all practical purposes identical for a given age and culture? What is chiefly important for the moral progress of humanity is the apprehension by experience which occurs apart from systems and on a different logical basis—assisted by such systems when they awake the conscience to knowledge of itself, hampered by them when they dim the apperceptions of spontaneous reason, or when they cast suspicion on a genuine acquisition of moral experience by linking it with some error of theory or false philosophy.

Finally, it is the speculative and interpretative approach, as such, which, in the present book, will afford the reader the chief food for thought. For the texts here collected bring us the testimony of men specially well qualified to give an authoritative exposition of the main currents of contemporary thought. It is profitable to know those currents, however severely we may censure those which are not our own, and however legitimate that censure may sometimes be. Whatever school of thought we belong to, the comparison of our own ideas with those of so many distinguished minds will perfect and broaden our views on the nature and basis of human rights, on what enumeration of them should be attempted at our present stage in historical evolution, and on the scope—indeed on the gaps also—of the new declaration being prepared in the councils of the United Nations.

From the point of view of philosophic doctrine, it may be said, without over-simplification, that, as regards the question of human rights, men are today divided—as the readers of this collection will easily perceive—into two antagonistic groups: those who to a greater or lesser extent explicitly accept, and those who to a greater or lesser extent explicitly reject 'Natural Law' as the basis of those rights.

In the eyes of the first the requirements of his being endow man with certain fundamental and inalienable rights antecedent in nature, and superior, to society, and are the source whence social life itself, with the duties and rights which that implies, originates and develops. For the second school man's rights are relative to the historical development of society, and are themselves constantly variable and in a state of flux; they are a product of society itself as it advances with the forward march of history.

Such an ideological contrast is irreducible and no theoretical reconciliation is possible; it could however be lessened to some extent, insofar as it was possible for the supporters of 'Natural Law' to stress that, although certain fundamental rights meet a prime necessity of that law while others meet only a secondary necessity or are merely desirable, nevertheless our knowledge of both is in all circumstances subject to slow and irregular growth, so that those rights only stand forth as acknowledged rules of conduct as moral consciousness progresses and societies evolve; and insofar as it was possible for the opponents of 'Natural Law' to stress that, though many rights are seen to be conditioned on the evolution of society, other more primitive rights stand out as a condition of society's very existence. However, it is by no means certain that the 'fundamental rights' of the first group would always coincide with the 'more primitive rights' of the second. . . .

If thereafter we adopt a practical viewpoint and concern ourselves no longer with seeking the basis and philosophic significance of human rights but only their statement and enumeration, we have before us an entirely different picture, where no theoretical simplification is any more in question: then, as I have explained above, not only is agreement possible between the members of opposing philosophic schools, but it must be said that the operative factors in any historical introduction to a joint assertion of human rights are less the schools of philosophy themselves than *currents of thought*, which are doubtless linked more or less closely to those schools, but where the principal part has been played by the lessons of experience and history and by a kind of practical apprehension, bringing with them a greater dynamic force and simultaneously a wider liberty relatively to the principles and logic of abstract systems. In consequence, it cannot be too strongly emphasised that admission of a particular category of rights is not the exclusive possession of any one school of thought: it is no more necessary to belong to the school of Rousseau to recognise the rights of the individual than it is to be a Marxist to recognise the 'new rights', as they are called, economic and social rights. The gains of the collective intelligence under the influence of its several cross-currents go far beyond the disputations of the schools.

It is legitimate to suspect that the antagonism which many contemporary authors see fit to postulate between 'old' and 'new' human rights is partly artificial and derived either from the liking of theorists for ideological conflicts or more, perhaps, from the absolutist concept of human rights held by the philosophy—or better the rhetoric—of the eighteenth century, whose after-effects still in some measure give rise to misunderstandings today, and taint certain sacred formulæ of the vocabulary of human rights. If each of these rights is in itself absolute and not susceptible to any limitation, in the same way as a divine attribute, clearly any conflict between them is insoluble. But in practice everyone sees that these rights, being human, are subject, like every other human thing, to modification and limitation. Even where rights are 'inalienable', a distinction must be made between possession and exercise, the latter being subject to the modifications and limitations dictated in each instance by justice. If a criminal can justly be condemned to lose his life, it is because he has, by his crime, deprived himself, not of his right to existence, but rather of the possibility of demanding that right with justice: morally he has cut himself off from membership of the human community, as far as concerns the use of that fundamental and 'inalienable' right which the penalty imposed prevents his exercising. Again, the imparting by teaching and upbringing of the heritage of human culture is a fundamental right: in practice it is subject to the physical capacity of a given society, and justice may forbid its enjoyment by all being demanded *hic et nunc*, if such enjoyment is only conceivable through the dissolution of the social body, as in the case of the slave-owning society of ancient Rome, or the feudal society of the Middle Ages; the claim nevertheless remains a legitimate goal to be achieved in time. It then remains to endeavour to change the social order in question. Incidentally, this instance shows us that at the root of the hidden urge which impels us ever to the transformation of society, there lies the fact that man *posesses* 'inalienable' rights and that nevertheless he is deprived of the possibility of justly claiming to *exercise* certain of them by such inhumanities as subsist in the social structure in each age.

It is only normal that the various acknowledged rights of the individual should be mutually limitative, and in particular that economic and social rights, the rights of man as a social animal, cannot take their place in human history without some restriction upon the freedom and rights of man as an individual. Where the difficulties and arguments begin is in the determination of the scale of values governing the exercise and concrete integration of these various rights.

Here we are no longer dealing with the mere enumeration of human rights, but with the principle of dynamic unification whereby they are brought into play, with the tone scale, with the specific key in which different kinds of music are played on the same keyboard, music which in the event is in tune with, or harmful to, human dignity.

Conceivably the advocates of the liberal-individualist, of the Communist and of the co-operative type of society might draw up similar, even identical, lists of human rights. But their exercise of these rights will differ. All depends on the ultimate value whereon those rights depend and in terms of which they are integrated by mutual limitations. It is in terms of the scale of values which we thus acknowledge that we establish the means whereby, in our eyes, human rights, economic and social, as well as individual, shall impinge on life; it is from these different scales of values that spring mutual accusations of misunderstanding certain essential rights of the human being levelled by those for whom the mark of human dignity lies firstly and chiefly in the power to appropriate individually the gifts of nature so that each may be in a position to do freely what pleases him; by those who see it in the power to place those gifts under the collective control of the social body and thus deliver man from the tread-mill of labour and gain control of history; or by those who see it in the power of bringing the gifts of nature into service for the joint attainment of an immaterial good and of the free self-determination of the person. It remains to be decided which has a true and which a distorted vision of Man.

By following this line of thought, the extent and limits of the practical agreement on human rights, so often mentioned in the pages of this Introduction, would become clear. It would be understood that to go beyond a mere list or enumeration of rights and to produce a true Charter determining a common way of action, the agreement must also cover the scale of values, the key in which in their practical exercise in social life, the acknowledged rights of man must be harmonised.

Thus, we must not expect too much of an International Declaration of Human Rights. Yet does it not, above all, bear witness to what the peoples await today? The function

16

of language has been so much perverted, the truest words have been pressed into the service of so many lies, that even the noblest and most solemn declarations could not suffice to restore to the peoples faith in human rights. It is the implementation of these declarations which is sought from those who subscribe to them; it is the means of securing effective respect for human rights from States and Governments that it is desired to guarantee. On this point I should not venture to express more than the most guarded optimism. For to reach agreement, no longer merely on the definition of human rights, but on arrangements for their exercise in daily life, the first necessity, as I have pointed out above, would be agreement on a scale of values. For the peoples to agree on the means of securing effective respect for human rights, they would have to have in common, however implicitly, not necessarily the same speculative concept, but at least the same practical concept, of man and life, the same '*philosophy of life*' if I may for once be allowed to use the word 'philosophy' in the outrageously improper sense of the popular pragmatism of today.

Does the testimony collected in this volume give grounds for hope that, despite the clash of theory, a few scanty features of such a practical ideology, sufficiently defined and resolved to be effective, are in the course of taking root in the conscience of the nations? Does it give grounds for hope that one day agreement may be reached throughout the world, not only on the enumeration of human rights, but also on the key values governing their exercise and on the practical criteria to be used to secure respect for them? We do know that, though the crisis of civilisation which rose with this century has offered to our gaze the gravest violations of human rights, yet simultaneously it has led the public mind to a keener awareness of those rights, and Government propaganda to pay to them—in words—the most ringing tributes. Pending something better, a Declaration of Human Rights agreed by the nations would be a great thing in itself, a word of promise for the downcast and oppressed throughout all lands, the beginning of changes which the world requires, the first condition precedent for the later drafting of a universal Charter of civilised life.

A letter addressed to the Director-General
of Unesco by MAHATMA GANDHI

Bhangi Colony
New Delhi
May 25th, 1947

Dear Dr Julian Huxley,

As I am constantly on the move, I never get my post in time. But for your letter to Pandit Nehru in which you referred to your letter to me, I might have missed your letter. But I see that you have given your addressees ample time to enable them to give their replies. I am writing this in a moving train. It will be typed tomorrow when I reach Delhi.

I am afraid I can't give you anything approaching your minimum. That I have no time for the effort is true enough. But what is truer is that I am a poor reader of literature past or present much as I should like to read some of its gems. Living a stormy life since my early youth, I had no leisure to do the necessary reading.

I learnt from my illiterate but wise mother that all rights to be deserved and preserved came from duty well done. Thus the very right to live accrues to us only when we do the duty of citizenship of the world. From this one fundamental statement, perhaps it is easy enough to define the duties of Man and Woman and correlate every right to some corresponding duty to be first performed. Every other right can be shown to be a usurpation hardly worth fighting for.

Yours sincerely
M. K. GANDHI

Dr Julian S. Huxley
Director-General UNESCO
Paris

The Rights of Man

E. H. Carr

ARTICLE 62 of the Charter of the United Nations provides that 'the Economic and Social Council . . . may make recommendations for the purpose of promoting respect for, and observance of, human rights and fundamental freedoms for all.' The fact that this task is entrusted to the Economic and Social Council suggests that the framers of the Charter intended to lay stress on economic and social rights. In coupling with the idea of human rights the phrase 'fundamental freedoms' they will certainly have had in mind Franklin Roosevelt's 'Four Freedoms,' which by placing freedom from want and freedom from fear side by side with freedom of speech and freedom of worship forestalled any attempt to interpret the word 'freedom' in a narrow legal or formal sense.

The conception of the rights of man dates historically from the eighteenth century when it was particularly (though not, of course, exclusively) associated with the American and French revolutions. It was expressed at that time in wholly political terms. The more modern conception of the rights of man may perhaps be associated (though also not exclusively) with the Russian revolution and is economic and social as much as political. It is this modern conception quite as much as the classical tradition which must be considered as having inspired this provision in the Charter. What is implied in the transition from a purely political conception of the rights of man to an economic and social conception may perhaps be illustrated by a comparison between a fundamental document of the French Revolution, the Declaration of the Rights of Man, adopted by the French National Assembly in 1789, and the Declaration of Rights of the Toiling and Exploited Peoples adopted by the All-Russian Congress of Soviets in January 1918.

The declaration of 1789 lays down that 'men are free and equal in respect of their rights'; that 'the natural and unprescriptable rights of man . . . are liberty, property, security and resistance of oppression,' that 'political liberty consists in the power of doing whatever does not injure another'; that 'the law is an expression of the will of the community' and that 'any restriction of liberty must be in accordance with law'; and that freedom of religious opinions and 'the unrestrained communication of thoughts and opinions' should be assured, subject to responsibility for any disturbances of public order.

The declaration of 1918 describes its fundamental aim as being 'to suppress all exploitation of man by man, to abolish forever the division of society into classes, ruthlessly to suppress all exploitation, and to bring about the socialist organisation of society in all countries.' This is to be brought about by abolishing private property in land and in the means of production, by establishing workers' control of industry and by nationalising the banks. The declaration goes on to express confidence in the Soviets as organs representing the workers and adds explicitly that 'at the decisive moment in the struggle of the proletariat with its exploiters the latter can have no place in any of the organs of power.'

It would be a mistake to suggest that the new conception of the rights of man supersedes the old. In the Soviet Constitution of 1936 such familiar rights as freedom of conscience, freedom of speech, and freedom of the press and public assembly are assured to the Soviet citizen in addition to such more modern rights as the right to work, the right to material security in old age or sickness, the right to education, and equality of rights irrespective of sex or race. It would, however, be equally a mistake to suppose that the new and the old can simply be put side by side without reacting mutually on each other. By whom the political rights can be exercised, and within what limits they can be exercised, will depend on the extent to which the social rights are also assured. Will the holding of certain political opinions expose the holder to social or economic discrimination? Does freedom of speech include freedom for the worker to criticise his employer or manager? Or will freedom of speech so exercised expose him to penalties? The answer clearly depends on the nature of the social system prescribed under the category of social rights.

These considerations help to make it clear that what is involved in any declaration of rights is a definition of the relation of the individual to the society in which he lives. Such a relation is necessarily twofold and mutual; in other words a declaration of rights is *ipso facto* also a declaration of obligations. The eighteenth century declaration of rights was the revolutionary protest on behalf of the individual against an over-rigid social system still exhibiting feudal features; in this historical context, therefore, the declaration was likely to be one-sided and to lay more stress on the rights of the individual against society than on his obligations to it (these were for the most part firmly rooted enough to be taken for granted).

But even so the declaration of rights of 1789 clearly presupposes acceptance by the individual of the established social order. Liberty may be curtailed by law which is 'an expression of the will of the community'; and freedom of religious belief and freedom of speech are specifically made subject to 'responsibility for any disturbances of public order.' No bourgeois democracy has in fact ever tolerated the dissemination of opinions hostile to its fundamental tenets on any scale likely to menace its existence. Neither in Britain nor in the North American colonies was religious toleration absolute until religion had ceased to have serious political implications. The recent example of Regulation 18B in Great Britain shows that the most cherished liberties will be curtailed if their exercise is felt to be dangerous to the community. There may be significant differences of degree and of practice which can be explained in various ways. But on the issue of principle that the exercise of political freedom cannot be tolerated up to a point where it menaces the foundation of society there is no difference at all. The obligation of loyalty to the established order is implicit in any declaration of political rights. Such a declaration may be a programme, an announcement of an intention, or the consecration of a policy. But if it is embodied in a constitutional or legal enactment, it will always carry with it its 'escape clause,' written or unwritten. The government of the day always in effect has the reserve power of withdrawing any right which is exercised in a manner which threatens the overthrow of the existing order.

The issue of the correlation of rights and obligations arises in a far acuter form when social and economic rights are in question. The correlative obligation to political rights is the mainly passive one of loyalty to the political order under which those rights are enjoyed. The correlative obligations to social and economic rights are active. If the new declaration of the rights of man is to include provisions for social services, for maintenance in childhood, in old age, in incapacity or in unemployment, it becomes clear that no society can guarantee the enjoyment of such rights unless it in turn has the right to call upon and direct the productive capacities of the individuals enjoying them. It is no accident that the biblical warning 'He that doth not work neither shall he eat' has found so prominent a place in Bolshevik writings and in the Soviet Constitution. A declaration of rights which placed on society the obligation to furnish certain material goods and services to the individual citizen without placing on the individual the obligation to produce his required share of those goods and services would be a hollow sham.

The drafting of an International Declaration of the Rights of Man should, however, in my view, be preceded by an enquiry which has in it a large factual element. What rights are in fact now enjoyed, in theory and in practice, by the individual citizen, and to what rights does he or she attach the highest importance? (The answers would certainly vary from country to country.) When we have drawn up a provisional list of minimum rights which, in our view, ought to be assured to the individual, what obligations must the individual accept in order to put society in a position to accord those rights? Until we are in possession of some sort of answer, however provisional and imperfect, to these questions, any declaration that may be drafted seems likely to remain abstract and unrealisable.

The conclusions which I draw from these observations are:

(a) that any declaration of rights which would be felt to have any validity today must include social and economic as well as political rights;

(b) that no declaration of rights which does not also contain a declaration of correlative obligations could have any serious meaning;

(c) that any declaration of rights and obligations of the individual in society should at the present stage be regarded as a declaration of intention or as a standard to be aimed at rather than as an internationally binding engagement.

A Fragment of Thoughts Concerning the Nature and the Fulfilment of Human Rights

Arnold J. Lien

IT is not surprising that mankind, horrified by the unspeakable atrocities of recent régimes equipped with all the destructive know-how of modern science and technology, has despairingly cried out for an international bill of the rights of man, just as in the critical revolts against the tyrannies of other eras demands were launched for national or local bills of rights. For bills of rights are always monumental indictments of régimes of the past, as well as promised safeguards against the same abuses by régimes of the future.

Since rights exist only in the sphere of the relations of man to man, the occasions for asserting them arise mostly when they are threatened, restrained or suppressed. Bills of rights, therefore, never have been and probably never can be complete and definitive catalogues of the rights of man. The Declaration of Independence of 1776 mentioned specifically only a few 'among these' rights. The Bill of Rights of the constitution of the United States warns that 'the enumeration in the Constitution, of certain rights, shall not be construed to deny or disparage others retained by the people.' The lists to be found in the Atlantic Charter and other recent documents are similarly only fragments.

Human rights are universal rights or enabling qualities of human beings *as human beings* or as individuals of the human race, attaching to the human being wherever he appears, without regard to time, place, colour, sex, parentage or environment. They are really the *keystone of the dignity of man.* In their quintessence they consist basically of the one all-inclusive right or enabling quality of complete freedom to develop to their fullest possible extent every potential capacity and talent of the individual for his most effective *self-management*, security and satisfaction. In this one transcendent human right, all others are implied, or, of it, all others are phases, each receiving a position of prominence or an emphasis dependent upon the particular temper or trend of the times.

From the primitive to the contemporary, education (not to be confused with propaganda or indoctrination), has had as its central aim the guidance and training of the individual for the responsible and successful exercise of this right. Nowhere is there any principle of nature or religion or science or reason which assigns prenatally one man to be master and one to be slave, one to be pauper and one to be prince. Yet under one pretext or another, implemented with the necessary military, economic, religious or political force, these human rights have been wantonly disregarded and suppressed throughout the history of man by all sorts of absolutist tribal, feudal, monarchical, industrial and other dictatorial régimes.

The great political revolutions of the late eighteenth century came as an explosion of the accumulated discontent of the oppressed. The phases of human rights which had been most abused at that time were formulated into declarations and bills of rights the reverberations of which in the next century were felt around the world.

But more important than the statement of the rights of man was the new doctrine that the main purpose of every government should be to preserve these rights and guarantee them against encroachment. Universal human rights were henceforth to be accepted as basic privileges of citizens of the state and be given the full protection of all the sanctions set up by the government. No longer were they to remain merely pitiable natural rights which the individual could proclaim as sacred but for which he could offer no sanction or authority other than his own feeble assertion.

With its beginnings even before the wars at the close of the eighteenth century, but its greatest momentum attained only in the late nineteenth and early twentieth centuries, another revolutionary movement encompassed the world and transformed society from a comparatively simple agricultural one into a complex and highly industrialised one. This industrial revolution brought infinite possibilities for the elevation of the standard of living and the promotion of the welfare of men; but it also involved new opportunities for oppression and abuse. Its tempo, complexities and magnitude threatened to reduce the individual to a babe, clinging to its toy-bank, in the woods of the giants of mass production and, periodically, mass destruction, with their billion dollar wallets.

To add still further to the bewilderment of mankind there flared up in Russia in 1917 a political revolution comparable in intensity and far-flung effects to the American and French revolutions a century earlier. Since then the earth has been ravaged by two world wars with unprecedented dimensions of costs, destruction and dislocation and with an almost incredible resurgence of old hatreds, autocratic disregard of human rights, and bestiality.

The new formulations of the rights of man in the twentieth century, as found in numerous bills of rights in recent consitutions and in the many documents growing out of the last war and the movement for international co-operation, are different from the old especially in the large emphasis placed upon the economic and social phases. The basic rights are the same; but the stresses peculiar to the new age have brought a change in emphasis from political to economic, from liberty to equality, from freedom to security.

Basically, the right of every human being as an individual of the human race remains that of complete freedom to develop to their fullest possible limit all his talents and capacities with the aim of effective self-management, security and satisfaction. Every man lives in a very complex society. With a few exceptions, every one is a member of a political unit or state. These states are on widely varying levels of economic, social, political and cultural advancement. While the basic rights must everywhere be the same, the degree to which they can be made operative and the extent to which they can be fulfilled must vary from one state to another—and continue to vary for a long time, in spite of the accelerating processes now developing through the United Nations.

The first essential is that all States accept the basic human rights as constitutional rights for their peoples and their observances as an international obligation, with the right of an ultimate appeal to some international tribunal, although it would be premature and unrealistic as yet to consider them as the privileges of citizens of a world state.

The second requirement is that these rights be gradually implemented with the goodwill and the techniques necessary for their effective operation. In many States, certain phases of these rights cannot be put into practice at once. The imperative requirement in such a case is that the State must take constructive steps at once to formulate and carry out a long-range programme through which to prepare its people for the participation required of them to make the rights operative. For instance, if the people are illiterate, let them be given an *education*; if they are starving, let them be *fed*; if they are irresponsible, let them be *educated for self-discipline*.

Within each State, what every individual is entitled to first is an opportunity for the development of a sound, healthy body and mind—a *safeguarded heritage*, adequate food, shelter and clothing, physical education, medical care, and all the other indispensables.

He must have the opportunity to get the *training and the guidance* to enable him to earn a living through productive activity and to ensure a modicum of security against old age and misfortune. He is entitled to an education to equip him with methods, techniques and information with which to work and perform his duties and to enable him to discover what his best talents and capacities are and to acquaint him with his place in and relation to society and the universe. Without these physical and intellectual foundations, the right of the individual to a free and full progress in *self-management* becomes a mere husk. He must have these basic assurances of freedom from want and fear.

Another cornerstone in the basic rights of man is the right to a status of equality with all other individuals who are citizens of the same State. This applies to every sphere of activity of the society to which the individual belongs—to the economic as much as to the political. In the *opportunities* offered and *services* rendered by organised society, he is entitled to share equally with others. Whatever freedoms are guaranteed must be available equally to all. Whatever burdens and responsibilities are assessed must be distributed equally among all. If there are resources they must not be monopolised or exploited by the few to the disadvantage of the welfare of the many. The diversity of opportunities must be made as extensive as the diversity of talents; for the operative principle of equality leaves ample room for infinite variation.

Nor is there any conflict between the principle of equality and the principle of liberty or the several freedoms. Rather they supplement and give substance to each other. In fact, no other application of equality is as vital as that which requires the equal distribution of freedoms or liberty among all. Liberty and equality are merely two phases of the one multiple-phased all-inclusive and universal human right of *self-realisation*. Other phases should, no doubt, be listed when an international bill of rights is written, but their connection with this basic one should never be lost sight of.

These human rights are rights of the individual. Within the State which guarantees them, they are balanced with a corresponding list of duties; but, quite apart from these, there are responsibilities implied in the rights themselves. No individual born today finds himself in an uninhabited world. His environment, consequently, immediately demands of him a sense of responsibility, first, to himself and, second, to the society in which he lives. His main law is that of self-interest; but that law can operate on many levels and, on the top level, may come very close to coincidence with the law of the common interest of all. Self-discipline and self-regulation may thus be resorted to as means of self-advancement.

If these responsibilities are not assumed by the individual and his rights are abused to the detriment of society as a whole or of other individuals, society itself (that is, all individuals acting collectively), imposes restrictions and prescribes regulations. These are intended to protect those who assume responsibilities against the derelictions of those who do not and are, in principle at least, temporary expedients to serve until the educational system can achieve a larger success in developing more effectively the universal sense of responsibility.

In a State, all institutions and organisations and individual activities are subject to the tacit or express sanction of the society as a whole. As long as private initiative and enterprise contribute to the common weal and adequately meet the needs of society, there is no occasion for collective or public action; but whenever they resort to the injurious or fall short of the standard of adequacy, society stands ready to restrain or suppress, to supplement or supersede. Thus there may be a combination of private and public or collective initiative and enterprise, as now in the majority of States, or there may be a plan in which all major enterprises are publicly or collectively owned and operated, as now in an occasional State. In either case, the people or the State is the ultimate authority on what is and what is not for the general welfare. The sense of responsibility on the part of institutions and organisations of every kind is of the same vital importance as that of individuals.

The problem of determining when a right has been abused to the detriment of others or of society as a whole must remain a difficult one, depending upon the crystallised national and world opinion of the time for principles and standards suitable to its solution. If a trial is required in a regular court and, with adequate safeguards, an ultimate appeal can be made to an international tribunal, a reasonably satisfactory solution should be possible.

The authority to suspend basic rights in the case of critical emergencies may best be placed in a small representative body in which all parties and minorities have members. The safeguards must include very severe restrictions on the duration of the suspension and a provision for ultimate appeal to an international tribunal.

Until these guarantees of individual rights have become traditional and certain, colonial peoples and minority groups of various kinds—racial, cultural, religious—will, no doubt, also have to be assured certain basic collective or group rights. These can logically take very much the same forms as those concerned with individual rights and be made subject to the same responsibilities.

The scientists are smashing atoms to set free new energies for the advancement of human welfare. Humanists are somewhat behind in their attempt to educate all to a sense of responsibility and a social consciousness sufficient to ensure a constructive use of these energies. Education seems to be the only key that can release the creative energies of the individual for the new era. Self-interest is the force of gravity which draws individuals together. That is the force on which the new order must be built. As individuals grow in knowledge, understanding and wisdom, their perspectives will be more complete, their horizons wider and their vision clearer. Their self-interest will find itself on ever higher levels until it ultimately coincides with the common interest of all.

Human Rights in the World Today

Luc Somerhausen

A PART from any question of the relative values of different political systems, the problem is essentially to determine:

    (a) Whether the rights proclaimed have so far been fully and effectively attained;

    (b) Whether there are new rights which should be proclaimed;

    (c) Whether the attainment of the old and new rights is compatible with the maintenance of the present forms of social organisation.

On point (a) it appears indisputable and mainly undisputed that under the present economic organisation of society, human rights have not been fully attained. Whether it be the right to own property, the right to personal freedom, the right of personal security, freedom of association or freedom of the press, it is found that apart from the limitations on all rights arising from legal enactments freely agreed to or grudgingly acquiesced in, such rights are limited as a consequence of the system of ownership in force, in which the profit motive and hence the exploitation of man by man is involved. It is symptomatic that all that has been said in the last century and more particularly in our day on the subject of human dignity, was stated by Marx, notably in his famous theory of alienation: Society, he said, may be defined as the consubstantiality of man and nature; man must be able to produce freely, to enjoy the fruit of his own work and to live in fellowship with other men and in harmony with himself.

Of this basic analysis we still retain today the concept of the precarious nature and the relative ineffectiveness of declarations of right which have in mind only 'man, the egoist' as he exists in a society based on the profit motive, man at odds with the community, 'turned in on himself, solely preoccupied with his personal interests and obedient to his private whims.'

Without underestimating the importance of declarations and formulations of human rights, it must be admitted that in contemporary society the strongest links between men are not the rights and duties to which appeal is commonly made, but material requirements, private needs and interests, the preservation of their property and of their individualism.

It may also be said that, wherever there has been conflict between material interests and human rights, the latter have been sacrificed either overtly or indirectly. Freedom of the press, which is mentioned in the memorandum, is a typical case. It is hardly necessary to re-emphasise the precarious nature of the principles of equality of freedom, of assembly or association.

It may thus be said that up to now there has been and still is a number of restrictions of varying severity on the full exercise of those human rights proclaimed as long ago as 1776.

(b) Not Soviet constitutional theory or practice, but the whole trend of modern thought has led to recognition of the need for distinguishing between political and economic human rights. It is a socialist platitude to say that no true human independence will exist until the individual's economic and social as well as his civil and political rights shall have been proclaimed. To put it another way, it may be said that traditional human rights will not become a reality until they have been completed by a social organisation which will make it possible for man to protect himself against exploitation.

It is purposeless to say that man is entitled to respect for his personality and to freedom in its development, if at the same time those essential rights are not proclaimed which in fact enable man to achieve the development of his personality and to secure respect for his dignity. This was the spirit behind the French Constitution of 1946, when it proclaimed the right to work, with the right to strike involved in it, the right to leisure, the right to proper conditions of work and to joint management, the right to health, the right to culture, the right ot society's help where anyone is unfit for work, etc.

(c) It must be conceded with regret that in those areas where democratic effort has been directed towards political rights, the social and economic rights of man are still not recognised.

It is worth stressing that, as developments tend to ensure the progress of economic democracy, there may be noted, even in Western Europe, attempts to limit certain rights once insisted on as essential. For instance, one can hardly fail to be struck by the reasoning of a French politician of advanced views, who said that in nationalised undertakings the substitution of public for private ownership must involve a modification of the workers' rights. Under pretence that the further we advance along the path to economic democracy, the more inconceivable becomes the idea of industrial conflict, many people in the West have come (for quite a different purpose, of course) to recommend the ideological conceptions which they disapprove of in the U.S.S.R., where one notes that the new social conditions have completely overthrown the old concept of human rights.

Obviously assent cannot lightly be given to the establishment of relative scales of human rights varying with the social legislation or economic evolution (or revolution) achieved. New human rights, like the old ones, will have meaning only in so far as the conditions necessary to their free exercise will be insured and secured.

It is quite otherwise as regards the question of deciding whether the values prevailing in a democracy should not be reassessed and the principal place be given to certain human rights which in the past have been denied or under-valued. However, in our opinion, the best course would be to proclaim equal rights while simultaneously evolving means to secure respect for them.

To sum up, it is our view, in opposition to that generally held, that the course of history is today tending to a more or less perfect synthesis between individualism and collectivism. A more difficult matter is to ascertain the norm on which can be based the proclamation of rights implying a direct curtailment of the right to own property.

Our views can best be summed up in Jaures' general statement of human rights:

'We must ensure the fullness and the universality of the rights of the individual. No human being at any stage must be left outside. None must be exposed to the risk of being the prey or tool of another. None must be deprived of positive means to work in liberty without servile dependence on anyone at all.' ·

The Philosophic Bases and Material Circumstances of the Rights of Man

Richard McKeon

THE problems faced in framing a declaration of human rights are basically philosophic. The difficulties involved in resolving them may therefore be recognised in the paradox that the resolution of practical problems involves philosophic commitments but agreement concerning actions to be taken need not presuppose philosophic agreement. The philosophers of the seventeenth and eighteenth centuries prepared the intellectual instruments by means of which bills of rights and declarations of rights were framed and, eventually, written into the constitution of most of the states of the Western World. Yet agreement in the promulgation of those declarations of rights, far from signifying a general agreement on a single basic philosophy, provided a framework within which divergent philosophies, religious, and even economic, social and political theories might be entertained and developed. The same paradox presents difficulties of a different order in the framing of a declaration of rights for the twentieth century. The fundamental problem is not found in compiling a list of human rights: the declarations of human rights that have been prepared by committees and groups who have undertaken the study of the problem and the declarations that have been submitted to the Commission on Human Rights are surprisingly similar, and little difficulty is encountered in the mere statement of the rights that ought to be included in the list. The differences are found rather in what is meant by these rights, and these differences of meanings depend on divergent basic assumptions, which, in turn, lend plausibility to and are justified by contradictory interpretations of the economic and social situation, and, finally, lead to opposed recommendations concerning the implementation required for a world declaration of human rights.

These three sources of differences concerning the meanings of human rights render nugatory any agreement concerning the list of human rights, and indeed, once they are raised, make even agreement concerning the bare enumeration impossible. The faith 'in fundamental human rights, in the dignity and worth of the human person, in the equal rights of men and women' which is re-affirmed in the Charter of the United Nations stands in need, if it is to be significant, of some resolution of these differences. The effectiveness of a Declaration of Human Rights, such as is urgently needed in the world today, depends precisely on (a) its clarity in formulating an ideal which will promote and encourage respect for human rights and for fundamental freedoms for all without distinction as to race, sex, language, or religion, (b) its pertinence and adaptation to the social, economic and cultural conditions of the present, and (c) its implementation in social and political agencies. These three conditions of the effectiveness of a declaration of human rights, moreover, are not independent of one another. Opposed philosophies lead to opposed interpretations of history and of the present. Opposed conceptions of historical processes and historical methods, conversely, are used to supply the criticism of, or to lend justification to, opposed philosophies. Political institutions are adapted to circumstances and also change them; they are consequences of philosophic principles as well as instruments of ideological control. The debates concerning a modern declaration of rights will turn, not on questions concerning what the rights are, but on questions of basic assumptions, actual fact, and appropriate implementation. The difficulties will be discovered in the suspicions, suggested by these differences, concerning the tangential uses that might be made of a declaration of human rights for the purpose of advancing special interests rather than establishing universal truths or promoting general welfare.

The focus of these oppositions and debates is, in part, determined by the tradition of human rights which received its classical expression in America and Western Europe in the eighteenth century and, in part, a result of changes in the circumstances and in the ideas of men since that time. The history of human rights is long, for it is possible to trace concern with them back to the Greeks and the Romans and most of the philosophic devices by which they were developed and on which they were grounded, like the doctrines of natural law and social contract, have like origins and evolutions. But the history of declarations of human rights is short.[1] The differences in those two histories may serve to separate the respects in which philosophic differences are unimportant in the resolution of practical problems from the respects in which they are of crucial importance. 'Natural law' does not designate a single philosophic doctrine: it receives different definitions and developments in the philosophies of Aquinas, Hobbes, and Locke, to mention only three of the numerous natural law philosophers; and in the controversies concerning the relation of Church and State in the late Middle Ages, the doctrine of natural law was employed to defend opposed positions of papalists, imperialists, and conciliarists. The conception of natural rights, sacred and inherent in man, was written into the constitutions of the eighteenth, nineteenth and twentieth centuries, not because men had agreed on a philosophy, but because they had agreed, despite philosophic differences, on the formulation of a solution to a series of moral and political problems. It is as easy to make a case for the derivation of the conception of human rights from the philosophy of Aquinas, Suarez and Bellarmine as for its derivation from the philosophy of Locke, and it is easy to question the historical accuracy of both derivations. What is indisputable is that the declarations of human rights separated inalienable human rights which were to be protected from governmental interference from alienable rights which were delegated to the government for due

---

[1] The brevity of the history of declarations of human rights justifies the treatment of the problem against the background of the classical statements of Western Europe. The problem in China, thus, is one of the constitutional movements influenced by or comparable to those of the Western World (*cf.* Chun-Mai Carsun Chang, 'Political Structure in the Chinese Draft Constitution,' *The Annals of the American Academy of Political and Social Science,* vol. 243 (1946), p 67), the Islamic tradition was crucially influenced by the Western formulations (*cf* Majid Khadduri, 'Human Rights in Islam,' *ibid* p 80), and in general the problem of declarations of human rights, as distinct from their philosophic bases, have had everywhere similar constitutional evolutions.

compensation in the form of just and effective government.[1] The discussion of human rights has as a consequence been couched in a series of simple oppositions: 'rights' have been related, or opposed, to 'wrongs,' to 'duties,' and to 'laws,' and the discussion of rights has been in the tradition of constitutionalism.

The use of these oppositions has become so traditional that they are accepted as inevitable or as statements of fact; and indeed they are statements of fact, but based on unnoticed philosophic assumptions which are emerging in the present discussion of human rights to revive forgotten or unexplored differences. When Mr Ribnikar, the member of the Commission on Human Rights from Yugoslavia, expressed his conception of human rights at the first session of the Commission, January 27th-February 10th, 1947, he stressed the basic differences between the economic, social, and national life of the eighteenth century and the present underlying the opposition between the ideology of individualism and the spirit of collectivity, and he argued that it is 'obvious that this common interest is more important than the individual interest, and that man can liberate himself only when the mass of a population is free.' Dr Malik, the member of the Commission from Lebanon, on the other hand, sought human rights, during the same session, in the essence of man and found the chief problem of human rights in a new tyranny which has been rising in the last few decades, 'the tyranny of the masses, which seems to have an inevitable tendency of ultimately embodying itself in what I might call the tyranny of the State.' This is only one of the many conflicts developed recently from the fertile opposition of man and State which had served earlier to protect man from unwarranted infringements on his freedoms. It could be supplemented by a long list of further conflicts or by a long list of philosophic, religious, moral, economic, or social recommendations for their resolution. The problem of human rights has, in this fashion, become a philosophic problem in which differences of basic conviction make seemingly simple distinctions deceptively complex.

[1] Charles H. McIlwain, 'Bills of Rights', *Encyclopaedia of the Social Sciences*, vol. II, pp 544-6.

There are two ways in which such a problem may be treated: a philosophic solution may be sought in an agreement which resolves the basic differences, or a political frame may be sought within which agreement is possible concerning common action toward common ends and within which basic disagreements are more likely to be removed when mutual suspicions have been lessened by successful common action. The utility of a declaration of human rights depends on the possibility of separating the political from the philosophic question. The resolution of philosophic differences would require the definition of basic terms—like freedom and right—and the balance of oppositions—like tradition and novelty—which have been variously defined and variously related in the philosophic traditions of the world. There is, among the philosophies of the world, a 'utopian' or ideal tradition of analysis in which 'freedom' is conceived to be a power based on knowledge of the truth; and in that tradition, which on this point is shared by philosophers as different as Augustine and Marx, to express or to follow what is false is not to be free. There is also a 'circumstantial' or material tradition of analysis in which freedom depends on the power of choice and the power to follow either of alternative modes of action; and in this tradition, in which philosophers as different as Aristotle or Mill might be found, freedom is found in a region of indifference, deliberation, and choice.[1] Likewise, what is revolutionary in the context of one set of philosophic assumptions is counter-revolutionary, subversive, or even traditional in another.

The eighteenth century did not resolve these basic philosophic oppositions, but the declarations of rights which were formulated in the philosophic language of the eighteenth century did succeed in stating ideals which had a profound influence in improving the relations of men and in advancing the practice of justice. The basic problem to which the declarations of human rights were addressed was the injustice of feudal rulers and governments. They were expressions of the revolutionary movements of the century:

---

[1] *Cf* R. McKeon, 'Discussion and Resolution in Political Conflicts,' in *Ethics*, vol. 54 (1944), pp 246-7

they reserved certain inalienable rights to man and forbade governments to infringe them; they were part of a constitutional movement in which governments were conceived to depend on the consent of the governed. In like fashion, contemporary discussions of the rights of man will not resolve the basic philosophic oppositions which have continued unabated since the seventeenth century, unless philosophers, professional and lay, have discovered unexpectedly a new versatility in terminologies and assumptions or a new susceptibility to the claims of reason. But a declaration of human rights could achieve an effect on the political and social practices of the next century comparable to that of earlier bills of rights, provided it is recognised that the problem has changed. A world declaration of human rights must, like the national bills of rights, be conceived within a constitutional frame, such as the Charter of the United Nations; and the basic problem then turns not merely on the relation of men to governments but on the relation of groups of men and of states to each other. In the framework of the United Nations, it is the problem of how men with basically different philosophic convictions and religious beliefs, associated in divergent political organisations and committed to divergent economic systems can co-operate in the maintenance of peace, the promulgation of justice, and the protection of fundamental human rights. The nature of that problem is seen both in the opposed assumptions implied in efforts to resolve it and in the nature of the additions that have been made in recent years to the list of human rights.

The fundamental issue of our times is probably to be found in the opposition of two assumptions, made implicitly and explicitly in policies advocated for the determination of the relations of the nations of the world. On the one hand, it is assumed that there are several basic ideologies, probably reducible to two, which are in necessary conflict and opposition and which are dividing, or will eventually divide, mankind into two worlds until one overcomes the other. On the other hand, it is assumed that means can be found by which men of different basic convictions in philosophy, religion, political theory and economic doctrine may co-operate to common ends in a single world of shared values. The first is a solution in which peace and human rights depend on the successful inculcation of a single basic philosophy throughout the world, and the failure of efforts towards universal indoctrination in the past, even in the case of basic doctrines which seem in retrospect more attractive than the rough outlines presented by either of the opposed doctrines to one who does not share it, make it highly probable that pursuit of that solution must lead to war. The second is a solution in which the establishment of a constitution, like that of the United Nations, and of agencies, like the specialised agencies associated with the United Nations, might preserve the peace of the world by furnishing the means by which to reach agreements concerning the equitable solution of problems and the achievement of human welfare and the common good, and which, in so doing, might facilitate the advance of common understanding and basic intellectual agreement. In the pursuit of the second solution the formulation of a declaration of human rights is of basic importance and the nature of such a declaration takes its form from the assumption that it is possible to come to agreement concerning the rights of man and to implement such an agreement short of arriving at philosophic unanimity.

The change in the problem of human rights which is seen in this opposition of basic assumptions is further exemplified in new additions to the list of human rights. As human rights can no longer be formulated effectively on the simple opposition of man and State or on the assumption that freedoms and rights will be safeguarded adequately if governments can be persuaded to desist from certain actions, so too, many of the rights which have become of basic importance in the nineteenth and twentieth centuries have burst through the classical definitions and safeguards of human rights. In even so brief an enumeration as the Four Freedoms, only two—freedom of speech and expression and freedom of religion and worship—fit the frame of the earlier conception of rights or the guarantees provided for them, while two—freedom from want and freedom from fear—require a different analysis and different implementation. The treatment of problems involving rights of the latter kind during the nineteenth and early twentieth centuries is indication and symptom of the change in the basic problem of human rights, and the clarification of that difference will serve also to suggest the appropriate means for the implementation of such rights.

When rights are to be protected from the possible tyranny of governments, the problem may be solved by recognising that certain rights are inherent in the very nature of man and by specifying the constitutional safeguards under which other rights may be delegated to the various organs of government. The rights of man are closely related. The rights of the citizen and civil rights are both precondition and consequence of political rights. The specification of rights proper to man and the formulation of the manner in which rights proper to citizens may be exercised determines a complex relation between them, for they are, on the one hand, different in their implementation and yet, on the other hand, involved in a process of mutual delimitation which is usually expressed in the opposition of rights and duties. Civil rights are designed to guarantee the individual against arbitrary treatment: they are formulated in terms of equality before the law and the operation of due process of law; they can be defended by providing access to court decisions when they seem to be violated. Political rights are designed to relate the government to the consent of the governed: they are formulated in the institutions of government and in the conditions, such as 'free elections,' by which consent is expressed; they are defended only by the constitutional frame which determines the manner of their exercise. Civil rights, like freedom of conscience and freedom of speech, were justified by their early defenders on the grounds, not only that they may be granted without danger to the public peace, but also that they may not be withheld without danger. The freedoms of association, assembly, press, and communications have like grounds, and, although a limitation might be set on any such freedom by invoking the interest of *salus publica*, the general tendency seemed, until recently, to be towards the spread and universalisation of such freedoms. Similarly, although the manner in which a citizen may influence the government under which he lives varies with the forms of government, the trend toward democracy seemed, until recently, universal. The change that has come into these problems in recent years is not so much due to a change in these tendencies as to the introduction of differences in the interpretation of what constitutes 'freedom' and 'democracy'.

These changes became apparent in the discussion of rights which were not part of the eighteenth century formulations and which are not easily reduced to the formula of rights inherent in the nature of man requiring only protection from governmental interference. The problem of the new rights arose from the changed social and economic conditions due to the advance of technology and industrialisation which brought fundamental and obvious rights into conflict with extensions and interpretations of 'property' rights. They have been posed variously. In practical action they have been treated by legal devices, like those by which 'in the United States' problems in labour regulations and public health were solved by making what had been rights of which individuals could not be deprived without due process of law proper subjects for the exercise of police power. They have been the occasion for political change, for legislative action, and for revolution. In abstract analysis they have seemed to some thinkers to involve a moral problem, in the need to relate rights to functions and obligations and to discover criteria and purposes for society,[1] while to others they have seemed to pose an intellectual problem, in the need to constitute a kind of knowledge which does not now exist for the resolution of the problems of the 'public'.[2] This variety of approaches, practical and theoretic, is indication of the nature of the problem and the diversity of implementation which is required for its solution. Even if it is stated in terms of the relation of man and the State, it is no longer a problem of rights of individuals reserved from interference by government or of rights by which individuals may secure proper influence on government, but rather a problem of how far opportunities to which men have a right must be secured by governmental action. The

---

[1] R. H. Tawney, *The Acquisitive Society* (London, 1937), pp 44-5, 82-3

[2] John Dewey, *The Public and its Problems* (New York, 1927), pp 157, 166

economic and social rights, which have a place in recent formulations of the rights of man—the right to work, the right to education, to social security, to recreation, cultural opportunities and a fair share of the advancing gains of civilisation, and, in general, the freedom from want and the freedom from fear—all are rights which require that something be done if they are to be secured for their recipients. The promulgation of economic and social rights has therefore brought them into conflict with civil and political rights, for the planning and control essential to the former impinge on some of the freedoms of choice and action that had seemed defensible under the latter. As a consequence one of the fundamental oppositions in the discussion of human rights is between those who hold that the preservation of civil and political rights is basic even to the establishment of economic and social rights and those who hold that, unless economic and social rights are first secured, civil and political rights are an empty sham and pretence.

The means by which to secure both sets of rights, and indeed the very meanings which they assume as their interdependences are examined, present problems which would be difficult to resolve without recourse to the other aspect of our present situation and another related set of rights. The advancement of science and technology, which gave rise, as a result of changes consequent on it, to the problem of economic and social rights, has had a direct effect in the new significance that has been given to a fourth set of rights—the freedom of communication and thought. For as political rights afford a safeguard and significance to civil rights, and as economic and social rights provide means essential to the exercise of political rights, so the rights of communication and thought may prepare the resolution of differences concerning economic and social rights. The advance of science gives promise of completely transforming the conditions by which the welfare of man is secured, and the extension of information and knowledge may lead to mutual understanding and even to the removal of conflicts found in the basic assumptions of groups, cultures, and nations.

The formulation of the philosophic bases and material circumstances of human rights would be important in an effort to remove the conflicts that have arisen in the conception of human rights. It is no less important to the preparation of a declaration of human rights, even though such a declaration need not await the resolution of fundamental problems, but should precede it, for the philosophic bases of human rights provide an analysis of the problem preparatory in the one case to resolution and in the other case to implementation and action. A world bill of rights is possible, if it is recognised that both the definition of the rights and progress in their achievement depend on implementation, and that implementation in the case of a world bill of rights means not merely the recognition of agencies by which to protect rights or resolve conflicts among them, but also recognition of the fact that within the constitutional frame of the United Nations, rights will have different legal implementation and different philosophic interpretation in the various sovereign nations of the Organisation. What is proposed, as an immediate step, is the formulation of a Declaration of Human Rights and Fundamental Freedoms to be adopted as a General Assembly Resolution. This declaration might serve as a standard to be observed by Member States, and might be incorporated in their constitutions and legislation. Most of the Member States already possess provisions in their constitutions for civil and political rights expressed in forms that are similar even when the interpretations are highly diverse. The economic and social rights, on the other hand, have the international aspects that are already subject to the operation of the United Nations and its various agencies. Civil rights could be given an international character only if they were assigned to the juridiction of a world tribunal, and political rights would be internationally effective only if the citizens of the nations of the world were made citizens of the world by a change in the structure of the United Nations. In the case of economic and social rights, on the other hand, the Security Council and the Economic and Social Council are already engaged in establishing the freedom from fear and the freedom from want, and specialised agencies like the World Health Organisation, the Food and Agriculture Organisation and UNESCO are engaged on the problems of health and education. Finally, the problems of communication, international understanding, and the use of educational, scientific and culture instruments in the maintenance of peace are among the chief concerns of UNESCO. The promulgation of a world declaration of rights depends, as bills of rights seem always to have depended, on the existence of a broad region of interpretation within which court decisions and administrative and legislative action have worked progressively to a practical definition and within which divergent philosophies have worked to less ambiguous or conflicting theoretic bases. The declaration will not remove the sharp differences in interpretations of civil and political rights, but it will provide a ground within which they may be brought into closer approximation, if economic and social rights are established sufficiently firmly to provide a minimum welfare and security, and if freedom of communication and freedom of thought are advanced enough to contribute to universal welfare and mutual understanding. Agreement can doubtless be secured concerning the list of human rights only if an ambiguity remains, both because of the absence of a uniform manner of administering them and because of the absence of a single basic philosophy, but that ambiguity is the frame within which men may move peacefully to a more uniform practice and to a universal understanding of fundamental human rights.

Rights of Man or Human Relations?

Don Salvador de Madariaga

I

No discussion of 'the rights of man' can yield fruitful results when the subject is so limited both to the rights and to the individual; and the very form of words is to be avoided. It dates from the era of the French Revolution, which bred a combative, biassed and therefore limited outlook. Historically this attitude was only too natural and even justified. A similar attitude has been fostered by the cruel oppression millions of men and women have suffered in the last two decades. But true constructive work in the field of *Social nature* can be achieved only if and when the matter be approached objectively and not aggressively. The first result of this change of outlook is that the word and concept of *rights* is found to be too narrow, for it only represents one aspect of the relations between the individual and the society in which he lives.

It is a commonplace—but an often forgotten one—that there is no such thing as an absolute individual, i.e. that no human being exists who does not contain a social element as well. Man is a synthesis which might be described as *individual-in-society*; and an individual without a society is no more thinkable than a society without individuals. It seems, therefore, that the right approach to the problem usually defined as that of the 'the rights of man' should be that of the right political relations between the individual and the society to which he belongs.

In our day, the political society in which we are set has become one. For a number of well-known reasons, nations, the separate societies of the past, have become merged into a world-society; and the chaos in which we all live is due to the fact that this world society being still without its State, or governmental institutions, the several nations seek to meet the trouble by the disastrous expedient of strengthening their respective authorities. The recrudescence

47

of governmental regulations and the raising of frontier barriers of all kinds are direct, though paradoxical results of the growth of world solidarity.

This paradox can be solved easily once the distinction has been made between objective and subjective solidarity. The owners of—or passengers in—all the cars in a traffic jam are in as 'thick' solidarity as the drops of water in a pipe: but their subjective solidarity is probably *nihil*, and each and every one of them is perhaps wishing the others were dead and in hell. The present chaos is due to the fact that while the objective solidarity of nations has rushed ahead with the increase in the speed of physical and mental communications, their subjective solidarity has lagged behind.

Of the three stages of social nature, man, nation, mankind, it is therefore the middle stage which most requires control and restraint. For it is the nation which, both towards the individual and towards the world society, turns an absolutist face. Towards the individual, the nation, once absolutist on the strength of the divine right of kings, remains absolutist on the strength of 'the will of the people.' Towards the world society, the nation remains absolutist entrenched as it is in the doctrine—and practice—of national sovereignty.

The problem first understood as that of 'the rights of man' thus reveals itself as one of the proper relations between man, nation and world community.

II

This conclusion raises a fresh problem: what is meant by 'proper relations'? In other words, what are the standards which are to guide us in our enquiry? The complete answer must ultimately depend on the faith, the philosophy or the *Weltanschauung* of the enquirer. The atheist-materialist-marxist, the agnostic-liberal, the undogmatic Christian, the dogmatic Catholic will each provide a different answer. This fact might of itself render illusory any hope of agreement on so capital a subject were we to insist on a thorough-going definition of our criteria and a rigid formulation of their consequences. Yet, the door remains open for some kind of compromise or common ground of all doctrines;

and it is as a contribution to this compromise that the following observations are put forward.

The atheist-materialist-marxist asserts that there is no life after death; the believer puts this life after death as the forefront of his philosophy. We need not decide the point. If we base our conclusions on the assumption that we do not know and do not prejudice the eschatological issue, we need conflict with neither of the two extremes and dogmatic schools. All we need is the agreement of both on the principle that every individual human being is a singular and precious unit of life with a fate of his own, and with rights and duties towards himself. True, when we come to define what this unit-of-life's chief aim is, differences appear: 'the pursuit of happiness' proclaim the fathers of the American revolution; 'the salvation of the soul' preach the fathers of the Church. Could we again bring them together on a non-commital ground? Let us define man's chief right-duty in life as that of seeking, and if possible, finding himself in experience, *i.e.* of understanding as much as he can of the world, of himself and of the true relation between the two.

This conclusion leads to the first political right of man: that of freedom to live and learn in his own way. It is a primary right, inseparable from that of merely living. For in fact when we lay down the right to live as the first and fundamental right of man, we assume that what is to live *is* a man; and therefore the right to learn by experience is no attribute super-added to, but part and parcel of the right to live which no society can deny its members.

It will be seen therefore that liberty of personal experience —with all the consequential rights that flow from it—is at the very basis of all rights of man, and that it need never be justified, but follows automatically from the very fact that man lives.

All limitations to this fundamental right must be justified before they can be accepted. They fall under three heads:

> limitations of individual liberty for the sake of the individual liberty of others;
> limitations of individual liberty for the sake of the nation;
> limitations of individual liberty for the sake of the world community.

III

If we come now to consider the first of these limitations, we might be tempted at first to dismiss all discussion of the subject on the ground that a balance could and would automatically be struck between all those equivalent rights. The matter is, however, more subtle than that. For the rights of the individual are of different qualities and values, and it is important that a scale should be set up and agreed upon so that no limitation of the higher or of the essential rights is permitted in favour of lower or less important ones.

It is clear from all that precedes, that the first right of man is to live; and that this right includes: that of living as a body, *i.e.* of ensuring his subsistence, and that of living as a mind and soul, *i.e.* of ensuring the freedom of his experience. In the exercise of their remaining rights, other individuals must not overstep the boundaries of these two primary rights, and should they attempt to do so, we know in advance that their claims cannot be legitimate.

It should be noticed that the two primary claims might, and, in fact, do enter into conflict, and not merely as between man and man, but even when one only individual is considered. For the body can be, and often is, the enemy of the mind and soul; and, particularly in our day, the trend of things favours the right to live as a body against the right to live as a spirit, or, in other words, the claims of security against those of liberty. This trend is unfortunate and decadent: a minimum guarantee against starvation is to be proclaimed as the *first* right of man; but the *foremost* right of man is a guarantee that he will be free to live his life in his own way.

IV

No other limitations of individual liberty can be admitted from the point of view of the nation than those required by the very existence and healthy life of the nation itself. Chief among them are internal order and external peace, both indispensable also for the exercise of individual liberty. But in this respect two important considerations arise:

one, mostly connected with order, touches on the administration of justice and the police; the other, mostly connected with peace, refers to the army and to military service. Order cannot be of the healthy kind which allows the free use of individual liberty if it does not rest on a wide basis of national assent. It follows that the rights of man must include: *government by the spontaneous, free and well-informed consent of the majority of the citizens, and with adequate guarantees for the freedom and opinions of the minorities. This implies objective justice and a non-political police.* The point need hardly be elaborated that, in their turn, these conditions require a *free press.* Without a free press no rights are worth the paper on which they are written.

The second point refers to the rights and duties of man with regard to international peace. When we admit the right of the nation to limit individual liberty for the sake of national defence, we have to bear in mind that nations have a way of covering under those words any designs, however aggressive, they may harbour. The problem thus created in the individual conscience was first discussed in the sixteenth century by Francisco de Vitoria in his *De Indis*. It is possible to adapt his conclusions to a modern setting. The citizen has the right, indeed the duty, to refuse military service if and when he is satisfied that the issue is against his conscience; but the decision is so grave that the citizen must not take it without listening first to the advice of the wise men. That is Vitoria's doctrine. In his day, when an orthodoxy was recognised by the overwhelming majority of Europeans, the 'wise men' were eminent churchmen. In our day, we must endeavour to find some objective standard. The solution might be to lay down the right of all citizens to refuse military service in any war in which his country's side would have been declared in the wrong by a majority vote of the Security Council of U.N.

It is clear that a country ready to go to war in defiance of the international authority can hardly be expected to respect the right of its citizens to refuse service for such a war. Nevertheless the right must be stated, for it may act as a deterrent, particularly if, the war over, the statesmen responsible for its violation are made to pay for their guilt. Furthermore, persons having authentically expressed their unwillingness to serve would, if falling in the hands of the other side, be treated as friendly aliens, and not as prisoners of war.

V

The discussion of the relations between the citizen and the nation does not exhaust the problem set by the existence of these two forms of human life: nation and man. What, for instance, of the right of immigration and emigration? This question is only too often discussed with a background and an understructure of feelings which deprive it of clarity. The point of view of the nation should be borne in mind, both on grounds of theoretical justice and of practical politics. *A nation has a right to exist.* And this might well be the best moment for establishing it on objective grounds. We start from the individual as the only tangible and concrete thing there is; and we re-assert that his chief purpose in life is to find himself in experience, *i.e.* to acquire a *culture.* Instruction, information, craft, are all excellent for earning a living and as elements of culture. But culture—a merely relative concept—is the degree of realisation, of awareness of adequate relationship between himself and the world a man has reached.

Now, the nation is the best setting for most human beings to rise up the slope of culture. It is the depository of tradition, the 'cup' in which the subconscious life of a community is held and accumulated; the setting of individual experiences. This function it is which gives the nation its *raison d'être.*

It follows that the nation has the right to persevere in its being, as Spinoza would have said. And therefore it is plain that the right of moving about and settling anywhere of any one man must be balanced against the right of any nation to remain what it is or to become what it wants to become.

VI

There remain the limitations to individual liberty to be accepted in the name and for the sake of the world community. They include barriers against acts injurious to the healthy life and peace of the world community as a whole;

and checks on individual acts against nations. In both cases, it is extremely unlikely that individuals, without the backing of a powerful nation, may threaten the peace or interests of the world or of another nation; so that this section practically merges with the next.

VII

A section on the rights and duties of nations towards each other and towards the World Commonwealth should be considered as an integral part of the projected Charter. This field has been already covered twice; by the Covenant of the League of Nations and by the Charter of U.N. Neither recognised the existence of the World Commonwealth, the logical outcome of the World Community. The problem turns on the issue of national sovereignty.

This issue is too often simplified into what is known as 'surrender' of national sovereignty to a higher authority. Such a thing can never happen except under duress as the outcome of a defeat. National sovereignty can be enlarged so as to include wider territories and populations, but only when the awareness of a common solidarity and destiny is so enlarged first. Surely this is a process which *must happen in life*; no 'Charter' can bring it about. The projected charter should therefore be limited to a modest outline of the rights and duties between nations and the co-operative of sovereignties U.N.O. may be said to represent.

On Human Rights

John Lewis

IT is now generally held that the conception of absolute, inherent and imprescriptible rights based on man's orgins and nature and antecedent to society, is not only a myth but involves a misleading conception of the meaning of human rights.

A more satisfactory approach would consider rights as based upon human needs and possibilities and the recognition by members of a society of the conditions necessary in order that they may fulfil their common ends.

The original view was appropriate to the eighteenth century and its rising industrialist class; the second view, which includes what is of value in the first, arises with the broad popular demands for social justice and human betterment characteristic of the nineteenth and twentieth centuries.

Rights are claimed when in the course of social development a section of the community whose strength and importance is increasing finds its needs circumscribed by the restrictions imposed upon it by a privileged class. These rights are asserted in relation to the obstacles interposed between them and the satisfaction of these needs.

In the eighteenth century the demands of the rising bourgeoisie were reinforced by appealing to the authority of 'Nature,' to a certain 'natural right' inherent in man, which could be opposed to the 'divine right' of kings and similar buttresses of privilege. The assertion of these rights had the very practical aim of widening the freedoms of an important social class in the economic sphere. In politics, they were at the mercy of the aristocratic ruling class, which used political power to interfere with their business interests. These practical needs, rather than an imaginary state of nature, are the real origin of the rights claimed, and their only validity.

But the challenge to such bourgeois rights can come not only from the existing ruling class, whose privileges are thus diminished, but from below. In England, America and France the demands of the bourgeoisie were expressed in terms which aroused hope and insistent claims which seriously threatened the very rights of property, at that time being with difficulty established.

When at a later period these claims are conceded under popular pressure the resulting reforms are felt by the propertied class as a diminution of their rights and a restriction of the area of liberty, a loss of the very rights formerly won. The anxiety therefore of many people today is to set a limit to the encroachment of government on individual liberty and the rights of property.

We see therefore that in their origin 'natural rights', while they have an appearance of being general and absolute, are really particular (defending or asserting concrete needs) and strictly relative to the occasion. They are not general rights appertaining to man as such, under all conditions and for all time.

The view of 'natural rights' first set forth by T. H. Green regards them as *the assertion of human purposes to be fulfilled in the future* rather than characteristics belonging to man as such; and so far from believing them to exist prior to society and to require society in order that they may be safeguarded, he holds that they arise out of society and broaden with the development of society.

Such rights cannot be considered as permanent and absolute. They are by their very nature constantly changing with human needs and widening opportunity. They do not look back to what is eternal and unchanging but forward to what changing circumstances require. These are *rights to pursue and realise values*. The supreme right to human freedom becomes then not mere absence of restraint, the detachment of the individual *from* all relations and bonds, but freedom *to* achieve things, made possible only (a) by the overcoming of obstacles, (b) by assuming the obligations of co-operative effort.

The historical circumstances in which the 'rights of man' were first advanced required a demand for more individual freedoms and less government interference. This has given a permanent cast to the idea of human rights, which persists, although we have long ago entered a new period in which the rights of property are not the most important and in which new functions are found for government every year. We know today, what was not clearly realised then, that society is not a social contract to secure property rights but an organism through which men pursue a common good to be shared. We now know that rights are not invaded and lessened by social obligations and common enterprises, but are only made effective *through* acceptance of social duty. This is well seen in the constraints willingly accepted by players in an orchestra, through which alone the achievement of a performance is possible. In such a performance the individual himself achieves self-realisation not possible in the freedom of complete isolation.

Such rights have, as their correlative, duties. If we are to have our rights, others must accept duties; if others are to have rights, we owe them duties. If we have a right to education, then our parents have the duty to see that we are educated. If we have the right to health, then society has the duty of preventing infectious disease. Rights and duties are inseparable. We have to recognise that, since the rights we claim are claimed by all, we can only obtain them through accepting a common task and common responsibilities.

It is essential therefore to break free from a formulation of the doctrine of human rights which separates them from joint activity and does not think of them as reflecting changing and developing human needs.

As Whitehead says, freedom is 'the practicability of purpose'; but our purposes are only made practicable by accepting certain limitations on absolute individual freedom; in the first place freedom is not escape from organisation, it depends on organisation. In the second place the needs with which man is most urgently concerned are unobtainable without the final destruction of certain long-established sectional and individual freedoms—the freedom to own slaves, for instance.

A comparison of the American Bill of Rights of the earlier

period with the Economic Bill of Rights, embodied in Roosevelt's message to Congress in January 1944, is instructive. The earlier Bill thinks exclusively in terms of what fields might not be invaded by the sovereign power in the life of the individual. Thus Article IV: 'The right of the people to be secure in their persons, houses, papers and effects, etc.' Roosevelt's Bill on the other hand speaks of 'the right to earn enough to provide adequate food, clothing and recreation.'

The more limited aims of these earlier 'rights,' however, must not obscure the fact that they came to have a wider significance. Firstly, the commercial interests of these times were in harmony with the general interests, and the freedoms demanded by this section of society increased the freedom of everyone and the general well-being. Secondly, the individual safeguards against the invasion of their rights are of permanent value. They are now however indefeasible.

As society developed, the wider aims which grew out of bourgeois rights and to which indeed they always pointed— life as well as liberty, the pursuit of happiness as well as the sacredness of property, were more insistently urged and were found to be in conflict with the narrower middle-class rights.

The result was that to fulfil these wider aims the earlier rights had actually to be attacked. To take an example: the rights of man included the right to property; property once consisted of negro slaves as well as the land they cultivated; but the wider conception of the rights of man requires the abolition of slavery, which involves the violation of property rights. Today the more the rights of man are seen to be the right to achieve wide human ends, the more it becomes apparent that earlier rights standing in the way of these wider social aims must be overridden, and are not final and absolute. This is not a mere opposition of incompatible rights, however; firstly, because the gain is infinitely greater than the loss; secondly, because the realisation of these aims requires and points to a social order lying beyond the slave order and all forms of exploitation in which the welfare of the emanicipated is harmful to no other section of the community. Such an order will exclude not only slavery, but capitalism. Under capitalism the rights of workers and the interests of employers frequently conflict. The aim of social organisation should be to secure an identity of self-interest and the interests of others. We achieve this in many human associations, clubs, families, colleges, musical societies, sports organisations, etc. It by no means follows, as well-intentioned people hope, that it is as easy to obtain in industry today. Hard experience may show a fundamental clash of interests in a fully developed capitalism like our own. The task of finding the correct pattern of social and industrial organisation within which all interests are potentially harmonious is one which involves us in the controversy for and against socialism. Socialists contend that such an order cannot be brought into existence without the abrogation of eighteenth century property rights. A public water supply is a common project, in which the good of each is identical with the good of all, and within the system no one suffers. Yet to establish the system it may have been necessary to override private pumping rights and it certainly requires limitations and invasions of private rights when it comes to laying pipes and mains, making regulations and fixing charges. All this is clear in simple cases and in principle, but not to most people in the general economic field.

II

Turning now to the document proposed by UNESCO,[1] the central issue will be found to be wrongly posed. The result is not, as intended, to make a reconciliation possible. It creates an irreconcilable contradiction.

An attempt is made so to formulate two contrasting views of human rights as to show that they are really complementary, and then to unite them eclectically. (This is quite wrongly described as an example of Marxian dialectic! It is not even Hegelian.) Neither view however is correctly set forth. This is because a confusion exists between the conception of 'natural rights' as the inalienable possession of man, as absolute principles which man gradually comes to recognise; and rights as goals, as arising concretely and

---

[1] See Appendix I

historically as different classes rise to importance and power. This is understood where the document itself refers to 'the rise of early capitalism' as giving rise to those rights, but is missed when elsewhere the same rights are spoken of as absolute and imprescriptible.

Clearly if the absolute rights of the eighteenth century are to be maintained there is no reconciliation possible, only a hopeless conflict, a permanent antagonism of interests. On the other hand, if rights are seen as human striving for the satisfaction of needs, the whole problem becomes tractable. To exalt the needs of the rising commercial class of the eighteenth century into permanent rights for all time, leads straight to conflict when another class seeks in due course its own historic aims and finds them in contradiction with the rights of its predecessors or when the aims and welfare of society as a whole are found to be incompatible with the rights of capital. This is clearly brought out when we consider some of the formulations in greater detail.

i. *Eighteenth century freedom 'by no means guaranteed economic or social freedom'*[1]

This is correct. The freedoms sought in the eighteenth century, although they carried wider implications, were essentially limited. The aims sought by those mainly responsible for advancing these demands did not include the lofty ideals of Rousseau. Both in America and France, after the defeat of the main enemy of the revolutionary commercial classes and farming interests, energetic steps were taken to see that the revolution did not continue. (For example, the 'whiff of grapeshot' of 1795.) The wider freedoms do not so much arise out of the bourgeois demands of 1788 as reflect the new needs of the growing working class. The *actual* rights first fought for in the eighteenth century were from the first inconsistent with the rights of the workers, and were felt to be so on both sides. Indeed the more the industrialist made good his rights and achieved his liberties, the more helpless and exploited the worker became. 'Rights'

---

[1] See Appendix I

and 'liberties' meant not only freedom for industry but the disappearance of old safeguards and restrictions which protected labour, the 'freeing' of the peasant from the land and the artisan from his hand loom. The 'free' wage contract between the propertyless and the property owner was a leonine contract. Therefore when social reforms are at last won, it is after a hard fight with the libertarians, and at the expense of such freedoms. New freedoms are appearing—freedom from long hours and hunger, the freedom afforded by some measure of security and so forth which can only seem to the employer to be the lessening of freedom—of *his* freedom. Reform is at the expense of bourgeois freedom and is attacked as 'grandmotherly legislation', 'government interference', 'loss of liberty' and so on.

So far is the new freedom from being a mere extension of the old that the more you have of one, the less you have of the other.

And far from being essentially the same—the one just another form of the other—the old is essentially *negative*, the right not to be interfered with; the new is *positive*, the right to overcome any obstacle, even the most sacred 'rights', which stand in the way of human welfare. That is why today the controls which ensure that millions have a sufficiency of rations at reasonable prices and without which there would be starvation at one end of the social scale and luxury at the other seem to the privileged nothing but a wanton interference with their liberty. Therefore the earlier rights, so far from being the source of the later rights, have become their main obstacle, and will remain so if they are considered as inalienable, as absolute. It is only when they are seen as a stage in the development of human freedom, as establishing certain important principles and pointing forward to wider freedoms, as giving place to quite different principles in a later age, that the old and the new can come to terms.

We must therefore re-define our terms. Liberty must be conceived in terms of the values of the masses who lack them and demand them. Hence the obstacles to their achievement of such aims become the centre of attention. The removal of such obstacles becomes the achievement of liberty and the vindication of human rights.

ii. *Soviet Russia misses the phase of individual freedom but may eventually come to recognise its importance.* *It does call attention to 'one new right, freedom from exploitation'* [1]

Soviet Russia is not at all likely to accept at any time the typical *laissez-faire* principle of liberty, which is the purely *negative* form of freedom, reflecting the desire of the bourgeoisie to escape from interference in economic matters by a semi-feudal government representing other interests than theirs. Indeed it believes that by finally repudiating such principles it attains a greater personal, social and economic freedom, and that only in such a society is political freedom a reality. This is the freedom of a planned economy, which can work to capacity without inevitable crises, and which is driven by a far more effective motive than that of selfishness, namely, a common good which all share. Nor does it lose what is of value in the old libertarian conception, for those are included, not denied, in the wider freedoms. The individual freedoms thus achieved include the freedom to work, social security, equal opportunity, etc. There is no essential freedom that is lost in the process; the only loss of freedom is to the industrialist and the kulak, whose right to employ others for their profit is taken away. The Russian citizen would say that, by excluding certain eighteenth century freedoms, he attains the freedoms we seek but only partially achieve, because obstructed at every turn by the freedom of property, freedom from government interference.

And now what is this solitary freedom which Russia has discovered? It is freedom *from* exploitation. But in the Russian Constitution this is put in a different way. They say that freedom *to* exploit has been taken away. It is this *cancellation of freedom* which is the condition of a vast range of new freedoms, not one only. Now that being so they are not likely to come eventually to recognise the value of the freedom to exploit, and reinstate it.

This prohibition will not 'wither away', nor are any of the other essential prohibitions on which Soviet liberties rest. *They are the permanent condition of those liberties.*

These conditions are plainly laid down in the Soviet

---

[1] See Appendix I

Constitution. They are the obligation to work, the *abolition* of capitalism, the *abrogation* of the right to own land privately, and the *abolition* of exploitation.

Such *permanent limitations of freedoms* hitherto regarded as sacred seem to many indefensible, but, as Bernard Shaw says: 'All civilisation is based on a surrender of individual liberty in respect of totalitarian agreements to do or not to do certain fundamental things.'

There is no question of any of them being withdrawn or of any opportunity being given for overthrowing them, since they are the *sine qua non* of all the liberties that matter.

This is what has to be seen before the question of political liberty can be considered. This vast social change is comparable with the foundation of democratic government in Europe and America. On such changes we do not go back. You cannot unscramble the eggs. We do not contemplate a reversion to a slave society or to cannibalism or to feudalism or to grand monarchy. And socialism cannot contemplate the possibility of a return to capitalism. It is the one closed question, just as in the United States to return to subjection to the British Crown is a closed question.

Until such advances have been completely consolidated, all freedom to agitate for a return is denied. Such consolidation is possible and is eventually achieved if it is the kind of change which does not leave interests permanently conflicting. That *was* the case under fascism, it was *not* the case when Britain expelled the Stuarts or when America broke free from Britain. In the latter two cases therefore the wounds are healed and the issue becomes a dead one. In a socialist society the dispossessed class is not exploited. It becomes unnecessary and dies out. Therefore no class within the new society suffers exploitation. Therefore the wounds can heal. The intractable are merely refusing their rights in the new order because they would prefer to deny others theirs in the old. The black market operator has no real grievance. Society can get on without him. Society offers him the same chance of working for and profiting by the common good as everybody else; but he refuses.

Therefore the new conditions can be gradually accepted, so that it finally becomes unnecessary to *enforce* them. But the freedom to re-open the question is never restored. It becomes academic.

The victory of bourgeois democracy in Europe and America was in this way achieved by the Cromwellian, the Jacobin and the Washingtonian dictatorships. This involved the forcible and final suppression of unrepresentative and tyrannical government. Every constitutional government retains the right to prevent the subversion of its constitution. Only when there is no serious danger are extremists allowed a certain latitude. This is seen in the unrepealed Sedition Laws of George III, still on occasions invoked, 'to prevent the established institutions of the state from being brought into hatred and contempt,' and in the American Espionage Act against those who 'wilfully utter, print, write or publish any disloyal, profane, scurrilous or abusive language about the form of government of the United States or the Constitution.'

Professor E. H. Carr has indeed pointed out that the toleration by a democracy of any movement for its overthrow can justly be regarded as implying a disbelief in democracy rather than an exceptionally fervent faith in it. Hence in liberated Europe, which unlike Britain and America, has known what it is to lose democracy and fall under the yoke of fascism, the permanent exclusion of fascism is generally accepted as essential to democracy.

Maritain concedes without hesitation the right of the State 'to resist the spread of lies and calumnies; to resist the spread of ideas which have as their aim the destruction of the State and of the foundation of common life' as not only consistent with democracy but as necessary for its preservation.

In the Soviet Union they are in the same way preserving their own society, the foundations of *their* common life, and they do not regard the political measures necessary, and the final exclusion of parties and principles hostile to what they regard as civilisation itself, to be in any way a departure from the principles of liberty or a restriction of freedom.

III

The particular questions covered by (B) SPECIAL in the Document[1] are really covered by what has been said

---

[1] See Appendix I

above. But it may lend clarity to some of these arguments if one or two of these questions are taken up.

Limitations to Freedom of Speech and Freedom of Opinion

Such limitations as we have already mentioned do not imply a *general* control of opinion or general censorship of the press, the repression of every kind of divergence from official policy and of all criticism. It is a *limited* repression, which does not apply at all to ordinary people. The point is that all societies ban subversive and anti-social minorities when the political situation is unstable or the minority a real menace. Such coercion is relaxed just so far as the danger recedes. But there is unlimited discussion and criticism *within* the society which is thus preserved, *e.g.* all of Mill's principles of liberty would operate, because none of these were concerned with the establishing or the overthrow of society but only with what goes on within it.

The new democratic order, which removes from the political, financial, industrial and civil control of all concerns and institutions an owning class, achieves and preserves a much wider measure of freedom of expression by doing so than existed under such class rule. The permanent exclusion of control over opinion by such elements removes the obstacles to the fullest expansion of real freedom of expression. It does not curtail the total quantity of such freedom, it increases it. 'The right to accurate information' is more fully satisfied if the power to control the sources of information is denied to capitalist groupings and if the control of broadcasting is similarly taken from the narrow and unrepresentative circles who exercise it at present.

If it is asked who then is to control the press, the answer is: any kind of association you like except a minority whose class and economic interests are hostile to the general welfare.

The existence of the *formal* right to freedom of expression which we now possess masks the absence of the *reality*.

> *e.g.* the limitation of Marxist publishers to one half of
> one per cent of the paper available for books;
> the immense financial resources needed to start a
> full-size paper;

the *proportion* of time allotted to the Left for broadcasting, and other methods of censorship.

A nominal freedom, an occasional opportunity to broadcast, exonerates the governing class from the charge of suppressing the other side. In point of fact the overwhelming weight of government and ruling class propaganda is calculated easily to cancel out any impression which may have been made by occasionally allowing the 'left' to make its voice heard. Even this limited freedom only exists on sufferance. Under conditions of emergency it disappears. *The right to limit freedom of expression to any extent deemed necessary is the prerogative of every liberal government in the world.*

This is clearly seen in war. It is also seen in such cases as India, Malaya, Palestine, etc. The best example is denazification in Germany, which in specific terms aims at 'preventing Nazi propaganda in any form, and removing of Nazism from German information services and media— such as the press, radio, the theatre, and entertainment, and also from education and religion.'

What then are *the theoretical grounds* of freedom of speech? Freedom of speech, freedom of assembly, association, access to information, organisation of political parties, etc, are necessary if the masses of the people are to obtain and effectually to use political power to attain human goals. This necessity is the sole ground of these rights.

'*The practical extent*' of such rights will be limited only by the strength of those elements which are able to resist the popular forces. Hence their extent is seriously limited in capitalist countries today. Where such elements are finally excluded from all power, the practical extent of such rights is unlimited.

'*The guarantees*' of such freedom are then the permanent exclusion of parties and opinions whose avowed aims are incompatible with the realisation of social democracy. Only the removal of such obstacles makes the power of the people effective and enables them to fulfil the programme of true democracy.

The successful utilisation of political power for this end is a further guarantee that it will not be relinquished.

It is an *effective* democracy, making real social progress, that endures. It is that half-democracy, which baulks at obstacles and allows itself to be compelled by class intimidation to leave its major tasks undone, that is swept aside by reaction, because the people have no good cause to believe in it. But effective democracy is the democracy which fulfils its social and economic aims and does not stop short with the achievement of formal political rights.

But the 'practical extent' of democracy must also be widened to bestow the first elements of political democracy upon those communities which do not yet possess it, the negroes of the Southern States of America, the unenfranchised Indians and natives of South Africa, and other colonial territories, and by the return of these rights to those communities which have been deprived of them or among which they exist in merely nominal form (Spain, Portugal, China).

Democratic rights cannot however be extended to those parties which exist to destroy them and hence frequently attempted to do so. It may subsequently be found that sections of society now enjoying economic privileges intend to interpose permanent obstacles to the full attainment of social democracy. Should that happen, they will place themselves in precisely the same position, as far as social democracy is concerned, that fascism occupies in relation to political democracy.

There can however be no limitation of the extent of democracy determined by differences of opinion as to how democratic aims are to be attained, and there must be room for all parties who pursue such aims. Limitation only comes into effect when it becomes clear that some parties or sections of opinion do not intend that democratic aims shall be achieved. The question then arises whether the barrier to all future democratic advance is to remain or be removed.

The more negative freedoms, such as freedom from want, exploitation and insecurity, etc, are based on the positive freedoms, which the document does not emphasise because it is thinking throughout in libertarian terms.

The positive freedoms are the right to work, to health, to personal property, to justice, to full opportunity, etc.

These stress what men want freedom *to do*, the former think of freedom as protection *from* some invasion of man's rights. The 'grounds' of such positive rights are simply man's personal values, constituting what Aristotle called 'the good life'; the 'extent' is limited only to such goods as can be shared, *i.e.* which all can enjoy without excluding others; its 'guarantee' is the final removal of social privilege based on private ownership of the means of life. Its further guarantee is the perpetuation of common ownership.

IV

Conclusion. Here we show in what way opposing views of democracy and democratic rights are compatible and what forms are incompatible with the fulfilment of human aims.

All agree upon the validity of the human rights to 'life, liberty and the pursuit of happiness' set forth in the eighteenth century, and to the fundamental rights of political democracy. The task still remains to extend these everywhere. We are still in the position of having to defend them against violent overthrow and to restore them where they have been lost.

All are agreed that such rights have not to be diminished or cancelled but on the contrary used energetically and continuously.

But the earlier emphasis—the 'liberal' emphasis,—misses the promise of social emancipation involved in such rights. Only in our century, because economic development for the first time makes it possible, and not only possible but necessary, can the fulfilment of human rights be properly placed upon the agenda of reform. Hence today we stress the next development in the struggle for human rights—social democracy, the right to control the external world, economic power and natural resources, for human welfare, the right to secure opportunity, health, education, cultural enjoyment, etc.

But just as the first period of struggle for rights was a period of political conflict, which only ended with the final defeat of autocracy, so the second period also proves to be a period of struggle. This struggle itself consists of two stages:

(a) the stage of compromise, in which social and property rights are compelled to make mutual concessions. The general result, however, is the pushing back of negative libertarian and property rights and the advance of social rights at their expense;

(b) the stage where compromise is more difficult, because property sees its very existence threatened and social reform finds that the solution of its most urgent and desperate problems, economic security, freedom from starvation, the end of economic wars, requires a more comprehensive and complete annulment of older property rights than had ever been contemplated.

This brings mankind to the same position socially, *vis à vis* property, as was formerly taken up politically, *vis à vis* autocracy. In the first case human rights could not be established without the final defeat of autocracy; in the second case human rights cannot be fulfilled without the final defeat of liberalism, *i.e.* the absolute rights of capital. In both cases it is social development leading to a new and critical situation that poses the question and makes it urgent.

Political advance required the removal of those parties and elements which were unquestionably bent upon the prevention of political freedom. Today the same position holds with regard to those sections of the community whose interests unquestionably conflict with those of the community, are inconsistent with democratic purposes and therefore implacably hostile to real democracy.

As Lincoln said, 'In fundamental things severe difference may destroy the community. A house divided against itself cannot stand.' Lincoln referred to slavery and himself looked forward to 'a new birth of freedom,' even if it required death as its prelude, a freedom which in his own words 'would lift the weight from the shoulders of all men.' This is what he called the great task remaining, the unfinished work.

So, for us, history decrees that the period of concessions

and compromise (which in the slave controversy for so long postponed a final settlement), must end.

The reason is not impatience but the plain fact that the overwhelming magnitude of the world crisis and the imminence of the perils it brings with it cannot permit us to endanger the very existence of civilisation by allowing sectional interests finally to block the way to the only means of salvation. It is as though a private interest insisted on some legal right to turn off the water supply needed to extinguish a raging fire, or as if the winning of the war against Nazism were dependent upon the removal of some political influence putting its own interests before the safety of the country—a state of affairs that actually existed in more than one country.

All previous advance has really been towards democracy; we have passed through the stages leading to it. We do not possess it yet. The crisis can only be solved with full democracy; that is, with the final release of popular power to control economic resources and to accomplish human ends. That requires the entire removal of all sectional interests whose aim it is to prevent or paralyse popular power.

We have discussed the 'extent' of democracy. As Professor Carr has recently pointed out, an essential of full democracy is *mass participation* in political, social and economic affairs. Sir Ernest Barker has described the main function of democracy to be the enlisting of the effective thought of the whole community in the operation of discussion. Our democracy is limited because lack of effective control results from division of effective power, *i.e.* from the clash of hostile sections of the community, and that again rests on a division of ownerships and interests. Soviet democracy, because it excludes all power and interests conflicting with social aims, can and does set the whole community on to the job of running the show. Socialism needs the whole-souled co-operation of the masses. Not alone opposition but even indifference is fatal to it. 'What we build,' said Zhdanov, 'cannot be built with passive people.'

It seems likely that our own problems cannot be solved with passive people, that indifference will be fatal for us too, and that only the fulfilment of the essential conditions of full democracy will give us the freedom, the understanding, the responsibility and the power to overcome the dangers which now confront us.

Liberal democracy does not in principle allow absolute liberty; on the contrary, it accepts the principle of excluding absolutely whatever in essence is hostile to and inconsistent with political democracy. Communist democracy makes no different claims. There may of course be considerable difference as to what may or may not come under this ban. That does not affect the principle.

Communist democracy, which is simply social democracy fully developed, also bans whatever is fundamentally inconsistent with human rights. Here again the question whether capitalism is inconsistent with human rights is a debatable one, but that does not affect the principle that what *is* inconsistent and finally prevents their realisation must go. Neither this nor any other disagreement on when and what to ban implies a rejection of the principle.

That being so, we do not, on the one hand, regard the liberal suppression of anti-democratic movements as a departure from principle due to pressure of circumstances, so that eventually the ban will be lifted and principle restored. Nor do we, on the other hand, regard communist suppression of anti-democratic classes and privileged groups as inconsistent with democracy though perhaps excusable in an emergency. On the contrary, it is allowable in princ- ciple where justified by the circumstances. Of course there will inevitably be considerable difference of opinion whether in any case the circumstances do justify such action. But even total disagreement on the latter issue implies no disagreement on the principle.

If, on the other hand, it is held that to apply it at all is a surrender of principle, then we are on opposite sides of the fence. Those who seek to excuse advanced democracy on the grounds that they have only temporarily given way on principle are on very weak ground and only succeed in strengthening the case of those who sincerely believe that the very essentials of democracy have been betrayed. The advanced democacies will not go back on this issue or give any ground for beliving that their action is only a temporary measure.

That is why it is necessary to secure agreement on the essential point that the basic principle is maintained by both political democrats and advanced social democrats.

On the Philosophy of Human Rights

Jacques Maritain

THE effects of the historic evolution of humanity and of the advance—be it never so precarious—of moral consciousness and reflection, have resulted in men apprehending today more clearly than heretofore, though still very imperfectly, a certain number of practical truths about their life together, on which they can reach agreement, but which, in the thought of the different groups, derive, according to types of mind, philosophic and religious traditions, areas of civilisation and historical experience, from widely different, and even absolutely opposed, theoretical concepts. Though it would probably not be easy, it would be possible to arrive at a joint statement of these *practical conclusions*, or in other words, of the various rights recognised as pertaining to the human being as an individual and a social animal. But it would be quite useless to seek for a common *rational justification* of those practical conclusions and rights. That way lies the danger either of seeking to impose an arbitrary dogmatism, or of finding the way barred at once by irreconcilable divisions. While it seems eminently desirable to formulate a universal Declaration of Human Rights which might be, as it were, the preface to a moral Charter of the civilised world, it appears obvious that, for the purposes of that declaration, *practical* agreement is possible, but *theoretical* agreement impossible, between mind and mind.

Now that these basic truths have been made clear, I have less hesitation in saying that as a philosopher I am concerned with the principles as much as, and more than, with the conclusions, and with the rational justification of human rights as much as, and more than, with a more or less effective practical agreement thereon. In embarking on the question of that rational justification, I am fully aware that, viewing things from a certain philosophic standpoint, which is for me the true one, I cannot hope for the agreement of those who hold to other philosophic principles.

I disagree with the view that the eighteenth century's concept of human rights was an extension to the individual of the idea of the Divine right of kings or of the indefeasible rights which God granted to the Church. I should be more inclined to say that that concept ultimately traces its ancestry from the long history of the idea of natural law and of the law of nations evolved by the ancient world and the Middle Ages, and more immediately springs from the one-sided distortion and rationalistic petrifaction which those ideas, to their great despite, have undergone since the time of Grotius and the birth of a mechanistic ratiocination. Thus there arose the fatal misconception of natural law —which is interior to the creature and precedes any explicit expression—as a *written* code to be proclaimed to all, whereof every just law would be a copy and which would decide *a priori* every detail of the norms of human conduct on lines claiming to be dictated by Nature and Reason, but in fact arbitrary and artificial. Moreover, the end of the matter was that the individual was deified and all the rights to which he was deemed entitled were looked on as the absolute and unlimited rights of a god.

To my mind, any attempt at rational justification of the idea of human rights, as of the idea of right in general, requires that we rediscover in its true metaphysical connotations, in its realistic dynamism and in its humble dependence on nature and experience, that concept of the natural law which was defaced by the rationalism of the eighteenth century. We then understand how an ideal order, with its roots in the nature of man and of human society, can impose moral requirements universally valid in the world of experience, of history and of facts, and can lay down, alike for the conscience and for the written law, the permanent principle and the primal and universal norms of right and duty.

Simultaneously we understand how the natural law calls for completion, according to the needs of time and circumstance, by the contingent dispositions of human law; how the human group's awareness of the obligations and rights implicit in the natural law itself evolves slowly and painfully in step with the evolution of the group, and despite all errors and confusions yet definitely advances throughout history along a path of enrichment and revelation which has no end. Here we see the immense influence of economic and social conditioning and, in particular, the importance for the men of today of the new viewpoints and new problems, transcending liberal or bourgeois individualism and touching the social values of human life, which are being brought to birth by the crises and catastrophes of the capitalist economy and the emergence into history of the proletariat.

No declaration of human rights will ever be exhaustive and final. It will ever go hand-in-hand with the state of moral consciousness and civilisation at a given moment in history. And it is for that reason that even after the major victory achieved at the end of the eighteenth century by the first written statement of those rights, it remains thereafter a principal interest of humanity that such declarations should be renewed from century to century.

Lastly, a reasonable concept of natural law allows us to understand the intrinsic differences distinguishing natural law as such, the law of nations, and positive legislation. We then see that any declaration of human rights necessarily involves a concatenation of rights differing in degree, of which some meet an absolute requirement of the natural law, such as the right to existence or the right to profess, without interference by the State, the religion one believes true (liberty of conscience), others responding to a need of the law of nations, based on natural law, but modified in application by human law and the requirements of 'common use' or the common good, such as the right to own property or the right to work—others again meeting an aspiration or desire of the natural law confirmed by positive law, but with the limitations required by the common good, such as the liberty of the press or more generally liberty of expression, freedom of exposition, and freedom of association. These last types of liberty cannot be erected into absolute rights, but constitute rights (conditioned by the common good) which any society that has attained a condition of political justice is required to recognise. It is modern liberalism's misfortune to have made that distinction impossible for itself, and thus to have been obliged either to contradict itself or to have recourse to hypocrisy, in order to limit the practical exercise of rights which it has confused with the fundamental natural rights and which theoretically it proclaimed as absolute and sacrosanct.

The concept of natural law has been so much abused, so much pulled about, distorted, or hypertrophied that it is hardly surprising if, in our age, many minds declare themselves weary of the whole idea. Yet they must admit that since Hippias and Alcidamas, the history of human rights and the history of the natural law[1] are one, and that the discredit into which positivism for a period brought the concept of natural law inevitably involved similar discredit for the concept of human rights.

Certainly, as Mr Laserson wrote recently: 'The doctrines of natural law must not be confused with natural law itself. The doctrines of natural law, like any other political and legal doctrines, may propound various arguments or theories in order to substantiate or justify natural law, but the overthrow of these theories cannot signify the overthrow of natural law itself, just as the overthrow of some theory or philosophy of law does not lead to the overthrow of law itself. The victory of juridical positivism in the nineteenth century over the doctrine of natural law did not signify the death of natural law itself, but only the victory of the conservative historical school over the revolutionary rationalistic school, called for by the general historical conditions in the first part of the nineteenth century. The best proof of this is the fact that at the end of that century the so-called "renaissance of natural law" was proclaimed.'

It remains true that a positivist philosophy based on observed facts alone, or an idealistic or materialistic philosophy of absolute Immanence is powerless to establish the existence of rights inhering by nature in the human being, antecedent and superior to written laws and agreements between governments, which the civil community is

---

[1] *Cf* Heinrich A. Rommen, *Die Ewige Wiederkehr des Naturrechts* (Leipzig, Hegner, 1936); Eng. transl. *The Natural Law*, Herder, St. Louis, 1947

required, not to *grant*, but to *recognise* and enforce as universally valid, and whose abolition or infringement no consideration of social utility can even for a moment authorise. Such a concept cannot logically seem other than a superstition to these philosophies. It is valid and rationally defensible only if the rule of nature as an aggregate of facts and events includes and invents a rule of nature in the form of Being transcending facts and events, and itself based on an Absolute greater than this world. If there be no God, the only reasonable policy is that 'the end justifies the means'; and, to create a society where man shall finally enjoy his full rights, it is today permissible to violate any right of any man if this be necessary for the purpose in hand. It is an irony stained with blood to think that, for the revolutionary proletariat, the atheist ideology is a heritage from the most 'bourgeois' representatives of the bourgeoisie, who, after calling on the God of the Deists that they might base their own demands on the natural law, rejected that God and the God of the Christians alike when they were come to power and sought to free the all-embracing exercise of proprietary rights from the shackles of the natural law, and to close their ears to the cry of the poor.

I think that two further general remarks are necessary. Firstly the family group is, under the natural law, anterior to the civil society and to the State. It would thus be important in a declaration of rights to indicate precisely the rights and liberties deriving under this head and which human law does no more than acknowledge.

Secondly, if it be true that the foundations of human rights lie in the natural law, which is at once the basis of duties and of rights—these two concepts being correlative—it becomes apparent that a declaration of rights should normally be rounded off by a declaration of man's obligations and responsibilities towards the communities of which he is a part, notably the family group, the civil society and the international community.

In particular, it would be important to bring into the light the obligations incumbent on the conscience of the members of a society of free men, and the right of that society to take suitable steps—through accepted institutions for the guarantee of justice and rights—to protect liberty against those who seek to use it in order to destroy it. The question was put in a form which we shall long remember by the activities of those who, before the second world war, became the propaganda tools of racialist and fascist perversion, to disrupt the democracies from within and to arouse among men the blind desire to deliver themselves from liberty itself.

On the enumeration and formulation of rights which logically follows, I take the liberty of referring the reader, for a fuller exposition of my ideas than I can give here, to the outline in my small book on *Les Droits de l'Homme et la Loi Naturelle* (Paris, Paul Hartmann), where I tried in particular to show the need of complementing the declarations of the eighteenth century by a statement of the rights of man, not only as a human and a civic personality, but also as a social personality (a part of the process of production and consumption), and especially of his rights as a worker.

I would point out, too, that many valuable suggestions and lines of thought may be found in Georges Gurvitch's essay, *The Declaration of Social Rights* (New York, Ed. de la Maison francaise, 1944).

Finally, on the special question of freedom of the press and of the means for the dissemination of thought, it seems to me impossible to deal with this fully without reference to the work of the *Committee on the Freedom of the Press*, which in the United States has during the last few years investigated exhaustively all aspects of the problem and of which I had the honour to be one of the foreign members.

Towards a Universal Declaration of Human Rights

Harold J. Laski

IT is of the first importance, if a document of this kind is to have lasting influence and significance, to remember that the great declarations of the past are a quite special heritage of Western civilisation, that they are deeply involved in a Protestant bourgeois tradition, which is itself an outstanding aspect of the rise of the middle class to power, and that, though their expression is universal in its form, the attempts at realisation which lie behind that expression have too rarely reached below the level of the middle class. 'Equality before the law' has not meant very much in the lives of the working-class in most political communities, and still less to Negroes in the Southern states of the United States. 'Freedom of Association' was achieved by trade unions in Great Britain only in 1871; in France, save for a brief interval in 1848, only in 1884; in Germany only in the last years of the Bismarckian era, and then but partially; and, in a real way, in the U.S.A. only with the National Labour Relations Act of 1935; this Act itself is now in serious jeopardy in Congress. All rights proclaimed in the great documents of this character are in fact statements of aspiration, the fulfilment of which is limited by the view taken by the ruling class of any political community of its relations to the security of interests they are determined to maintain.

It must be remembered, further, that one of the main emphases which have underlain past declarations of rights has been the presumed antagonism between the freedom of the individual citizen and the authority of the government in the political community. It is not merely that the rights of the citizens have been conceived in individualist terms, and upon the political plane. There is the deeper problem that has arisen from the unconscious, or half conscious, assumption of those who wrote the great documents of the past that every addition to governmental power is a subtraction from individual freedom. Maxims like Bentham's famous 'each man is the best judge of his own interest,' and that 'each man must count as one and not more than one' have their roots in that pattern of social organisation so forcibly depicted by Adam Smith: in which, under any 'simple system of natural liberty,' men competing fiercely with one another in economic life are led, each of them, 'by an invisible hand to promote an end which was no part of his intention,' and that end, by some mysterious alchemy, is the good of the whole community. Even if it be argued, and it is at least doubtful whether it can be argued, that this liberal pattern was ever valid, it is certainly not valid today. There are vital elements in the common good which can only be achieved by action under the state-power —education, housing, public health, security against unemployment; these, at a standard acceptable to the community in an advanced society in Western civilisation, cannot be achieved by any co-operation of citizens who do not exercise the authority of government. It becomes plain, on any close analysis, that so far from there being a necessary antagonism between individual freedom and governmental authority, there are areas of social life in which the second is the necessary condition of the first. No statement of rights could be relevant to the contemporary situation which ignored this fact.

It yet remains true that there are certain areas of life where human rights depend, in all normal circumstances, on the limitation of governmental authority. The principles underlying the writ of habeas corpus, of double jeopardy, of what the American Constitution calls 'cruel and excessive punishment,' are obvious examples of such areas. It is more difficult to define with any precision the limitations which ought to be placed upon governmental interference with rights such as freedom of speech, freedom of association, and freedom of religious belief; yet, on experience, limitations upon the power of government when such rights as these are involved are of profound importance. Each of these, however, is acquiring a new and intricate context in the light of social and economic, including technological, change. The nature of modern weapons, the power of wireless, any concentration of the ownership of the press or the cinema in private hands, may be as dangerous even more dangerous, to the fulfilment of rights than when they are in the hands of a government. General principles in these areas have little meaning except in terms of their application.

Nor must we forget that most attempts, since the classic declarations of rights at the end of the eighteenth and in the first part of the nineteenth centuries, to safeguard society against the abuse of power, especially economic power, by individual citizens have been gravely unsuccessful. This is true, for example, of the Fourteenth and Fifteenth Amendments to the American Constitution. It is true also of most of the social and economic clauses of the German Constitution of 1919; Articles 121 and 151 are examples of this. It is a pretty fair historical generalisation to say that no right is likely to have effective operation in any society unless the citizens of that society have a broadly equal interest in the results of its fulfilment; whereas, in Soviet Russia, private exploitation for profit has been abolished, it is, for example, immensely easier to prevent racial discrimination than it is in the United States of America, where both Negroid and Asiatic peoples have never been admitted to a status in which equal cultural opportunities obtain. The fact that the economic system permits them to be exploited for profit by American Whites is a powerful lever to persuade the latter to continue the discrimination now practised to their own advantage.

There is the further difficulty that we are now in the midst of a vast world-revolution which has brought with it one of those deep crises of values, both individual and social, in which, as Thucydides pointed out over two thousand years ago (Bk. II, 82-4), men ceased to understand one another because 'the meaning of words had no longer the same relation to things, but was changed by them as they thought proper.' It is obvious that 'democracy' does not mean the same thing to the chairman of the National Committee of the Republican Party in the United States as it does to Generalissimo Stalin; and it is equally obvious that each has a different conception of terms like 'freedom' and 'right.' The economic system, indeed, which the United States business man calls 'free enterprise' is unrecognisable under that description by a British socialist. The nature of the state-power itself, moreover, appears quite differently to a British socialist than it does to a British Tory. Any statement of human rights would encounter inescapable problems of understanding and interpretation which would either make it so vague as to be worthless, or so composed as to be a threat to that concept of value in any particular area it appeared to reject. It is bound to be a doubtful matter whether a Declaration of Human Rights will be universally acceptable until there is a real prospect of resolving the crisis of values before which we stand. Anyone who reads the debates, three centuries ago, in the Army Council over which Cromwell presided during the English Civil Wars will see at once that, within the confines of a national community, the assurance of peace is vital to a common recognition of values and, therefore, of rights. We are, as yet, far from having attained this assurance.

The absence of the assurance of peace on the international plane is still more striking. However true it be that there is no government in the world today which wants war, there are governments pursuing objectives which other governments would not permit them to realise except under the compulsion of defeat in war. What one government calls 'indefensible imperialist expansion' another government regards as 'necessary strategic protection.' The atmosphere of doubt and suspicion leads to the development of what may fairly be called 'client nations' whose sovereign control of their own affairs has become a myth without the power even to edify its exponents any longer. Any discussion of human rights must involve the discussion of the rights of those nations recognised as states. For their governments exercise, in greater or lesser degree, not only direct power over their own citizens, but also indirect power over the lives of the citizens of other nations. A loan from one government to another, the limits placed on emigration and immigration, the level of a tariff, currency policy, methods and amount of taxation, all these help to make differences, which may be important, in the well-being of one nation through the decisions of another. Before our eyes is the grim fact that the shortage of coal in half a dozen countries may settle problems of life and death. Unless, moreover, we agree swiftly on the international ownership and control of fissionable materials essential in atomic power, it may well become true that any territory which possesses those materials will become as grave a source of contention, in which itself it is a helpless spectator, as weak countries have become, in the last three quarters of a century, in the soil of which oil has been discovered. The assurance of peace on the plane of international relationships is a vital condition for achieving reality in any formulation of human rights.

The swift pace of change, especially of technological change, adds to the burden of our problem. It has the twofold result of intensifying inequalities within nations and between nations. On the evidence, there can be little doubt that one of the consequences of mass production in a highly industrialised community upon all save the exceptional worker is a conditioning to submissiveness and irresponsibility; and this is increased where dismissal, with the prospect of unemployment, is the penalty for any failure in the adaptation required by a machine-technology which is always seeking to reduce as much as possible the initiative the worker must contribute to the performance of his job. We are becoming increasingly aware that the less the initiative the job calls for in working, the less likely is it that the worker will desire to use his leisure creatively. He gets drugged, as it were, by the routine of monotonous repetition in the hours of work; and the effort to think, in the hours of leisure, becomes continually harder save where the worker has exceptional force of character or of intelligence. The bearing of this on education is clear. It may very easily produce workers who, unless deliberate precautions are taken, cannot, in any serious way, become responsible citizens in a democratic society. The pace and character of technological change, moreover, give the rich and highly industrialised nation an immense advantage over the poor, especially the mainly agricultural nation, whenever any issue arises which involves the possibility that force may be employed in its determination. A nation which can afford to manufacture atomic bombs, and is prepared to use them, is bound to have its way against another nation which lacks the means, financial and material, necessary to their manufacture.

In the light of such considerations as these, any attempt by the United Nations to formulate a Declaration of Human Rights in individualist terms would quite inevitably fail.

It would have little authority in those political societies which are increasingly, both in number and in range of effort, assuming the need to plan their social and economic life. It is, indeed, legitimate to go further and say that if the assumptions behind such a declaration were individualistic, the document would be regarded as a threat to a new way of life by the defenders of historic principles which are now subject to profound challenge. Its effect would be to separate, and not to unify, the groping towards common purposes achieved through common institutions and common standards of behaviour which it is the objective of such a declaration to promote.

Nothing, in fact, is gained, and a great deal may be lost, unless a declaration of this character notes the fact of important ideological differences between political societies and takes full account of their consequences in the behaviour both of persons and institutions. To attempt to gloss them over would be to ignore completely the immense changes they involve in the attitude that a socialist society, on the one hand, even a society beginning to embark on socialist experiment, and a capitalist society, on the other, is likely to take to things like private property, law, both civil and criminal, the services of health and education, the possibility of living, between certain ages, without the duty to earn a living, the place of the arts—of, indeed, culture in its widest sense—in the society, the methods of communicating news and ideas, the ways in which citizens adopt a vocation in life, the conditions of promotion in the vocation adopted, and the relation of trade unionism to the process of economic production. These are examples merely. When it is remembered that the Napoleonic Code, to take an outstanding example of law-making, set out deliberately to give the largest possible rights to the enjoyment and disposal oᵢ private property, so that the owner of a piece of real property is even safeguarded against having to recompense his tenant for improvements made by the latter; that there is, in the code, practically no protection for a contract of service; that, while usury in loans is prohibited, nothing is said of that usury which imposes excessive rents, or pays sweated wages; that trade unions and strikes are prohibited under heavy penalties, while employers are permitted to form Chambers of Commerce and their corporate agreement to enforce a lock-out of their workers is punished by the mildest of penalties; it becomes possible to understand why the French legal historial Glasson could write that 'to tell the truth, the worker was pretty completely forgotten in the Code.' Its character, indeed, could hardly have been better defined than by a phrase in the speech of Boissy d'Anglas, when, as *rapporteur*, he introduced the Constitution of the Year III to the Convention. 'A country governed by property owners,' he said, 'is a true civil society; one where men without property govern is in a state of nature.' It is only in precision of statement that the attitude here defined differed from contemporary attitudes in Great Britain or Germany or the United States. We take the social philosophies underlying the institutions to which we are accustomed so much for granted that, as de Tocqueville insisted, we confound them with eternal and unchanging truths. We are then outraged by their denial, or even by scepticism of them. Nothing is more difficult than to keep an open mind about the ultimate principles of social organisation. Yet an anthropologist who studied the habits say, of a society in Western civilisation, would frequently find that many of the 'rights' we regard as 'sacred' are not more rational than the taboos regarded with religious veneration by a savage tribe at a fairly primitive stage of social development.

Under circumstances such as these, the issue of a Declaration of Rights would be a grave error of judgment unless it set out deliberately to unify, and not to separate, men in their different political societies. It must, therefore, emphasise the identities, and not the differences, in the competing social philosophies which now arouse such passionate discussion. But even then it will have little value, even as a general expression of aspirations, unless it is both concrete enough and definite enough in character to seem clearly to possess the practical merit of being capable of application by the effort of those to whom it is addressed. It must, this is to say, be a programme and not a sermon. It must be a criterion of the actual practices of existing political countries, so framed that it is felt to be a living canon of their validity. No use, for instance, to argue today that such a declaration of human rights must insist that only in a political society where the principle of the separation of powers is regarded as sacrosanct can citizens hope to be free; for that principle was the expression of a half-truth, no doubt an important half-truth, which had special relevance to bourgeois society at a particular stage in its constitutional development, but has long ceased to have that relevance even in political communities where it is still venerated. The same is true of the 'right' to trial by jury; it is at least open to the gravest doubt whether the institution of a jury is the most effective way of arriving at a just verdict, and the more complex the evidence in the issue to be decided, the more doubtful it is whether the jury is a satisfactory instrument for arriving at the truth. Nor must we forget that it is as difficult to define a right as it is to define a crime. We can only say that behaviour is criminal when the law chooses to declare it so. But the law is not likely to be effective merely because it emanates from an organ of government formally competent to enact it. The experience of the United States in attempting to enforce Prohibition shows clearly that, in the absence of a government able, like the Nazi rulers of Germany, to terrorise its citizens into obedience, law is only likely to be effective when it elicits a pretty general consent to its purposes. What is true of law is true, also, of rights which at some stage require the power of law behind them if they are to be more than pious aspirations which do not affect the social behaviour of men.

This view has special relevance to the sphere of international relations. It is significant that, between the two world wars, no Member Nation of the League of Nations, with the partial exception of Czechoslovakia, made any serious attempt to respect the rights of those minorities within its territory it had undertaken to respect. It is significant, also, that certain states to which the League of Nations entrusted a mandate for colonial peoples did not hesitate to violate the terms upon which they had been given a mandate, without any apparent compunction. An international declaration of human rights must, in this aspect, take serious account of the fate of the Kellogg-Briand Pact which was introduced with an enthusiasm only surpassed by the contempt with which it was ignored by its signatories after the outbreak of the Italo-Abyssinian War. The danger is real that a declaration, which is written in terms too far ahead of the probable practice of governments to be expected, will deepen the mood of cynicism and disillusion which is one of the characteristics of a revolutionary age like our own. It is at least doubtful whether we can afford to risk the deepening of this mood.

It is difficult, moreover, to avoid the conclusion that was aptly formulated by Marx when he said that 'the ruling ideas of an age are the ideas of its ruling class.' From that conclusion it follows that, historically, previous declarations of rights have in fact been attempts to give special sanctity to rights which some given ruling class at some given time in the life of a political society it controlled felt to be of peculiar importance to the members of that class. It is no doubt true that they were often, even usually, written out in universal form; perhaps even their claim to the status of universality gave them a power of inspiration beyond the area in which they were intended to be effective. But it remains generally true that in their application the status of universality was always reduced to a particularity made, so far as possible, to coincide with what a ruling class believed to be in its interest, or what it regarded as the necessary limits of safe concession. That has been notably the case where there has been a formal abolition of the colour-bar; there is no limit to the ingenuity of the legislation by which the agreement to confer equal rights upon non-white persons has been evaded. Nor must it be forgotten that there are many political societies in which, on the formal plane, all the rights of democracy have been conceded without altering in a serious way the fundamental principles of the society's social and economic constitution. The fear, for example, that universal suffrage would result in the use of the private property of the rich for the benefit of the poor has been largely unfulfilled; and it is notable that, even near the middle of the twentieth century, the plebiscite, in a country like Germany, with a high standard of education, powerful trade unions, and a social democratic party with a long tradition behind it, was an invaluable weapon in the hands of the Nazi dictator and his supporters. It becomes difficult, in the light of European and American history since some such time as the French Revolution, to believe either that the institutions of political democracy are permanently safe, or that human rights essential to the life of a free man will be assured of respect, if there are wide divergencies of economic interest between citizens, if, to put it in a different way, the major division of any national society is between a class owning the instruments of production and another, invariably much larger, class which can live only by the sale of its labour-power. No doubt there are groups of persons intermediate between these two fundamental classes. No doubt, also, their interests are divided so as to obscure what is the essential cleavage even in capitalist democracy. But no one can seriously study the statistics of the increasing concentration of economic power in a few hands and above all the swift growth of that concentration in the United States of America—by so much the greatest industrial society in the world today—without seeing clearly that democratic institutions, and the human rights these are intended to safeguard, necessarily function within the limits of a framework imposed upon them by the purposes implicit in the relations of production which a concentration of economic power involves. The great industrial corporations of modern civilisation are, effectively, empires which deal with the state-power of government in a political society very much as one sovereign deals with another. The history both of Europe and of America since the French Revolution suggests that human rights are only effective either when the power of private ownership to make the profit that is the inherent necessity of a capitalist system is satisfied, or where the political solidarity of the majority of the community is so intensely felt and so strongly organised that an attempt at the invasion of rights would be successfully resisted and lead to a re-organisation of the economic foundations of a community. In the post-war world in which we find ourselves, important internal and external factors have combined to make the satisfaction of capitalist need for profit easily compatible with the realisation of human rights at the level of expectation which the workers, in any well-organised trade union movement, deem adequate. The contrast between capitalist need and democratic demand has become outstanding and momentous. This contrast is one of the major reasons for the revolutionary condition of our time. No delcaration that failed to take full account of its consequences would be more than an empty body of formulæ, receiving polite recognition but exercising no serious influence.

This is the central reason why a declaration of rights which aims at assisting the victory of social justice in the present crisis of values in our civilisation must take account of the fact that the private ownership of at least the vital means of production makes it increasingly impossible to maintain either freedom or democracy. Economic exploration, in the measurable future, is certain to be vertical, not horizontal. We have passed the frontiers of horizontal economic expansion; even in the United States internal migration has become more difficult as free land has ceased to be available. If we are, therefore, to make the relations of production in contemporary civilisation proportionable to the forces of production, the need for a basic revision of the foundations of private property, as these were conceived by all except persons of a socialist outlook, since 1789, has become imperative. Vertical expansion of production can only be obtained in a planned economy which is consciously aimed at the well-being of the whole community. Any continued reliance upon horizontal expansion, in times of private ownership, means the increasing use of the state-power to protect a privileged minority in a political community which, sooner or later, is bound to look beyond the territorial boundaries of the community both to maintain its own privileges and to satisfy the majority excluded from them. We ought to have learned this lesson from two world wars and, not least, from the implications of the history of the years between the wars. It is, for example, no use saying that there is need to recognise the right of the citizen to a secure job with adequate wages, and with reasonable leisure, if the only periods when this right has been fulfilled have been those of the two world wars. Nor is it any use proclaiming the right to adequate medical care if, first, the territorial distribution of doctors makes this unavailable to the citizen, and his standard of life does not permit him to take advantage of medical care even if it is available; no serious study of the problem of public health can fail to arrive at the conclusion that it is insoluble unless the medical profession is organised as a national service.

Freedom of speech cannot be seriously said to exist in any political society (a) in the absence of economic security, and (b) where the vital means of communication—the press, for example, the radio and the cinema—are all of them departments of big business, and tending increasingly towards monopoly in each instance. Without economic security only the very exceptional citizen will speak his full mind, for fear of losing his job; there is no safeguard for his job in a society where there is full employment; and there cannot be full employment in a capitalist society save when it is at war. A century ago, Horace Greeley could found the New York *Tribune* on a capital of a thousand dollars; today the establishment of a successful daily paper requires the expenditure of millions. Even where, as in Great Britain, radio is government owned (though in part independently controlled), unconventional opinions, in the field of religion for example, have the greatest difficulty in securing the right to be heard. It is well known that, in most countries, if the cinema is primarily a source of profit through entertainment, its second objective is propaganda in favour of the *status quo*: and far too little means exist for utilising it either as an instrument of social criticism or as one of the most promising aids to the process of education.

Freedom of speech is, in fact, largely a function of economic power; even more so is the right to freedom of association, especially in the context of industry. The right to strike, for example, is, of necessity, severely limited in any vital area of a complex economic community. A government is compelled to intervene wherever a strike endangers food or health, communications or transport. If the services which provide these goods are privately owned, the inevitable result is that government intervention, save in the most exceptional circumstances, renders the power of the strike, as a weapon of effective protection for the worker, largely null and void.

Even political freedoms, such as the right to organise a political party with a view to winning governmental power by constitutional action, or the right of the individual citizen to exercise the franchise, are largely functions of economic power. Groups in Great Britain which preached socialist principles were incapable of serious political action until they secured the support, and therefore the funds, of the great trade unions; without independent political action, their authority in the economic sphere was threatened by doctrines of the English Common Law which they could only get changed by legislative action. There are wide areas of Europe in which a free election has, in fact, never been known; as there is a number of states in the United States of America where the Negro dare not exercise his vote and the 'poor white' is excluded from the register of voters by the imposition of a poll-tax which he has not the ability to pay.

If we make the assumption that a political society is only likely to seek through its government to secure social justice for its citizens, historical experience suggests that social justice depends upon the acceptance of two inescapable principles. The first is that each citizen must be recognised to have an equal claim upon the resources of the community; the second is that, where there is differentiation in response to that claim, it must be possible to show, to the satisfaction of those differentiated against, as well as of those in whose favour the differentiation is made, that the decision to make it does in fact lead to an increase in the resources of the community, and that this, in its turn, results in an increase in the standard of well-being for each individual citizen.

If we look at modern civilisation in terms such as these, it is obvious that human rights are not likely to be realised on any adequate scale if any class enjoys special privileges, which may be defined as the receipt of an income from the effort of others without the performance of a function regarded by the community as an addition to its welfare. It is not likely to be realised in any political society where the operations of government are confined to external defence and internal order, together with the provision of a postal service and the provision of such other public services as it would not be profitable for private persons to undertake. Nor can human rights be made effective in the absence of an educational system which makes possible the full use by the citizen of his instructed judgment, and in the absence of his systematic and continuous access to truthful news about the world surrounding him.

None of these conditions is likely to be fulfilled unless citizens have an equal interest in the results of the social processes of the community to which they belong, and those processes in our own day must be regarded as not less vital in their international than in their national aspects. None of them is likely to mean very much in communities which are economically, socially, or politically backward, unless the effort to bring them forward is an organised international responsibility. None of them is likely to mean very much, either, unless the rights of minorities who are distinguished from the majority of a national community by their colour, or race, or religious creed have the assurance of international protection. But that assurance means the existence of an international organisation to give protection; and the protection then depends upon the agreement of national communities that the authority of an international organisation, in those realms where the incidence of government action in one national community reaches beyond its boundaries, has primacy over the authority of the national government. Our situation, in a word, requires a world-order to which the primary allegiance of the individual citizen must be given.

It follows from this, first, that the relations of production require fundamental revision if human rights are to be satisfied at a level which offers the prospect of peaceful development. It follows, second, that the era when the national state could claim the right to sovereignty, in order that its government should be bound by no will save its own, draws swiftly to its close. An International Declaration of Human Rights which was based on these premises and built upon these conclusions, to which men and women all over the world might look for a programme of action, would be a valuable stimulus to the recognition of the need for reforms, any long denial of which is likely to result in violent revolution here, to violent counter-revolution there, and perhaps, even more grimly, to international conflict which may easily assume the character of a global civil war. To provide the appropriate inspiration, such a declaration would have to be both bold in its general character and concrete in its detailed conduct. It would have to take account rather of the possibilities which are struggling to be born than of the traditions that are dying before our eyes. It would be better to have no declaration than one that was half-hearted and lacking in precision, or one which sought an uneasy compromise between irreconcilable principles of social action. A declaration such as is proposed would do more harm than good unless it was issued in the confident expectation that the members of the United Nations gave to it an unquestionable faith and respect. An age like our own, which has seen the impotence of the League of Nations, the contemptuous disregard of the Kellogg-Briand Pact and the cynical violation of international law and customs, and has lived under the barbarous tyranny of régimes which made torture and wholesale murder the sanctions of their policy, cannot afford another failure of so supreme a significance as this failure would mean. They have no right to offer hope to mankind who are not prepared to organise the essential conditions without which it has no prospect of being fulfilled. The next betrayal by statesmen of what the common man regards as the basis of his self-respect as a human being will be the prelude to a disaster this civilisation is unlikely to survive.

The Rights of Man and the present Historical Situation

Benedetto Cruce

DECLARATIONS of rights (of the *natural and inalienable* rights of man, to quote the French Declaration of 1789) are all based upon a theory which criticism on many sides has succeeded in destroying: namely, the theory of natural right, which had its own particular grounds during the sixteenth, seventeenth and eighteenth centuries, but which has become philosophically and historically quite untenable. Nor can we argue from the moral character of such rights, for morality recognises no rights which are not, at the same time, duties, and no authority but itself—this is not a natural fact but the first spiritual principle.

This, moreover, is already implied in the report, where it says that these rights vary *historically*; thereby abandoning the logical basis of those rights regarded as universal rights of man, and reducing them to, at most, the rights of *man in history*. That is to say, rights accepted as such for men of a particular time. Thus, they are not eternal claims but simply historical facts, manifestations of the needs of such and such an age and an attempt to satisfy those needs. As an historical fact the Declaration of 1789 had its importance, since it expresses a general agreement which had developed under European culture and civilisation of the eighteenth century (the Age of Reason, of Enlightenment, etc,) concerning the certain urgent need of a political reform of European society (including European society in America).

Today, however, it is no longer possible to realise the purpose of the Declaration, whether of rights or of historical needs, for it is precisely that agreement on the subject which is lacking and which UNESCO desires to promote. Agreement, it is obvious, is lacking in the two most important currents of world opinion: the liberal current and the authoritarian-totalitarian current. And indeed that disagreement, though moderated in its expression, may be discerned in the report I have before me.

Will this agreement be obtained? And by what means?

By the reinvigoration of the current of liberalism, whose moral superiority, power of thought and persuasion and whose political wisdom and prudence will prevail over the other current? Or will it be through a new world war which will bring victory to one or the other side, according to the fortunes of war, the course of events or Divine Providence? And would the immortal current of liberalism emerge from its opposite, should the latter be temporarily victorious?

I assume that UNESCO reckons with the first alternative or hypothesis and I need not tell you that, for my part, I am heart and soul in favour of this endeavour for which each of us is bound to work with all his energies and for which I myself have been working for nearly twenty-five years in Italy and also further afield.

If that is so, however, a working organisation such as that you invite me to and in which representatives of all currents, especially the two most directly opposed, will participate with the same rights, cannot possibly proclaim in the form of a declaration of rights, a declaration of common political action, an agreement which has no existence, but which must, on the contrary, be the ultimate outcome of opposed and convergent efforts. That is the point to be carefully considered, for it is the *weak point*.

Nor do I even see how it would be possible to formulate any half-way or compromise declaration which would not prove either empty or arbitrary. It may be that you and your colleagues, when you get to work, will discover the futility and the impossibility of it and even, if you will allow me to say so, the danger of causing readers to smile at the ingenuousness of men who have conceived and formulated such a declaration.

In my opinion, there is only one useful form of practical work for UNESCO to do: namely, a formal, public and international debate on the necessary principles underlying human dignity and civilisation. In such a debate I do not doubt that the force of logic, culture, doctrine and the possibility of fundamental agreement would secure the triumph of free minds over the adherents of autocracy and totalitarianism, who are still reduced to reiterating the same slogans and the same sophistries to catch the public ear. Once that debate was held, it would no doubt be possible to formulate a declaration of certain historical and contemporary rights and needs in some such short form as the Ten Commandments or, if it were to include details, at somewhat greater length.

Reflections on some Declarations of the Rights of Man

J. Haesaerts

THE Memorandum on Human Rights dated March 27th, 1947[1] brings out, clearly and completely, the difficulties in the way of any general declaration today. Having as its object 'to reconcile by some means the various divergent or opposing formulations now in existence,' it must be not only 'sufficiently definite to have real significance both as an inspiration and as a guide to practice,' but also 'sufficiently general and flexible to apply to all men, and to be capable of modification to suit peoples at different stages of social and political development while yet retaining significance for them and their aspirations.' Is not this what is called squaring the circle?

Moreover, all the declarations which have played a part in modern history, from the 1776 Declaration of Independence down to the Fourth French Republic's declaration of rights in 1946, have stumbled, *mutatis mutandis*, against similar difficulties. Their authors were unable, more particularly, to solve the technical problem before them, a problem which the Memorandum has very properly stressed on the present occasion.

I am not speaking of the obscurities, misconceptions and contradictions which these documents reveal. Discussion of the documents, which generally began in an atmosphere of enthusiasm, more often resulted in votes dictated by exhaustion, in which such peccadilloes were passed over. There are more serious shortcomings than these, and they represent real professional mistakes.

I would mention the following:

1. These proclamations quickly dated. They were overtaken by events and their effects betrayed the intentions of those who drafted them. Freedom of labour in the United States of America opened the way to strikes which imperilled victory and are even today prejudicing a return to normality.

---

[1] *Cf* Appendix I

The freedom of the trade unions has been marshalled against the State. The freedom of the press has become the perquisite of a few magnates who, whatever one may say, make and unmake opinion. Adjustments have everywhere been necessary: the 116,000,000 working days which they lost in 1946 will perhaps lead the Americans to revise the National Labor Relations Act and to forbid collective abandonment of work.[1]

Other provisions in the declarations have remained a dead letter. Equality has been reduced to the narrow civic equality that we know so well. Political equality has barely begun and economic equality is not considered. Resistance to oppression is hunted down wherever it appears, but oppression itself is flourishing, thanks to the crises which pursue us, and it threatens rights the possessors of which have no means of defending themselves.

These facts are sufficient proof that all the work so far done has been ineffective. It has been ineffective because no realism, no sense of law and no professional skill were brought to bear upon it.

(a) In the first place, the authors of these declarations were fired by a political passion which was still hot, or had barely cooled, and concentrated their attention upon their own special position and the times in which they lived. The Virginia Bill of Rights (1776) is steeped in a pioneering spirit, which was itself fed by religious fervour. The principles of 1789 reflect the revolt of the Third Estate. Those of 1793 reveal the mind of the pure revolutionaries who viewed with suspicion the encroachments of authority. The Belgian Constitution of 1831 was a reaction against the Dutch régime, while the preamble of the 1946 declaration reflects not only the 1940 psychosis but the 'arrival' of the masses and their contradictory aspirations, bent as they are upon both freedom and planning.

These turbulent improvisers, with their blind concentration upon themselves, did not stop to think that a charter applies to generations to come and that, although the latter may in a general way converge in the long run, their

---

[1] This measure was actually taken since the text was written. (Editor's note.)

physiognomies and structures differ. This difference produces so many surprises that it would be better, on this subject, not to commit the future in matters of detail. It is hopeless, in any case, to attempt to do so; tomorrow will have no hesitation in releasing itself from today, and the new rebels can resort to unforeseen stratagems to evade precautions taken by earlier stabilisers. What is to be done? The answer is that the rules laid down must apply to factors that are constant. I do not mean that they should crumble away in abstractions. They must remain positive, but be elastic enough to absorb change. Charters should contain only what is essential. The rest is matter for the law, for regulations and above all for jurisprudence.

Under laws and regulations there is room for second thoughts, relaxations, adaptations and resistance to abuses. In the face of this constant give-and-take between rights and their limitation, no document could succeed in drawing a demarcation line which would cover all possible cases. It requires the intelligent intervention of the man who is able to weigh all the decisive factors and imponderabilia. The important thing is therefore to establish this office of arbitrator, and to establish it in such a way that it will be effective. This is the surest means of guaranteeing that the principle will remain constant through all the vicissitudes of history and that it will be protected against malicious attacks.

The general framework of this arrangement—the drafting of the principle and the setting up of a judicial body—must therefore be sufficiently wide to command all circumstances. A standard, therefore, is likely to be preferable to a rule.

The standard is commonly known to be a form of directive. It is a compromise between the need of a right to be secured and its need to develop. It indicates, in a general way, what the legislator wants to achieve. It develops according both to the subject-matter of the standard and the rank of the legislator; the development is greater in regard to the principle than in regard to the ways in which that principle is applied; it is greater for the constitution-maker than for the ordinary lawgiver. Articles 1 and 6 of the Soviet Penal Code, as well as Article 1 of the Soviet Civil Code, are classic examples of a standard; and there are several examples in American law, especially the *due process of law* so constantly invoked.

In the case we are considering, the subject-matter represents the very basis of social life and the legislator is represented by the member of a constituent assembly. The expansion of the formula must therefore be as wide as possible, though it must not cease to be a guide; to state, as in 1848, that the Republic is based on 'public order' has no practical significance.

(b) Moreover, on the occasion of each fresh social change, the new masters have advanced their own ideals by clothing them with the name of rights. This procedure reduces the charter to the level of a programme, or even of an electoral platform; it becomes no more than a catalogue of claims, ill-assorted and impassioned; additions or deletions are made as feeling dictates. The authority of the charter is thereby undermined.

The Constitution of 1789 mentions, in somewhat of a jumble, liberty, equality, property, security, resistance against oppression, the right to take part in drawing up laws and to occupy public positions, individual freedom, freedom of opinion, and the right to fix, vote and control taxation. The Constitution of June 23rd, 1793, more social in character, adds not only the right of assembly, but freedom of work, culture and trade, the right to public assistance and the right of petition. The Belgian Constitution, which had the benefit of considerable recent experience and approached the matter more soberly, suppressed the right of resistance to oppression, circumscribed the right of petition and introduced the inviolability of domicile, the free use of languages, the inviolability of correspondence and the right of association. The 1946 Declaration incorporated the principles of 1789 as a whole, and frenziedly added, with a stroke of the pen, the right of asylum, the right to work, the right to trades union activity, the right to strike, the right to the collective fixing of working conditions, the right to the management of enterprises and to the nationalisation of the most important of them, the right to the development of the individual and the family, and the right to health, material security, rest, recreation and culture. It then surpassed itself by guaranteeing the same rights to all men and women in the French Union. At which, the lawyer, the economist and the sociologist are left breathless and aghast. These declarations seem therefore to have been mere intellectual excursions. They take no account of ways and means; for them, everything has been achieved once the formula has been drawn up in more or less clear-cut terms. No matter what trouble it causes; no matter what the state of society is, or what means are available for putting the principles into practice; all this, to these visionaries, is trifling detail. The right to work and to manage enterprises is established, no matter whether the economy perishes as a result; when finances are exhausted, the right to leisure is proclaimed; every individual receives the right to vote, even if he cannot read and write. Circumstances, however, will not be jostled, hard facts remain hard facts. Society has its traditions, and demography its laws; economics exercises its sway, and even geography has not lost all influence. And all the while the historical situation proffers or withholds a chance, as the case may be.

2. These documents do not emphasise sufficiently that there can only be rights when they are accompanied by corresponding duties. Philosophers have always been careful to make this clear. Indeed, the *National Catholic Welfare Conference*, on February 1st last, began by defining man's duties, to fulfil which, it said, he receives certain rights. This is pushing matters too far, but it does emphasise a relationship between rights and duties in the absence of which rights alone constitute a public danger. Admittedly some declarations—for example, those of 1789 (Article 4) and 1793 (Article 6)—acknowledge this condition; others ignore it; but none gives it its due prominence.

The result has been that disorder which is now familiar to all and the discredit which has overtaken the vaunted individualism in these declarations.

3. The technical needs of legislation also demand a structural relationship which allows some to exact and compels others to fulfil this requirement. They presuppose sanctions where the obligation is evaded. Liberty and equality may be established, but fraternity is elusive. To

state in a charter, as the Americans did in 1776, that man has the right to seek happiness, is to confuse terms and to talk philosophy instead of legal regulations. It is idle to claim the right to progress or to health. Health is normally a natural gift, and progress is in the hands of fate, which walks like the blind and makes signs like the deaf.

Conclusion

In the case of every single State, declarations have proved, owing to the shortcomings we have described, incapable of adjusting themselves to social evolution. If we were to make the same mistakes on the international level, these would inevitably, and even more pronouncedly, produce the same results. A common formula must therefore be restricted to principles, in their widest possible application; for the rest, each State must translate them, as need be, into the legal measures which seem most indicated. But the formula will in any case provide for the establishment within each community of a jurisdictional organ to apply the law in question, *i.e.* to pass from the general standard to the rule deriving therefrom, and from the rule to the particular case.

Nowhere less than here does the rule suffice to prescribe conduct or settle a conflict; it is a mere instrument, and in order to be effective requires a man who can apply it discriminatingly. He alone can assess the actual situation properly and arrive at a suitable decision in full knowledge of the facts and according to a proper procedure. Since he will be a professional, he will have no difficulty in avoiding those technical mistakes which have made the declarations so vulnerable.

An international organisation cannot do more than this if it is not to run the risk of achieving something that is not only useless but dangerous.

The universal declaration would be confined to the following paragraphs :

I. Man has an indefeasible right to the respect and development of his physical and moral personality, to the extent that these are compatible with the essential needs and the potentialities of collective life; and he assumes responsibilities corresponding to those rights.

II. The law of a country decides, where necessary, how these principles are to be applied, and provides the sanctions required to ensure their effective application.

III. A special and independent court will, in each State, alone be competent in this matter. It may refuse to apply any measure that is contrary to the principles enunciated in Article I, whatever be the authority that has taken such a measure. Appeals will be heard before an International Court of Justice.

Comment

Article I

Personality: Every moment in civilisation reveals man in a particular form. The content of personality therefore varies according to the particular state of society at the moment.

This personality must be protected; under the above text, its value is fundamental. Once again, the assessment of this value, in importance and extent, is contingent; it can never be completely denied nor become absolute for the individual. It depends:

(a) on the *essential* needs of collective life. The existence of a society presupposes certain basic conditions which cannot be conjured away without the group itself being endangered. The individual is subject to these conditions, for apart from the community in which he lives he has virtually no existence. The needs, however, are *essential* needs and are few in number; as they are independent of the environment and the moment, they readily leap to the eye. They cannot therefore be defined arbitrarily. They may be summed up as: the optimum population, the means of subsistence, territory, public order and the political structure. They are necessary and inescapable. There are no others, however; so there is no danger of totalitarianism, which, on the pretext of acting on behalf of higher interests, is actually designed to profit those in power.

(b) *on the potentialities.*

The potentialities of a society vary from moment to

moment, and restrict its policy. One cannot spend more than one has. It is useless to claim an annual pension of at least $2,500 for every aged person; if the means are not to hand, this is a utopia. The right to work is no less sacred; but what if an international crisis closes the markets for it? Desires are of no avail where means are lacking; the latter govern the former. This provision eliminates the danger of demogogy.

Finally, Article I brings out the connection between rights and duties, without which liberty becomes licence, as has often been shown in the past.

Article II

Strictly speaking, it would seem superfluous to elaborate the principle by texts defining how it is to be applied in individual cases. In practice, however, this may be desirable; the task must be left to a legislator at a lower level than the constituent assembly, so as to permit progressive adaptation according to circumstances.

Sanctions apply to individuals as well as to those in power.

Article III

This article emphasises the special importance of jurisprudence, which, as the history of English law shows, is the best adapting instrument. The court concerned, however, must be independent of the other organs of the State and must have jurisdiction over them when freedoms are called in question. One thinks, obviously, of the Supreme Court in the United States, which decides as to the constitutional nature of laws.

Lawyers are well aware that laws are powerless apart from custom. But the peoples, for the most part, have neither the reflex of liberty nor the sense of solidarity which goes with it.

In short, the essential thing is not the law, but the general social habits of the community, of which the law is but the instrument. In most cases, indeed, the law is not a creative institution. In our context it is usually education alone that can establish liberty and show how it is to be rightly used. To look for formulæ instead of educating people is to court fresh disappointment; the most eloquent declarations in the world might with advantage be replaced by a spirit of the good neighbour, and it is more for the educator than for the lawyer to foster it.

Some Reflections on the Rights of Man

Pierre Tielhard de Chardin

As first expressed, in 1789, the rights of man were mainly an assertion of the desire for individual independence. 'All for the individual within Society,' implying that the 'human species' was created in order to expand and culminate in a multiplicity of units which would each, in isolation, reach their maximum development. This would seem to have been the principal concern and ideal of the eighteenth century humanitarians.

Since then, owing to the importance assumed in the world by collective phenomena, the fundamentals of the problem have changed considerably. There is now no longer any room for doubt. For numerous convergent reasons (rapid increase in ethnic, economic, political and psychic ties) the human individual is finally drawn into an irresistible process directed towards the establishment on earth of an inter-dependent organo-psychic system. Whether we like it or not, humanity is collectivising, 'totalising' itself, under the influence of physical and spiritual forces of a world-wide nature. Hence the new conflict, which is taking place in every human heart, between the human unit, who is ever more conscious of his individual value, and his social ties, which become ever more exacting.

On reflection, we realise that this conflict is only apparent. We now see that the human being is biologically not self-sufficient. In other words, it is not by self-isolation (as one might have thought), but by *proper* association with all other human beings that the individual can hope to achieve full development of his person (full development of energy and movement, and full development of consciousness particularly) since we cannot become completely 'reflexive', each of us, except by reflecting ourselves in and taking reflections from other human beings. Collectivisation and individuation (not autonomous, but personal) are therefore not two contradictory movements. The whole difficulty is to regulate the phenomenon in such a way that human totalisation is carried out, not under the influence of an external mechanising compression, but through inner harmonisation and sympathy.

From this new point of view it becomes immediately apparent that the object of a new definition of the rights of man must be no longer, as hitherto, to secure the greatest possible independence for the human unit in society, but to lay down the conditions under which the inevitable 'totalisation' of humanity is to take place, in such a way as not to destroy, but to enhance in each of us, I will not say independence, but—what is quite a different thing—the incommunicable uniqueness of the being within us.

The problem is to cease organising the world for the benefit, and in terms of the isolated individual, and to direct all our efforts toward the complete development ('personalisation') of the individual, by wisely integrating him within the unified group, which must one day become the organic and psychic culminating point of humanity.

When thus restated in terms of an operation with two variables (progressive, inter-dependent adjustment of the two processes of collectivisation and personalisation), the question of the rights of man does not admit of any simple or general answer.

At the least we can say that any solution envisaged must satisfy the following three conditions:

(1). Within a Humanity that is in process of collective organisation, the individual is no longer entitled to remain inactive, *i.e.* to refrain from developing himself to the greatest possible extent; because on his perfection depends the perfection of all the others around him.

(2). Society must, in its own interest, *tend* to create around the individuals it comprises the most favourable environment for the full physical and psychical development of what is most original in each of these individuals. This is admittedly a commonplace proposition, but the ways in which it is to be applied cannot be laid down uniformly for all cases, since cases vary according to the educational level and the potentialities for progress in the various human units to be organised.

(3). Whatever be the measures taken in this direction, one capital principle must be stated and constantly observed.

This is that in no case, and for no purpose, must the collective forces be in a position to compel the individual to distort or falsify himself (as he would do if he accepted as true what he saw to be false, *i.e.* if he lied to himself). If it is to be legitimate, any limitation or direction applied to the independence of the human unit by group force can only be applied *in conformity with* the free and inner structure of that unit. Otherwise a fundamental discord would be introduced into the very heart of the collective human body.

Each human being has an absolute duty to work and personalise himself.

Each human being has a relative right to be placed in the best possible conditions for personalisation.

Each human being within the social organism has an absolute right not to be distorted by outward coercion, but to be integrated within the organism by inward persuasion, *i.e.* in conformity with his aptitudes and personal aspirations.

These three points must be made explicit and guaranteed in any new charter of humanity.

The Rights of Man in Liberalism, Socialism and Communism

Sergius Hessen

I AGREE with you[1] that the unity of the world depends to a great extent on whether it would be possible to elaborate a 'common set of ideas and principles,' including a 'common formulation of the rights of man.' Hence the importance of effecting a reconciliation between the two apparently opposite conceptions of the rights of man—the Liberal and the Communist—in a higher synthesis. May the following reflections contribute to this important task.

I

Considering the development of the modern 'State of Law' in Western Europe, we can distinguish four main stages, each showing its own interpretation of the rights of man: (1) the Absolute, (2) the Liberal, (3) the Democratic and (4) the Socialist State.

Although the Absolute State did not acknowledge explicitly the rights of man, it laid down practically the first foundations for the rule of law, without which any realisation of these rights would be impossible. Together with the unification and codification of the law it proclaimed the principle of the security of law as well as that of the equality of all the subjects of the crown before the same common law. Besides the principle of equality thus emphasised we already have here the germs of such freedoms as the inviolability of the person of the citizen, of his property and of his dwelling. Such was Montesquieu's conception of liberty—liberty as the security of law, which can be ensured in reality only through the independence of the judicial authority. Through the postulate of the division of powers (or rather their 'balance'), Montesquieu indeed transcended the stage of the Absolutist State, though this already evolved in itself the germs of such division by the

---

[1] See Appendix I

strict delimitation of the competencies of its bureaucratic organs and agencies. Nevertheless Montesquieu was far from the conception of the Liberal State. He expressed rather the Absolutist State in its historical dynamics which, once accomplished, would already transcend its 'ideal type' in the direction of the Liberal State. Formulating these dynamics and the postulates of Montesquieu in the terms of 'rights,' we could say that the fundamental 'rights' implicitly acknowledged already in the Absolutist State were: the right to the security of law, the right to be equally treated by the law and the right to justice. For the advocates of the Absolutist State, and partly for Montesquieu himself, this 'firm basis of the law' was but a means of the *'raison d'état,'* an instrument of the efficiency of the state authorities. It was an attribute of an ordered state, a duty of the state authority against the state itself rather than against the individual. The latter was a mere subject of the state authority conceived as an earthly Providence, omni-competent, wise, benevolent and mighty, imitating the attributes of God who had created it for the welfare of men. The model of such a State was the office responsible only to a higher power which created it, not to the subjects for whose welfare it had to care, which it knew better than they did themselves. The fundamental relation in the Absolutist State was that of subordination, the subordination of the subject individual to the officer, of this latter to his immediate authority, etc, up to the King as the Chief Officer of the State, who had created his office and from whom came the power possessed by the officer.

Liberalism brought a new conception of State and liberty, obviously opposed to the theory and practice of the Absolutist State. The liberty of man is, in the Liberal State, liberty from the interference of the Government with the private life of the individual. This private sphere of activity of the individual is marked out by the set of so-called *civil freedoms*: freedom of conscience, of speech and of press, of assembly, of work and property, of movement and corre-spondence. Negative in its essence (not to be interfered with), this liberty assimilated liberty as security of the law (the inviolability of personality, of its dwelling and property being conceived, together with the freedom of movement and of work, as the freedom of an enlarged body of personality), and in the first half of the nineteenth century evolved some other freedoms of a similar kind, which enlarged the list of freedoms contained in the Declaration of 1789. Thus to the negative freedoms mentioned above were added the freedom of teaching, of scientific inquiry, freedom of association and, as the last of these freedoms, the freedom to strike proclaimed in 1848. The evolving from the general principle of negative liberty of just those and no other freedoms was conditioned historically. Each of these concrete freedoms energed from the principles of negative liberty as the reaction of this general principle to the kind of oppression which at the time was felt by most people to be most intolerable.

The stress laid in the Liberal State on the principle of negative liberty did not exclude the equality emphasised (though far from having been truly realised) by the Absolutist State. On the contrary, the principle of equality, under the influence of the principle of liberty, considerably expanded its meanings: in the Declaration of Rights it means not only the equality of all citizens before the common law, i.e. the abolition of feudal jurisdiction and legal privileges, but also the equal accession of all citizens 'to State offices, functions and honours on the basis of their capacity without any other distinction but their virtues and their abilities' (Article 6).

While the Absolutist State only acknowledged the duty of the subjects and not the rights of men, the philosophers of liberalism expressly understand the civil freedoms as the 'rights of man': the right to dispose of one's body and property according to one's own will, the right to express one's self in one's faith, speech and work, etc. These rights are inalienable rights because, rooted in the very nature of man, they transcend his social being as a citizen or a mere member of the State. The metaphysical conception of the pre-social, natural rights was only a rationalistic inter-pretation of a more original conception of man as a spiritual being, who is not only the subject of an earthly State but also the member of a higher, spiritual community —the Kingdom of God. Benjamin Constant was right when he asserted that the idea of liberty in the sense of negative freedom was a modern idea unknown to antiquity. The 'liberty of the ancients,' he pointed out, meant the participation of every free man ('citizen') in the exercise of State sovereignty, and by no means freedom from the interference of the State in the private life of man, the State being understood as the highest community bestowing on a man his dignity as a free being.

According to the classical liberal conception, the essential function of the State is to ensure the 'rule of law,' *i.e.* the security of citizens and their rights of negative liberty. If there could be a guarantee, says Benjamin Constant, that the Government will not misuse its power, the best solution would be to entrust the governmental function, by competition, to a company bidding the cheapest terms. However, the only method of ensuring such a guarantee being the control of the Government by those who pay for it, there must be a representative organ delimiting its competence and supervising its expenditure and efficiency. The franchise of the Liberal State is the right to elect the trustees and not participation in the exercise of sovereignty, as was the case in antiquity, which for this very reason did not know of the principle of representation. The franchise so conceived, and the independent judiciary likewise selected from the 'enlightened part of the nation,' were to be sufficient guarantees for the 'rule of law' in the sense of negative liberty, entirely satisfying the interests of the propertied classes.

The democratic conception of the rights of man, without denying the rights to negative liberty, lays stress on rights of a different kind, which may be described as *rights of positive liberty*. By this I mean such rights as the right to education, the right to work, the right to assistance or pension in case of illness, maternity, infirmity and old age. These rights, already proclaimed in the Declaration of Rights voted by the French Convention in June 1793, have a positive character, as they include the claim of every citizen to be assisted by the community and not only not to be interfered with in his own way of life. According to the Declaration referred to, these rights come from the principle of the 'social guarantee,' consisting in the action of the whole community (*action de tous*) designed to ensure for everybody 'the enjoyment and the preservation of his rights' (Article 23). Indeed, the principle of these rights seems to be rather the principle of solidarity or fraternity, not that of liberty. This is the actual opinion of the French 'solidarists.' According to them, these 'social rights' are rooted in the fact of a close interdependence between all members of modern society, a necessary consequence of the continually increasing organic division of labour. The success of one and the distress of another are interlaced, and the same elemental process, *e.g.* disturbances and changes in the market, may create unearned income for one and undeserved poverty for another. The individualistic fiction of a *'contrat social'* must be replaced by the solidaristic fiction of a *'dette sociale'* (social debt). In modern conditions the successful man owes his prosperity to a great degree not to his own work and talents but to the work and experience of his neighbours and of the community as a whole. It is therefore his duty to repay this debt in proportion to his income, and the 'social fund' thus formed must be so used as to ensure everybody the right to a human existence. According to this democratic conception the model for the State would be rather an insurance co-operative than the private police company of Benjamin Constant.

Far from abolishing the principles of liberty and equality, the principle of solidarity gives them a new, richer and deeper meaning. Classical liberalism regarded freedom as a finished substance, equal in each individual and acting in the interest of this individual as soon as all bondages have been removed and negative liberty ensured. The ten-year-old child contracting for work was presumed to act as freely as his big employer, exploiting his own and his parents' poverty and ignorance. According to the democratic conception, freedom is rather an inner potential force, inherent in every human being. This force of personality may grow and blossom, but it may also shrink and degenerate. The community has the duty of guaranteeing to every citizen the opportunity of the self-development of that inner freedom, to help him in this task of making his *potentia* an *actus*. The negatively and statically conceived liberty thus becomes a positive and dynamic process of liberation.

It is the same difference as that between the liberal and the democratic conceptions of equality. In the first case, equality meant: (a) the equality of all citizens before the codified common law (a postulate inherited by Liberalism from the Absolutist State) and (b) the abolition of all privileges of birth, denomination and race for the purpose of possessing property, holding State offices and honours, or entering public schools. It was a mere negative and static conception of equality. On the other hand, the democratic conception of equality as 'equal chances for everybody' is both positive and dynamic. It means the duty of the State to interfere in a positive way in the field of education, labour conditions, etc, in order to equalise the start of life and the conditions of competition, to make it 'fair play.'

A further step in the analysis of the democratic ideas of liberty and equality may show that the 'liberation' of personality and the 'equalisation' of the conditions under which different personalities develop are, in an even deeper sense, also merely negative. As a matter of fact, liberation means practically the removal, by the united action of the community, of various barriers and obstacles which may handicap, or even entirely frustrate all efforts of the poor aiming at self-realisation. And equal chances for everybody means, practically, the abolition of the privileges of the wealthy as regards entering public schools and thereby coming to hold State offices and honours. However, this removal of the barriers and privileges created by social (chiefly economic) conditions is attainable only through a positive united effort on the part of the whole community. In this sense, democratic liberty is really positive and deeply imbued with solidarity or fraternity, to use the phrase of the first pioneers of modern democracy. It is obvious that this democratic conception of the rights of man implies a change in the attitude to the State. The virtue of government no longer resides in its abstention from any activity and in its inexpensiveness. On the contrary, the government, realising the rights of positive liberty, must interfere with education, economy, public health, etc. To ensure everyone the rights to education, work, health, old age pensions, etc, the voluntary activity of the interested parties themselves is not enough nor is the activity of the organs of local self-government. The State must complete and co-ordinate all these voluntary and local efforts and give them its financial support. It must share responsibility for the fullest possible realisation of the rights of positive liberty, as well as for the collection and distribution of the enormous funds which this realisation requires. The efficiency of governments, both central and local, is to a great extent assessable from the amount and structure of their joint budget.

This is why participation in the control of government ceases to be irrelevant. Growing circles of the nation demand this participation in the control both of local and central government, because control by the people interested themselves is the only means of guaranteeing the efficiency of the local services (in education, health, etc) and the fairness of the schemes for social insurance (in regard to illness, infirmity, unemployment, old age pensions, etc). In modern democracy universal suffrage does not mean the immediate participation of every citizen in the exercise of sovereignty in the sense in which Benjamin Constant interpreted the 'liberty of the ancients.' The right to vote signifies rather the right to influence the government by electing persons, both to local and to central governing bodies, who share our own experience of life. For, as Professor H. Laski has rightly pointed out, 'the less we live in the experience of our neighbours, the less shall we feel wrong in the denial of their wants.' As long as security and justice were thought to be the only functions of the State, the lack of any experience of a large majority of the people, of their needs and wants, did not matter so much as when the realisation of the rights of positive liberty was acknowledged to be the fundamental function of government. As a matter of fact, until the political parties were, owing to the ever-enlarged franchise, put under the pressure of a growing multitude of voters, the rights of positive liberty were denied, as being contradictory to the very spirit of freedom.

The right to vote is but one of a set of concrete rights emerging from the new, democratic conception of the State and actualising what may be suitably called *the right to political action*. Apart from the right to vote, equal and secret, in order to be efficient, to these political rights belong also such as the right to organise political parties, both supporting or opposing the government in office, the right to criticise the government in and outside the parliament or local assemblies, etc. Concrete rights actualising the fundamental right to political action may vary from time to time and from country to country, depending on the constitution of a given State. They may include, *e.g.* the right to partake in the action aiming at dissolution of the parliament or of demanding the submission of a question to the referendum. On the other hand, in the States whose constitution does not admit the dissolution of the parliament or the referendum, there are other positive laws securing to every citizen the fundamental right to participate in political action in order to influence the government, both central and local, and to control its efficiency. These political rights often overlap and are closely interlaced with rights of civil freedoms emphasised by liberalism. Yet in a liberal State they were rather privileges of a wealthy minority, while the democratic State tends to make them actual rights of every grown-up citizen.

It was the great merit of thinkers like Woodrow Wilson and T. Hobhouse that they demonstrated once more the truth of the thesis upon which Condorcet had already insisted—that 'the new liberty is the old one,' which means that liberty, under changed conditions, must modify its own content if it is to save itself from degeneration. According to Condorcet the right to education is involved in the rights of liberty already formulated in the Declaration of 1789, in the same way as the right to justice. It is this that makes the civil freedoms and political equality real. Just as every encroachment upon the freedom of an individual gives the injured person a claim to be restored in his right by the court of justice, so the exercise of the right of liberty presupposes that every citizen 'knows and is able to understand and to realise his rights and duties, to perfect his work and to develop his abilities.' The rights of positive liberty are thus a logical consequence of negative freedoms limiting the arbitrary power of the government, just as the security of the law and equality before the law have already been germs of liberty, though not, as Montesquieu intended, its essence.

Logical consequence does not mean logical development, as was Hegel's idea. Concrete freedom from interference by the Government, as well as concrete right to assistance by the community, may be inherent, as latent, in the general idea of liberty. The authors of the Declaration of Rights of 1793 were right in regarding liberty as comprising both that freedom and that right as well as the security of the law as their foundation. It may be true that logically the security of law ought to come first, that the second step ought to be the realisation of the negative freedoms, and that only the third would achieve the rights of positive liberty. The historical development of the modern 'State of Law' (absolutist-liberal-democratic) did conform to this logical sequence. This development, however, would be impossible without real factors, such as the absolutist monarchy, the industrial revolution, and the middle and lower-middle classes, whose needs and interests played at various stages the rôle of a chemical developer, making a latent picture visible. The democratic ideal of Condorcet had to wait more than 100 years to realise in his own country, because of the lack of real factors powerful enough to act as such a developer. Both Marx and Lassalle well understood the necessity of such real power as the motive force of progress.

One could be induced to think that the democratic or the 'New Liberalism,' to use the terminology of Wilson and Hobhouse, is the last stage of development in the modern 'State of Law.' It could be demonstrated, as G. Gurritch tried to do it recently, that the idea of democracy is a dynamic tension between three principles—equality, liberty and solidarity (fraternity)—forming a kind of unstable equilibrium. Changes in social structure may bring about the hypertrophy of one or the other principle, which would lead to a deformation of the other two principles and to a degeneration of the whole. The reaction to this is that the stress is then laid on the most neglected or endangered principle. Thus in the middle of the nineteenth century Alexis de Tocqueville, while seeing in the principle of equality the very essence of democracy, feared that the hypertrophy of this principle in American democracy would undermine that of liberty. At the beginning of this century both French Solidarism and Anglo-Saxon New Liberalism emphasised the principle of solidarity as being the true kernel of democracy. The experience of totalitarianism at present induces many to emphasise the principle of liberty as being the essence of democracy. On the other hand the 'people's democracy' of the East-European countries rather lays stress on the principles of equality and solidarity, neglected in those countries in the pre-war period.

It would be easy to show that this modern idea of democracy is deeply rooted in the new attitude which Christianity has brought into the world. This is true not only historically but also philosophically. The three principles which form an unstable equilibrium within the idea of democracy are but three aspects of the 'greatest' (I Corinth., 13, 13) of Christian virtues—charity. For charity, indeed, presumes equality. Under this aspect of equality it is more than mere pity or compassion. It is a relation or rather a tie—the tie of love—between equals. True charity excludes every patronising condescension. It aspires rather to make the fellow-creature who is the subject of our loving activity a free being, no more in need of our help and standing firmly on his own feet. This is a task much more difficult than merely satisfying a need, or stilling a pain or even a grief, which is the objective of so-called philanthropy. True charity is an 'active love' (Dostoievsky) whose objective is the liberty of the fellow-creature. It is the love of this concrete 'neighbour,' not of an abstract ideal man. This neighbour may be a sinner, he may 'stink,' as Ivan Kara-mazov says. Charity excludes all contempt, even the slightest disgust. For he who loves his neighbour feels his own responsibility even for the sins of his fellow-creature. If I had more love, I would perhaps be able to prevent misdeeds, and even their contemplation. 'Every man is responsible for everybody and for everything,' says Father Zozima in *The Brothers Karamazov*. The feeling of solidarity between all fellow-creatures, of their fraternity as sons of God, is a necessary element in the very attitude of charity. True cherity includes therefore equality, liberty and fraternity as its elements. They are inseparable components of Christian love. But, falling on the surface of social life, the pure moral beam of love resolves into its components which become different principles, demanding a continual effort if they are to be kept in harmony.

2

If democracy is an equilibrium between the principles of equality, liberty and solidarity, which in their turn are but a social transcription of Christian love, does it not follow that democracy is rather an absolute ideal of the 'State of Law,' and not merely an historical stage in its realisation? The majority of the democratic liberals see, indeed, in the democratic State the last word in political progress, and even many socialists share, to some extent, the same opinion. These 'liberal socialists' conceive socialism as being the fulfilment of democracy and not its opposite. The question is, what does this fulfilment mean? Is there any new conception of the rights of liberty in the socialist idea of the State, or is the Socialist State nothing but a new technique for making effective the same rights of positive liberty which were already proclaimed by the democratic State, but, owing to the economic structure of capitalist society, were to remain in it sheer slogans?

Expressing the claims of Socialism in terms of the 'rights of man,' we could conveniently distinguish between two or even three kinds of such rights. To the first belong such rights as 'right to a job,' the 'right to education,' the 'right to a human existence.' For many Socialists the exercise of these rights of positive liberty is the very essence of Socialism. In his *Précis du Socialisme*, published in 1892, Benoit Malon advocated the creation of a ministry of social insurance as the chief aim of a Socialist State. He asserted that the realisation of a comprehensive system of social insurance was not possible under a capitalist economy. Fifty years later Lord Beveridge, the author of a comprehensive system of social insurance, came to the same conclusion. Though avoiding the term Socialism and disapproving even of the policy of thorough nationalisation, he advocated what he calls 'national planning' as the only means of ensuring full employment, without which the whole plan of social insurance would be unworkable. There is only a slight difference between the modern Fabian view and the standpoint of

F. D. Roosevelt and 'New Dealers' like Lilienthal and Wallace, for all their denial of 'planned economy' and their emphasising of the vital necessity for preserving private initiative and enterprise. It is the view of consistent democratic (or 'new') Liberalism which, being free from any capitalist doctrinairism, has an open mind and the courage to experiment with a view to making the rights ensuring the dignity of man effective.

Only one step further in the same direction and we reach the attitude of the British Labour Party. Though explicitly socialist in its policy, it is free from any socialist doctrinairism and sees in planned economy and nationalisation merely the technical means, the efficiency of which has to be proved in each particular case. The real aim of both is full employment, the raising of the purchasing power of the working class (the 'vertical' expansion of the market), and the raising of the efficiency of industry, all these and other similar aims being regarded as indispensable conditions for making the rights of positive liberty effective. While proving the case of nationalisation by the necessity of fighting monopolistic economic power in private hands as something dangerous to the progress and even the preservation of democracy, liberal Socialists are on the other hand no less anxious to avoid the concentration of economic and political power in the hands of an omnipotent government. In this respect they seem to share the view of the 'anarchist' Proudhon and the liberal Lord Acton that 'absolute power corrupts absolutely.' Their Socialism is firmly rooted in the idea of liberty, just as the liberalism of the consistent democrats is already transgressing the limits of more freedom.

The rights of positive liberty being closely connected with the negative freedoms, these latter are no less an objective of liberal Socialism than are the former. While agreeing with the argument of all the enemies of capitalism that civil freedoms are under capitalism a privilege of the well-to-do, Liberal Socialism will make them really universal and will not do away with them because of their worthlessness for the poor. If monopolistic tendencies in the publishing industry, especially in the daily press, make freedom of opinion more and more illusory, the right course is not to entrust the government with the monopoly of the press, but to break every monopoly in this sphere and to re-organise the press in such way as to ensure for everybody the 'right to impartial information.' This 'freedom from lies and from partiality,' applying not only to the readers of newspapers but also to radio listeners, is but one example of the changes which the old negative freedoms undergo under the complicated conditions of monopolistic capitalism. The socialisation of the press has nothing to do with the clumsy nationalisation which transfers the monopoly from the private firms to the government, but is rather an intricate technique, specially adapted to the solution of this complicated problem. According to liberal Socialism there is no single universal technique of socialisation, such as nationalisation, municipalisation or syndicalisation. The devices of socialisation are as manifold as are the rights of negative and positive liberties. These are the only fundamental ends, to which all the devices of socialisation are but more or less suitable means.

Yet even this conception of thoroughly liberal Socialism has its own logic, which leads it far beyond the idea of the Democratic State. The model of the latter is, as we have seen, the insurance association. Co-operation in it is limited to the distribution of the risk among a possibly wider circle of associates, as was really the case in all the schemes of unemployment insurance devised in the capitalistic democracies. Yet after the mere *distribution* of the risk comes necessarily, as a further step, the *fighting* of the real causes of the risk, as practised indeed by all insurance companies, *e.g.* in fostering fire-proof buildings, etc. If the risk which is the subject of the insurance grows, as it really does in the case of unemployment, the necessity of fighting the causes of it becomes more acute. The insurance association must then extend its scope by including among its functions the organising of the production and consumption of its members on the lines of a planned economy. The consumers-producers co-operative thus becomes the model of the Socialist State.

This brings us to the second group of rights of man involved in the Socialist doctrine, often described as 'economic rights' or as the rights of man as producer and consumer. The object of all these rights is what may be fairly called 'freedom from exploitation.' The right of the employed worker not to be exploited by the owner of the enterprise was formulated by many influential socialists of the past century as the 'right to the full product of one's labour.' This formula, being a crude simplification of the Marxian theory of the surplus value, has been abandoned by the majority of Marxists themselves and replaced by a less definite but a more realistic one: 'the right not to be treated as a mere commodity.' The rich experience of the daily struggle of the trades unions against exploitation has filled this genuine Marxian definition of exploitation ('treatment of labour as a mere commodity,' *cf*. Vol. I of *Capital*) with concrete meaning, drawn directly from life. Many special workers' or 'producers' rights' have been drawn from that fundamental principle of rights. The more important of these special producers' rights are: the right to a fairly paid job,[1] the right to a fair wage, the right to leisure, the right to healthy and secure conditions of work, the right to decent homes, the right (for women workers) to equal pay for equal work done, etc.

It is obvious that all these rights are subject to further individualisation, *e.g.* the 'fair wage' is dependent on the financial situation of the enterprise and the productivity of the work; the 'leisure' and the working day depend on the branch of industry, the kind of work, and the age and sex of the worker; the term 'decent home' includes communication and shopping facilities, etc. It is the proper function of the trades unions to see that the adjustment of the workers' right not to be exploited in relation to the concrete situation is fair in every individual case, and that leads us to a further group of producers' rights without which the right to be treated as a human being, not as a mere commodity, could never be carried out effectively.

---

[1] This producers' right to a 'fairly paid job' coincides only partly with the previously analysed 'every man's right to work.' The accent is laid here on mass unemployment as an inducement to exploitation. 'Full employment' means 'a state of things in which there are always more jobs looking for people than people looking for jobs' (G. D. H. Cole), as against the normal capitalist state of things, when 'for every two jobs available there are three candidates looking for them.'

The second fundamental right of man as a producer is the right to associate in free unions independent of any political or economic authority. This right involves such special rights as the right of collective bargaining, the right of unions to associate in regional, national and international organisations, the right to the free choice of a union, the right to strike, etc. All these special rights are also subject to an often minute individualisation, which may be very different in different concrete situations.

Yet apart from producers' rights, the 'economic rights' also include the rights of the consumer. The latter has likewise a claim not to be exploited. In its abstract form this claim was often expressed as the right of the consumer to his full share in the profit. But now even the most orthodox adherents of the 'Co-operative Commonwealth' see that the exploitation of the consumer cannot be identified with the surplus price extorted from him by the owner of commodities. It is rather as manifold and many-sided as is the exploitation of the worker, and includes analogous special rights. The most important of these consumers' rights are: the right to a fair price, the right to a free choice of commodities, the right to saving freely one's income (the two latter making what is often called 'freedom of consumption'), etc, as well as the right of the consumer to associate in free unions and the special rights involved in that freedom of consumers' co-operatives (the right to associate in regional, national and international unions, their right to possess their own enterprises, the right of the consumer to a free choice of his co-operative, etc).

One could argue that most of the above-mentioned economic rights already characterise the democratic State, and secondly that they are rather incompatible with the State as many socialists conceive it. The right to associate in free trades unions or co-operatives, their right to form regional and national organisations, etc, are indeed acknowledged rights in all democratic States; on the other hand there are many Socialists who doubt whether the right to strike, or the right to the free choice of a union or the freedom of consumption and of saving would be compatible with the principles of a socialist economy. As regards the first argument, it is true that in respect, also, of the 'economic' rights of man the democratic State anticipates a good deal of what the socialist State aims to realise when fully developed. Many of the economic rights quoted are really directly involved in the general rights of negative and positive liberty. Thus the right to association in free trades unions or co-operatives is a direct consequence of freedom of association, and the right to a fairly paid job is, as we have seen, only a variety of the 'right to work' already included in the democratic Constitution of 1793. In the socialist State, however, firstly they derive from the more comprehensible principle of the right of man to be treated in economic life as a human being, not as a mere commodity, and, secondly, all the manifold rights involved in this freedom from exploitation are to be developed to their possible extent and protected by means of planned economy, free from all capitalist prejudice.

Does this method really ensure man's economic rights and does it not rather endanger the freedom both of producer and consumer, as the liberal critics of Socialism insist? Take for instance the right to strike or the right to the free choice of a job, or on the other hand the right to save as one will. Will all these rights be upheld in a Socialist State? All adherents of liberal Socialism agree that they ought to be maintained, and can be ensured in a planned economy. After the admirable argumentation of Barbara Wootton, there is no need to insist on this. Of course they have to be re-adjusted to the new conditions, because all special rights, as we have seen, get their concrete meaning from the historical situation which they have to shape. In a Socialist State aiming at the utmost realisation of the workers' rights and ensuring for the trades unions wide legal possibilities for a fair settling of their disputes with the management, the 'right to strike' has necessarily a meaning other than when the strike was the only means of extorting from the reluctant capitalist owner somewhat fairer conditions of work. It ceases to be a normal weapon of a class struggle and becomes, as Harold Laski points out, the *ultima ratio* of the trades unions' freedom which can only be used by the official trades union authorities in the extreme cases where freedom is endangered, similarly to the 'right to rebellion' or the 'right of resistance to oppression' included in the Declaration of Rights of 1789. If, as Aneurin Bevan points out, 'in a Socialist society everybody should have a right to a job, but no man should have a right to a particular job,' it does not mean that the free choice of a job will there be more limited than under Capitalism, when for so many people looking for a job this right was a meaningless phrase. However, the 'right to a free choice of a job' has in Socialist society a real meaning as a safeguard against the compulsory direction of labour that a liberal Socialist abhors no less than the fiercest critic of Socialism. At the stage of the Absolutist State in which the freedom of work was proclaimed first, its real meaning was different; it meant the abolition of the feudal guild and class privileges which prohibited the majority of people from doing various productive jobs. And the same can be said about the 'right to save.' This right will be fully maintained in the Socialist society, though it will not involve 'the right to invest as one pleases.' In the last decades of Capitalism this latter right has become practically a privilege for the few and rather the greatest danger for the savings of many.

I have not yet mentioned such economic rights as the right of the workers, as well as the consumers (and users), to the control of industry. Many friends and critics of Socialism, conceiving it first and foremost as 'self-government in industry' or as 'industrial democracy,' have considered these rights to be the very essence of Socialism. Socialism was for them the abolition of the very relation of the 'employer' to the 'wage-earner' (of what French syndicalists call *salariat*), and the suppression of this relation of subordination by that of co-partnership and co-ordination. I do not believe that there are at present many Socialists or even Syndicalists who would still maintain this view. For Liberal Socialism at any rate 'the right of producers and of consumers to the control of industry' means hardly more than the partnership of the representatives of the workers and users in the exercise of some of the functions of the management of single factories and concerns, as well as in the regional, national and international organs of the planned economy. There can be no 'right' of a single worker or consumer to elect the management of the factory, as in a democratic State organisation, though the producers' co-operative may be one of the many various forms of enterprise in the Socialist society. If the right to workers' control means more than what is included in the right not to be exploited (*i.e.* not to be treated as a mere commodity) and in the special rights this general principle may imply, its real meaning, together with that of the right to consumers' control, can be nothing but the demand that the national economy be planned in a democratic way, from below, and not in a bureaucratic way, from above. The model of a Socialist State is, indeed, as I have already pointed out, the co-operative association based on co-partnership in a common task and fellowship in the common work, and not the office that was the model of the absolutist State, nor the liberal joint-stock company, nor even the mere insurance co-operative, the model of the modern democratic State. Yet all these postulates concerning the structure of the Socialist society cannot be conceived of in terms of the rights of man, and overstep the limits of our inquiry.

And how is it with the third kind of rights, associated with what may be called Communism rather than Socialism? The general principle of these rights may be stated as 'the right to satisfy freely one's needs'; that would be a fair transcription, in terms of rights, of the classical Communist slogan 'to everybody according to his needs.' In spite of the theoretical up-to-dateness of the 'economy of plenty,' I shall not discuss here the Communist principle of rights in its maximalistic version, based on the supposition of an economy of absolute plenty, knowing no scarcity at all and therefore being no longer economy but rather an omnipotent technology. The more so as such a utopian view excludes not only the notion of economic goods or 'commodities' but also the notion of any rights, as it is rightly inherent in the Marxian theory of the 'withering away of State and Law in Communist society.'

We shall rather confine ourselves to the conception of a relative Communism, claiming to satisfy only some definite, more or less elementary needs of each individual. Then, according to the needs selected to be freely satisfied, the Communist principle of rights will involve a number of special rights, *e.g.* the right to three decent meals a day, the right to decent shelter, the right to decent clothing, etc.

The difference between this Communist conception and the Socialist conception referred to above would be twofold. First, Socialism is anxious to guarantee everybody the right to a fairly paid job, as well as to a decent minimum for the unemployed, old and disabled who are unable to work through no fault of their own. The guaranteed minimum is thought of rather as an incentive to fair work, and not to idleness—in the sense of the slogan 'to everybody according to his work.' Communism, on the other hand, claims to guarantee everybody the satisfaction of his elementary needs quite independently from his work. Does it not mean that the Communist conception involves the 'right to idleness'? It would be certainly so, had Communism not tended to supersede all kinds of rights and laws by purely moral relationships implying amongst others the duty of everybody to work for common good 'according to one's abilities.'

The second point of difference would be that Communism guarantees the satisfying of one's needs in kind and not in money, thus limiting the freedom of consumption which belongs, as we have seen, to the most cherished rights in the Socialist conception. One could even be induced to assert, as Bernard Shaw admirably did, that the very essence of Communism consists in the free distribution of some commodities or services to everybody, thus excluding those commodities and services from the exchange market. A park or a beach open to all, a road that can be used freely by everybody without turnpikes and toll-collectors, and free water supply are elementary examples of such 'communism.' The realisation of rights both to education and to health already implies at present, in many democratic States with a capitalist economy, a good deal of communism in this relative sense. Not only are the services of teachers and masters distributed free to every child 'according to his needs,' but text and copy-books, paper, pens and pencils, etc, sometimes even milk or other foods. The same applies to the health service scheme recently introduced in England, everybody receiving freely 'according to his needs' the services of doctors and nurses, as well as all prescribed medicines, eye-glasses, etc. Why not replace the fare-collectors in the buses and tramways by another mode of financing these public services? Why not include the costs of the power supply for the home consumption in local expenditure, as is more and more becoming the case with water supply? Why not distribute to the schoolchildren work- and sports-clothes as well as daily meals? The boundaries of this 'communistic sector' of satisfying one's needs are obviously moving. The more elementary and the more standardised the needs are, the more 'ripe' they are to be included in the communistic sector. And one need not be a Communist in the present political sense of the term to forecast a state of things where everybody will have his elementary needs satisfied by the free distribution of a minimum of commodities and services indispensable for a decent life. For instance, according to Emanuel Mounier (*cf.* his *Manifeste du personnalisme*), this enlarged 'communistic sector' guaranteeing to everybody his right to have all his elementary needs satisfied free, may be to a large extent financed by the compulsory work of the youth during the twelve to eighteen months after he leaves school. The youth would take over the most automatic, dull work, not qualified as a permanent job because of its depersonalising character. Yet, as it lasts some months only, it can so be organised that it would have a great educational value. To the right of everybody to have his elementary standardised needs freely satisfied would thus correspond the duty for everybody to share, on the eve of his adult life, in the exercise of the standardised automatic work indispensable to the community.

Communism in the relative sense of the term is, therefore, not the alternative to liberal Socialism, but rather its constituent. It is not a higher and more distant ideal than that of Socialism, but only a technique of the realisation of the rights of man, a technique that was already first applied at the beginning of the modern State, when the toll-collectors on the highroads and bridges were removed and replaced by other methods of financing public services. The enlarging of the 'communistic sector' of satisfying the needs of the public is therefore a question not of principle but of calculation. Its natural limit is the freedom of consumption, which it ought not to be allowed to endanger by eliminating money through supply in kind. For to everybody who attaches value to the rights of man, freedom of consumption seems to be an indispensable component of liberty.

3

We have seen that the Communist principle 'to everybody according to his needs' begins to play an increasing part in liberal Socialism. In doing so it ceases to be a principle and becomes the mere technique of a fulfilment of the rights of man and his liberty in modern industrial society. Would is not be permissible, to say that an analogous development characterises economic and political progress in the Soviet Union, only that the development here goes in an opposite direction—from the Communist principle first exposing all liberal 'rights' and 'freedoms' as either sham in capitalist or unnecessary in communist society, to a progressively greater acknowledgment of them as an indispensable technique of the building up of Socialism as the first stage in the realisation of an integral Communism?

The first years of the Bolshevik Revolution had not only an heroic but undoubtedly also an eschatological character. The Communism they tried to realise was later justly called a 'War-Communism.' But then the great majority of the average members of the Lenin Party and many of its leaders shared the belief that they would see in their own lifetime the implementation of the Communist principle. Such measures as the closing of the shops, the abolition of the market, the general rationing of all commodities, free school attendance and sometimes free transport, the practical elimination of money through rationed products and services in kind, all these and other analogous measures, later declared to be mere emergency measures, were then believed, both by friends and enemies of the Soviet Government, to be genuine steps in the realisation of true Communism. By introducing audaciously the N.E.P. (New Economic Policy) and declaring that the road to Communism was a very long one, that it implied many transitional stages and many, many years of strained work, Lenin gave the first decisive blow to what may be called Communist doctrinairism.

This doctrinairism, filled with genuine enthusiasm for the great task of the social Revolution, was an excellent explosive, very effective for the purpose of a radical upheaval of all traditional institutions and old ways of life. It was an admirable expression of a hope and a powerful weapon in the struggle. But it could contribute nothing to a positive programme to build up a new social order. With its maximalist, both revolutionary and utopian, attitude it was rather an obstacle to those who were willing to stop fighting and try to embark on the positive work of building, even if only to make a later fight more successful.

Let us remember the chief features of that utopian conception of the Communist society. In his last book, written on the very eve of the Revolution, Lenin himself gave it classical expression. He emphasised here the identity of the Communist ideal with that of Anarchism. The point of division between Communism and Anarchism, says Lenin, is not the conception of the ideal society, which is just the same, but exclusively that of the way leading to the ideal. Anarchists limit themselves to the destruction of all kinds of power—political, economic, religious. They believe that the mere destruction of the existing power machine would suffice to realise their ideal. Communists, on the contrary, think that the masses of the working people under the leadership of their political party must first conquer the State authority in order to destroy the economic power of the capitalists. This task will be completed during the transitional period of the 'proletarian dictatorship.' After the destruction of the economic power of the propertied classes and the abolition of the actual divisions between classes the process of the 'withering away' of the State will necessarily begin. With the State, both its weapons for enforcing the obedience of the exploited—Law and Religion—are also doomed. According to Engels, their place will be in museums, 'by the side of the stone axe and the spinning wheel.' For State, Religion and Law are nothing else but instruments of class rule. They have no other function to fulfil.

State, Law and Religion form the most immediate layer of the so-called 'ideological superstructure,' which is a 'reflection in the minds of men' of the 'economic basis,' the primordial reality of all social and historical life. Law is not only the most immediate, *i.e.* the nearest to the basic layer of the ideological superstructure, but it even permeates the economic basis itself. Marx used to distinguish between what he called *Produktionsweise* and *Produktionsverhältnisse*. By the former ('methods of production) he meant a certain combination of 'productive forces' (*Produktionskrafte*), *i.e.* of natural energies, raw materials, tools of work, man-power, all this being the technical aspect of the process of production. This aspect concerns the attitude of men to nature, while the 'relationships of production' mean the social relationships amongst men which arise on the base of the former. These relationships are the relations of power, and they find their expression in the so-called rights, especially in the rights of property, possession, succession, and paternal rights, and in such legal relations as marriage, servitude, serfdom, the relation of wage-earner to employer, etc. Law and rights are, therefore, a necessary constituent of the economy, the essence of which are 'relationships of production,' *i.e.* power relationships between men. The so-called economic laws imply a good many social laws, which are historically changing. They formulate in the last resort changing relations between men, and not constant relations between things, this latter, 'fetishistic' conception being a fundamental error in classical political economy. Through that, legal constituent economy differs from mere technics, what is economically profitable being different from what is technically perfect. As the Law, with all the 'rights' it implies, withers away in the ideal Communist society, the economy will coincide with technics, and considerations of profitableness will no longer handicap the application of what is technically the best. To use the terms of Saint-Simon, whose influence was decisive on this point of Marxian doctrine, 'the power of men over men will be superseded by the power of united mankind over nature.' For this very reason Russian Communists aimed, in the early stage of the Soviet State, at eliminating political economy, as an exclusively bourgeois science, and substituting for it the pure technical science of the work organisation.

The belief that the liberation of technology from the bondage of profitableness would bring about the state of absolute plenty strengthened the suspicious attitude towards the Law as a mere instrument of class rule. Even after the conquest of power this attitude remained for a long time unchanged, law being regarded as the mere command of the rulers, and not as an agent limiting their arbitrary power. Very effective for the upheaval of the old bourgeois law, such an attitude could not foster respect for any new law. As a matter of fact it was, indeed, responsible for many shortcomings in what has been called 'revolutionary legality' or 'proletarian dictatorship.'

But it would be an unfair misrepresentation to label this revolutionary attitude in Marxian Communism 'totalitarian tyranny.' It is true, indeed, that both fascism and nazism see in the law, like Marxism, nothing else but the instrument of power, the mere command of the rulers denying that the individual has any rights independent of State authority. Without subscribing to economic materialism, they also maintain that spiritual life (knowledge, art, morality) is but the ideological superstructure of a harder social reality where the decisive factors are force and power. What idealistic philosophers call the 'universal validity' of spiritual values (truth, beauty, goodness, justice) is nothing else but a mere fact of social acknowledgement; something is being acknowledged in a social group as true or good or beautiful, first and foremost because of its utility in the existence of the group, its inner coherence and its external power. This sociological point of view may be common to Marxism and fascism, and it is, indeed, shared by some other trends of a doubtlessly liberal character (e.g. the doctrines of E. Durkheim and L. Duguit). But while the essence of fascism and nazism is their imperial or racial particularism, fiercely denying such sentimental ideas as humanity, the most essential feature of Marxism is its universalism, whereby it advances beyond its sociological starting-point.

Marxian universalism goes far deeper than its slogan of proletarian internationalism. It manifests itself first and foremost in the conception of the ideal Communist society. While state, law and religion are doomed to wither away, science, art and morality will become what until now they only pretended to be—the pure expression of truth, beauty and goodness themselves. Until now, in societies divided into antagonistic classes, science, art and morality belonged to the ideological superstructure. They expressed the interests of propertied classes and were instruments of class rule. But after all class divisions, and with them all particular class interests, are abolished, they will become autonomous.

Not only men, but science, art and morality will be freed from all exploitation. They have been mere tools in the class struggle; they will become expressions of pure humanity. This is the deeper meaning of Engels' well-known formula that Communism 'will mean a jump from the kingdom of necessity into the kingdom of freedom.' It means, indeed, a breach in the original conception of economic materialism itself. As in the ideal Communist society there will be no 'economy' (*i.e.* power relationships among men, limiting the application of technology), there will obviously be no more economic 'basis,' 'reflecting itself in men's consciousness' as its 'ideological superstructure.' Instead of only 'reflecting' real economic relationships, the spirit of man will be free in its search of truth, in its expression of beauty, in its relations with other men which will be relations of sympathy and mutual aid and not of everlasting struggle for power. Through technics as applied science, the spirit of man will freely mould its relations to nature, so that science will shape the methods of production, and not instead be shaped by them through the medium of the relationships of production. The individual, instead of being moulded by authorities according to a given social pattern, will realise himself as a free personality. He will freely follow the appeal of truth, beauty and justice, being attracted by their intrinsic value (which is the real meaning of their 'universal validity') and not forced to conform to what is acknowledged by this or that social group as true or fair.

In the perspective of this humanistic and idealistic breach in the doctrine of Marxism, we can better understand the deep gulf between Marxian Communism and totalitarianism. It is true that Marx and his most orthodox followers did see in the law nothing else but the instrument of class rule, and that fascists likewise saw in the law but the command of the rulers. Yet Marx despised the law because he dreamed of a state of things in which men would obey, not the arbitrary rules of men, but either the necessity of nature (in order to override it) or the inner voice of conscience. He shared with the anarchists their ideal of a society based on sympathy, equity and mutual aid, not on rivalry, struggle and rights. For all rights mean delimitation of the spheres of possession, and they are of no use where the motive of possession has yielded to that of creation. Even granted that this contempt for law in favour of a higher morality has in practice all too often turned out to be arbitrariness (according to the proverb that the better is the enemy of the good), it is something very different from the cynical and arrogant treatment of law as the mere instrument of a deificated authority.

It has often been pointed out that there is a flagrant contradiction in the Marxian doctrine between the anarchistic ideal of an almost unlimited freedom of spiritual life and the complete lack of economic liberty. The liberty of cultural activities, say the critics of Communism, can not exist without economic liberty, just as the development of fascism has taught us that private initiative, praised by fascism as the best means to the prosperity and the power of the State, cannot co-exist with total lack of any political and cultural freedom. However strong this argument of the indivisibility of liberty may be as regards fascism, it does not affect Communism at all. In the view of Marx as well as of Lenin, Communism does not suppress economic or political liberty, but, abolishing Economy and State, makes these liberties purposeless. There is no contradiction in thought. The triumph of liberty is complete, because after the substitution of Morality for Law and of Technology for State and Economy man's whole life will be spiritualised. There is also no contradiction as regards the period of transition. In the period of 'the dictatorship of the proletariat,' as is openly acknowledged, all liberties will be suppressed and all rights suspended.

However consistent and noble in its final aim this doctrine of the withering away of State and Law may have been, it was decidedly hostile to the very idea of the rights of man and of the liberties of the individual. Very effective as a weapon of destruction, it was unable to provide a programme for constructive work. The dialectical gap between the anarchistic liberty of its ideal and the denial of individual freedoms during the dictatorial period of transition could only be widened by the consistently negative interpretation of Marx's theory. As up to now, and even in the transitional period, the whole ideological superstructure including science, art and morality are nothing else but the reflection in the consciousness of men of real class relationships, the social revolution giving the whole power to a new class, hitherto eliminated from a share in it, must necessarily involve a totally new ideology. On the ruins of obsolete bourgeois science, philosophy, art and morality an entirely new superstructure must arise, no less opposed to the old than is the new proletarian State and its socialised economy to the bourgeois State and the capitalist economy. The new ideology will hardly pay any regard to bourgeois cultural tradition, save that it may draw profit from its disparate elements, just as people often use the bricks and stones of a ruined building for a new one. The only exception will be the highly socialised technology of capitalist industry, but it too will soon be superseded by proletarian technology.

Of all the Communist leaders, Trotsky seems to have represented this point of view the most consistently. His conception of the permanent revolution was quite intransigent in regard to liberal tradition. He fought not only western capitalist democracy, but everything that could be called democracy either in the Communist Party or in the Soviet Trades Unions. He conceived the proletarian dictatorship on purely military lines: labour mobilised, trades unions entirely subjected to the government, and the Party hierarchically organised from above. And in his opposition to the bourgeois tradition he went so far as to try in a special pamphlet (*Voprosy byta*, Moscow, 1924) to outline the picture of a new everyday life from birth to death, substituting for the old individualist way of life and for obsolete religious symbols totally new ones, collectivist and proletarian. In Soviet educational theory it was the time of the radical upheaval of tradition and of various attempts to build something totally new on the ruins of the old. The most radical of all these attempts was the theory of the 'withering away of the school' in Communist society. It was tried on a large scale at the eve and at the beginning of the new constructive period inaugurated by Stalin with the first Five Year Plan, and was soon rightly exposed as a belated manifestation of 'Trotskyist leftism.'

Stalin's 'building up of Socialism in one country' (though this country was one-sixth of the globe) means a decisive break with the radical Communist conception. Not that Stalin has lost faith in the ideal of an integral Communism or ceased to be a revolutionary fighter. During the second World War he revealed himself, indeed, as a great organiser of victory. But to become such an organiser he has to substitute positive constructive work for mere revolutionary struggle. The final ideal had to be replaced by the realities of life. The industrialisation of the country and the rationalisation of industry and agriculture, on the basis of modern technology and without enslaving the country to foreign capital, have been declared to be the most urgent priorities. 'From everybody according to his abilities, and to everybody according to his work' was the slogan of this constructive socialism, which laid stress on production, not on consumption, as Communism had done in its principle: 'To everybody according to his needs.'

A great deal of courage, perseverance, sagacity and patience was required in order to change the attitude of the average Communist, who could not help seeing the advent of Communism in the Five Year Plan. How many Communists took the industrialisation and the rationalisation of industry for the 'withering away' of everything—profitableness, market, money—by which economy differs from mere technology. How many of them saw in the collectivisation of the farms not the means of raising the productivity of farming through rationalisation and mechanisation, but the achievement of the Communist ideal! The first great blow to this obsolete attitude was Stalin's 'ten points,' published on the eve of 1933. They introduced into the new state-owned industry the principles of business calculation and the responsibility of the management. Instead of thoroughly nationalised industry being regarded as a gigantic common pool, single enterprises received 'business autonomy,' property rights having been defined. The fostering of consumers' and producers' co-operatives was a further step towards introducing into the unified economy the principle of pluralism. The paying of the members of *kolkhozes* according to the size of the family was superseded by pay according to the number of working days and the efficiency of the work. The property of the *kolkhozes* and of the other co-operatives was declared inviolable, and the land-marks delimiting their land irremovable. Inviolable were also declared to be the contracts between enterprises, whether nationalised or co-operative, most of them even including clauses on the payment of damages. Rationing and payment in kind were each year progressively superseded by money wages, even in the *kolkhozes*. When in 1937 rationing was definitely abolished (to be reintroduced as an emergency measure during the war) the Communist press rightly praised this as the triumph of Socialist reconstruction work. It would be overstepping the limits of our subject to enumerate here all the ways in which present Soviet Socialism differs from the original Communist ideal. We have mentioned some of them merely to show that the building up of a Socialist economy (according to Marx and Lenin there is no such thing as a Communist economy) meant the reintroducing, though on new lines, not only of market, money, profit, even credit and interest, but also of Law and Rights. Marx's theory that Law and Rights are a necessary constituent of economy, its formative element, proved true once more. The triumph of this process of the consolidation of the legal framework of the new Soviet society was the Stalin Constitution of 1937. Officially labelled as both socialistic and democratic, it enumerates, among the rights guaranteed by it to all citizens of the Union, the right to work ('and to be paid according to its quantity and quality') and to rest ('forty-hour week, yearly leave and other leisure facilities'), the right to old-age pensions and insurance against illness and infirmity, the right to education (ensured by 'a system of scholarships'), and the right of women to equal treatment and special privileges in cases of maternity. Beside these democratic rights of positive liberty, the Stalin Constitution emphasises (an an 'inalienable right of every citizen') the equality of all citizens without any racial discrimination in economic, political and cultural life, as well as the rights of negative liberty: freedom of religion (and of atheism), freedom of speech and press, and freedom of assembly and meetings, even of 'processions and demonstrations.' A special article guarantees all citizens of the Union the right of association, *i.e.* the freedom of all kinds of organisation (professional, co-operative, sporting, cultural) with the exception of the Communist Party. Further articles guarantee the inviolability of the person, his dwelling and his correspondence. And as regards the right of property, the

Constitution guarantees, besides the property rights of state and co-operative organisations, the right of 'individual property of citizens' ('on their work-earned income and their savings, house, etc'), as well as 'the right of inheritance to such property.'

As regards the rights of positive liberty, the Soviet list of these rights seems not to differ substantially from that of liberal Socialism. The right of the worker not to be exploited, though not formulated especially, is implied in many paragraphs of Section I of the Stalin Constitution. The analogous right of the consumer is not mentioned, obviously because the authors of the Soviet Constitution did not pre-suppose the possibility of the consumer's exploitation by enterprises managed by public bodies and co-operatives. However, the freedom of co-operatives and their unions is guaranteed by the Constitution, as well as the freedom of trades unions. The more their practical independence of the government grows, the more will the trades unions' freedom become a real guarantee against possible exploitation, even though the right to strike is not mentioned in the Constitution, obviously on the ground that in a socialised economy there can be no conflict between workers and management which could not be settled fairly without such detrimental measures. While labelling all idleness as the exploitation of fellow-citizens, the authors of the Soviet Constitution proclaim work to be 'a duty and a matter of honour for every citizen.' They would obviously resist every attempt to establish 'the right to idleness,' and I do not think that their attitude would differ much from the attitude of the Western Socialists, provided the housewife's work is acknowledged as socially useful. The opposite view, popular in Communist circles in the first years of the Revolution, has long ago been exposed as 'leftist prejudice.'

As regards the negative freedoms, the freedom of private enterprise finds, of course, no place in the Soviet Constitution, though small individual enterprises 'based on the personal work of the owner and excluding the exploitation of labour' are allowed in both agriculture and trade. The development of the artisan co-operatives makes the use of the freedom of small enterprise more and more important. It is well known that in East European countries Communist parties, rather on the advice of their Soviet friends, went a good deal further in enlarging the freedom of small enterprise. While the freedom of saving (though, of course, not of investment) is specially mentioned in the Constitution, the Government paying high interest on State bonds, freedom of consumption is implied in repeated declarations by the Soviet Government that rationing is but an emergency measure which will be abolished as soon as the rise of production permits. These words were written in July, 1947. The abolition of rationing backed by a successful deflationary currency reform was carried out in December, 1947. Since then the freedom of consumption and the limits of individual property have been substantially enlarged.

The acknowledgement of the freedoms of negative liberty as necessary attributes of a Socialist State can be real only on the basis of the security of Law. Indeed, according to Stalin, there can be no real building up of Socialism without the 'atmosphere of security.' 'We need the security of Law now more than ever,' declared Stalin in his speech on the Constitution.

We thus see that the more the anarchist idea of the withering away of State and Law ceases to be actual, the more its place is taken by the conception of the rights of men, of negative freedoms and of the security of Law, one presuming the other. It is false to think that the withering away of State and Law would mean the growth of the security of Law and the Rights of Man. Rather the reverse; the fading away of the anarchist ideal has been the indispensable condition for the understanding of the part Law plays in social life, and for the changing of the negative attitude to the Law into the positive one. To yield a complex of concrete rights and freedoms the idea of Liberty, at first abstract and negative, defying historical reality, ought to descend from its absoluteness into the very depths of reality, ought to begin to permeate it and to shape it in a constructive effort. It ought to become clear that liberty, including liberty from exploitation, can not be achieved at once, at one stroke, but is rather a long process of liberation.

The building up of Socialism demands the security of Law, the negative freedoms and the rights of man, and demands democracy, just as it demands the appropriation of bourgeois technology and even of such institutions of traditional economy as market, money, credit, banking, profit and interest. Of course, in a Socialist society all these institutions receive another meaning, being liberated from their servitude to private profit and private power. Just as democracy, ceasing to be a mere instrument in the hands of private monopolies, becomes the people's real rule, the economy is being freed from the limitations to which it is subject under the yoke of capitalist profit-hunting, though it does not merge with mere technics and remains economy. It is Stalin's great merit to have understood this and, still more, to have had the courage and perseverance to carry it into effect.

The task was facilitated by the fact that Marx himself had rather a similar constructive approach to historical tradition. Indeed, his approach was a negation of the bourgeois tradition, but this negation was not exclusively destructive; it was, to use the terms of Hegel, not *Vernichtung*, but *Aufhebung*, *i.e.* a kind of negation in which only the limitations of a principle are denied, its essence being 'saved' and raised to a higher level of development. We have seen that, according to Marx, spiritual culture (morality, science and art) will cease, in the classless society, to be mere 'ideology' and will become in future the realisation of values having universal, not only class, validity. We have then spoken of a breach in Marx's economic materialism. There are many places in Marx's writings where this breach seems to be enlarged, also in the explaining of the past. Marx often points out that in the epochs of feudalism or capitalism there were periods where the feudal class, and later the class of the bourgeoisie, really did fulfil social functions useful and even indispensable for the community as a whole. Being a part of society, it represented society as a whole, just as according to Hegel's philosophy of history each 'historic nation' had its optimum stage of development when it was embodying humanity as a whole or when, speaking in Hegel's own terms, the 'national spirit' was vehicle of the 'world spirit.' There was a time when the feudal baron was really an organiser of the economy of his serfs, being also their protector against numerous robbers and pirates. He provided his tenants with tools of work, cattle, and grain, supplied them with products in times of bad harvest, etc. The justice administered by the baron was based on customary law that was not a mere command of the rulers, but was largely acknowledged as fair. Art and philosophy flourished, they possessed an intrinsic value far transcending their class origin. The same can be said about the bourgeoisie in the seventeenth and eighteenth centuries. At this time the class of feudal landlords had already ceased to play any substantial part in the economy of society. The important social functions it used to fulfil had been taken over by other classes and factors. It kept only its privileges. Thus the 'spirit of the wholeness' had abandoned it. Its philosophy and literature, lacking any elements of universal validity, had degenerated into a retrograde ideology, a vindication of narrow class interest. The place of the degenerate feudal class was taken by the bourgeoisie, which began to represent the interests of the whole of society. Even granted that the postulates the bourgeoisie fought for in the seventeenth and eighteenth centuries did express its class interests, they were welcomed and approved as just and right by an overwhelming majority in all classes of the nation, because of their universal character, transcending narrow class interests. And this could happen, because the 'third estate' was more and more becoming 'everything,' yet legally remaining, as formerly, 'nothing' (in the famous words of Sieyès). This ascendent and revolutionary period of the capitalist class was the time of its prime. Most, and the best of, spiritual culture at this period was of bourgeois origin, and favoured the economic and politic interests of the bourgeoisie. But over and above that, science, philosophy, literature and art; even the conceptions of Goodness and Justice, of Law and State, rooted as they were in the aspirations of the capitalist class, had a universal value transcending mere class interest. Indeed, they revealed and expressed truth, justice and beauty themselves, being far more than the mere reflection of class interest in the brains of men.

In publishing his *Communist Manifesto* (1848) Marx firmly believed that the capitalist class had already fulfilled its historical calling and from being formerly a creative class of society, was more and more becoming a parasitic one.

Its real functions of adventure and discoveries, of management and organisation were in a growing degree being taken over by proletariat, which from a nought was becoming everything. Thus the spiritual activity of the bourgeoisie was losing its freshness and originality of thought, its universal validity, and degenerated into a narrow ideology, defending class privileges and challenging every attempt at social change. Contemporary political economy and the theory of Malthus were, according to Marx, typical instances of such ideology. On the other hand, the proletarian ideology, though deeply rooted in the economic interests of the working class, is far more than mere ideology. As the proletariat becomes the bearer of the interests of the community as a whole, its ideology becomes the revelation of truth itself. It becomes exact science and that for ever because, the proletariat being the last oppressed class and its victory resulting in abolition of all class divisions, there is no more danger of degeneration of the pure new science into mere class ideology.

We see, therefore, that the breach in economic materialism, originally thought of but for the remote future, has also been widened gradually for the present and even for the past. In one of his last letters in the late eighties, Engels went so far as to maintain that the spiritual superstructure evolves its own logic and, by reflecting the 'relations of production,' does for its part influence the economic basis. That the rôle of ideology in shaping economic relationships is especially great in the period of transition, is one of the chief points of Leninism as interpreted by Stalin.

It is closely connected with the new, affirmative attitude towards historical tradition. According to it, there are in what has been created by the bourgeoisie, and even in the epoch of feudalism, elements of imperishable value. Their validity is not limited to a class, but is universal and human. Indeed, this tradition was deeply rooted in the social class relationships of the time. But these class relationships did not create those spiritual values as a mere reflection in the minds of men. They only limited the development of science and technology, of philosophy and art; they have too often lessened their discoveries and deformed their achievements.

While building up Socialism, Communists ought not to reject the cultural tradition of the bourgeois or even of the feudal past, but should only disentangle it from its class limitations. They must free it from its deformation, but also appropriate in it what was great and true.

Even if these briefly outlined philosophical consequences of the new constructive attitude are not yet explicitly acknowledged by Russian Marxists, held in check by the attitude of the revolutionary approach, the practical issues have been formulated clearly and unmistakably by both the most authoritative leaders of Russian Communism. 'To be a Communist,' Lenin said shortly before his illness in 1922, 'means to enrich one's mind with all the values humanity has created in the past.' And ten years later Stalin expressed the same thought in the suggestive words: 'The Proletariat is not a tramp without parentage and kinship. On the contrary, it is the proper heir of whatever great and valuable has been produced in the entire past history of mankind.' From 1933 onward the appropriation of tradition in Soviet Russia has made considerable progress. It began with the appropriation of technology, but was soon enlarged to include education, literature, art, economy, and even political and military tradition.

What kind of tradition was it? That of Byzantine Moscow or the tradition of Peter the Great, the tradition of the West European civilisation? Undoubtedly the latter, all the Russian Marxists being essentially 'Westerners' (*zapadniki*), notwithstanding their Eurasian achievements (consisting largely in the expansion of Western civilisation) and their Slavonic policy, imposed on them by the latest historical developments. Yet one of the greatest ingredients of the European tradition has been undoubtedly the idea of the rights of man. We have, therefore, every reason to expect that further progress in the rehabilitation of tradition, being but the other side of the building up of Socialism in the Soviet Union, will include a growing actualisation of the Rights of Man, and thus contribute to the synthesis we all are aiming at—provided, of course, that this progress will not be checked by armaments and the fear of a new war.

Relationship between different categories of Human Rights

Quincy Wright

HUMAN rights suggest rights which are alike for all human beings. Yet it is recognised that much of human nature is a product of the particular culture in which the individual has developed. Consequently, if all men have something in common which might provide the basis for a universal bill of human rights, it must reside either in common biological, psychological, or spiritual characteristics which persist in spite of cultural differences, or in those common elements of the many cultures which may be regarded as a world culture. The approach to human rights may, therefore, proceed from the analysis of the individual short of all culture, the seventeenth century concept of the 'state-of-nature,' or from the analysis of world culture to be found by abstracting those common elements in all cultures.

From the first point of view, the biologists tell us that all men share with the higher animals desires of varying intensity for life, for food, for sex, and for dominance. The psychologists add the desire for a home territory, for personal freedom, for movement and for society. The theologians and philosophers often insist that all men have also a sentiment of religion and a capacity for abstract thought, although some would derive this sentiment and capacity from culture rather than from original human nature.

From the second point of view, the sociologists and historians find in most cultures the germs of a recognition that human beings as such should be accorded some respect, that each personality should have some sphere of freedom to develop its own genius, that men can discover truth by observation and reason, and that compromise with persons of different cultures is possible. As civilisation has advanced, these principles have been more precisely recognised. The value of some form of human equality, of some measure of individual freedom, of the application of scientific method, and of toleration for cultural and personality diversities have been elements in the world civilisation which emerged with the development of contacts among all parts of the human race after the sixteenth century. These values were also recognised, in part or in whole, by earlier civilisations. Most of them also figure in the great religions, although religions have given greater emphasis to the specific religious value of mystic identity of the individual with the universe, or with the ruler of the universe, than to these more humanistic values.

To assert that men are men and that all cultures have something in common is far from a formulation of rights which may protect the needs and desires of men and may secure for all the values recognised by world culture. Any such formulation encounters circumstances in which individual needs and desires conflict with one another, or with universal values, and even circumstances in which universal values conflict with one another.

Every formulation of a human right that has been suggested raises the following issues: (1) of man *versus* the group; (2) of group *versus* group; (3) of group *versus* the world. These issues necessarily arise in the formulation of a bill of human rights and even more in the establishment of institutions and procedures for the enforcement of such a bill. If the final interpreter of human rights is the individual, society may dissolve in anarchy. If the final interpreter is the group, world society may dissolve in international or class war. If the final interpreter is the world, lesser groups may disappear and a universal tyranny may be possible. Consideration will be given successively to these three basic dilemmas in the formulation of human rights.

Man versus the Group

The issue of man *versus* the group was vigorously presented in the first meeting of the United Nations Human Rights Commission in February, 1947. According to Mr Ribnikar of Yugoslavia:

'The new conditions of the economic, social and national life of our time have tended to develop the spirit of collectivity, and the conscience, and the solidarity of the popular masses. We are more and more aware that real individual liberty can be reached only in perfect harmony between the individual and the collectivity. It becomes quite obvious that this common interest is more important than the individual interest, and that man can liberate himself only when the mass of a population is free.

'In our time the social principle comes first. If it has one purpose, it is to create conditions necessary to the fulfilment of the interest of every individual. The social ideal is the ideal of the enormous majority of the world and it is in the identity of the interest of society and of the individual, Therefore, when we desire to speak today of the rights of man, of modern men, we must not think of the social ideal or of a political ideal of another age. This ideal belongs to the past, and if it remains in some countries, it is the ideal of one class only of a society. . . .'

On the other hand, Dr Malik of Lebanon said:

' . . . the very phrase "human rights," obviously refers to man, and by "rights" you can only mean that which belongs to the essence of man, namely, that which is not accidental, that which does not come and go with the passage of time and with the rise and fall of fads and styles and systems. It must be something belonging to man as such. We are, therefore, raising the fundamental question, what is man? And our differences will reflect faithfully the differences in our conceptions of man, namely, of ourselves. . . .

'The individual human being, you and I, today may not be in need of protection against the despotism of the individual. The day of individual dictators and tyrants may be passed. But if man is no longer in need of protection against the tyranny of kings and dictators, he is desperately in need of protection against another kind of tyranny, in my opinion equally grievous.

'There has been rising in the last few decades a new tyranny, the tyranny of the masses, which seems to have an inevitable tendency of ultimately embodying itself in what I might call the tyranny of the State. If there is any danger to fundamental human rights today, it is certainly from that direction. . . .

'The real danger of the present age is that social claims are in danger of snuffing out any real personal liberty. It is not social security and responsibility that are going to lack advocates and therefore expression in our bill. It is rather the questions which relate to personal values and freedoms. May I express that what I ultimately mean is this. I am not setting an artificial antithesis between the individual and the State. I am asking this question. Which is for the sake of the other? Is the State for the sake of the human person or is the human person for the sake of the State? That, to me, is the ultimate question of the present day. I believe the State is for the sake of the person and therefore our Bill of Rights must express that for the sake of which everything else exists, including the States.'

This debate makes it clear that in spite of the effort of the sociologists to synthesise the individual personality and group culture, the potential conflict between the individual and the group emphasised in Herbert Spencer's *Man versus the State* has not been solved. Those who adhere to the Socialistic view expressed by Mr Ribnikar emphasise social and economic rights such as the right to work, the right to fair conditions of work, the right to social security, the right to education, or in more general terms the rights to freedom from fear and from want. On the other hand, those who share the individualistic thesis expressed by Dr Malik emphasise civil and procedural rights such as the rights of conscience and free speech, rights of association and property, rights of movement and choice of occupation, the right to prompt and fair trial for alleged transgressions of law, and the right to be governed by laws which do not discriminate arbitrarily—rights which contribute to the individual freedom of religion, opinion, expression, and action customarily guaranteed in the eighteenth century bills of rights. It is to be observed that these rights were usually expressed in universal terms, whereas the social and economic rights which have often figured in the bills of rights of twentieth century constitutions usually apply only to nationals of the State. This perhaps indicates that the economic and social rights are less susceptible of universalisation than are the more individualistic rights.

Most of the international bills of rights which have been proposed by private organisations during the last few years include both of these types of rights, and it may be that the alleged incompatability between them has been exaggerated.

146

It is true that States which emphasise social and economic rights have frequently neglected civil and procedural rights in practice. An emphasis upon individualistic rights has also led to problems.

Modern States have generally recognised the need of compromise of individual interests and social interests, and have sought to give some protections by law to both of these interests. Twentieth century Constitutions usually guarantee both of these types of rights to their citizens. They have, however, usually expressed both types of rights relatively rather than absolutely. Furthermore, they have recognised that the method of implementation of these different types of rights must be different.

Individual rights are in the main correlative to negative duties of the State, and social rights are in the main correlative to positive duties of the State. Individual rights require that the State abstain from interference with the free exercise by the individual of his capacities, while the social rights require that the State interfere with many things the individual would like to do, by the collection of taxes, the exercise of police power, the regulation of economic activities, and the administration of public services. Individual rights can, therefore, in large measure be enforced by judicial action, declaring laws and administrative decrees which violate them null and void. The social rights, on the other hand, require legislative, administrative, and executive action to make and to enforce new laws. The individual rights might, therefore, be expressed in an international bill of rights as rules of law susceptible of judicial application, while the social rights can only be expressed as goals or principles for the guidance of national or international legislation, or of international co-operation or administrative activity. Consequently, if both types of rights are included in a common statement, it should be understood that no common mode of implementation would be possible. The international bill of rights would be a declaration of purposes rather than an effective rule of law.

Even in this respect, however, the differences between the two types of rights may be exaggerated. Individual rights, while primarily correlative with the State's duty of abstention, may also require positive State action in establishing and maintaining courts with adequate jurisdiction and in providing criminal legislation and administration to prevent other individuals within the community from encroaching upon these rights. The maintenance of all human rights in the modern interdependent world also requires suitable international agencies and procedures to assure that States observe both the negative and positive duties correlative with the rights.

These considerations suggest that the initial statement of human rights should be in the form of a declaration by the appropriate authorities of the world community, stating the rights but without any formal provision concerning their implementation. It should be assumed that in application the rights are to be regarded as relative to one another and that each is to be implemented by appropriate and perhaps different methods of national and international activity.

Group versus Group

The issue of group *versus* group was less discussed in the meeting of the Commission on Human Rights than was the issue of individual *versus* group, but this potential conflict underlay the discussion as indicated by a statement of Mr Mora of Uruguay:

'The traditional bills of rights have a national character. It seems to me that in the twentieth century we must emphasise the international human rights, the international rights of the man. . . .

'The classic doctrine says that only States are subject to international laws. We need now to declare that man is the most important element of any kind of law, national or international.'

Why did the doctrine develop that only States are subject to international law and that individuals are subject only to national law? It was not because of a socialistic opinion that the group should dominate the individual, but because of the necessity of ultimate State control of its subjects in order to protect the State from outside States.

It is clear that this argument, which objects to human rights on the ground that their enforcement by world authority would qualify the freedom of the State in its international relations, is likely to prevail so long as conditions of power politics and the demand for the absolute autonomy of the national government, economy, and culture prevails. Confidence that the United Nations can assure security to all States may be a condition for the effective implementation of human rights. So long as international emergencies may develop in which State survival may depend on State unity, the State will hesitate to surrender ultimate control of the law applicable within its domain.

But in an interdependent world, security through even the most able playing of power politics may be impossible. Security may be obtainable only through collective security, and that may be obtainable only through the development of the world community. This, in turn, may imply the universal recognition and maintenance of human rights. World institutions which can give security may be impossible unless the world community develops a common culture and common standards of human rights.

The universal maintenance of human rights may create conditions in which these relations between groups may become ones of co-operation and the expectation of peace. The rules of international law, which have defined the relations of State to State, must develop to meet this new situation. The rights of States must be considered relative to the rights of individuals. Both the State and the individual must be considered as subjects of world law and the sovereignty of the State must be regarded not as absolute, but as a competence defined by that law. Such a development, however, implies that the world community is sufficiently organised and sufficiently powerful to assure the security of States under law.

Group versus the World

The issue of the group *versus* the world is recognised in the somewhat conflicting clauses of the United Nations Charter. On the one hand, the Charter forbids the intervention of the United Nations in matters which are essentially within the domestic jurisdiction of any State (Article 2, paragraph 7) and on the other hand, it pledges all the members to take joint and separate action in co-operation with the organisation for the achievement of universal respect for, and observance of, human rights and fundamental freedoms for all, without distinction as to race, sex, language, or religion (Articles 55, paragraph C; 56).

Does this mean that United Nations action to protect human rights is by the Charter placed outside the prohibited sphere of domestic jurisdiction of States? Or does it mean that the protection of human rights is at the mercy of the interpretation and exercise by each State of its domestic jurisdiction?

The resolution of the General Assembly in December, 1946, on the Indian complaint that South Africa was denying human rights to Indians within its territory, suggests the former interpretation. This interpretation is also suggested by the provision of the Nuremberg Charter, sustained as a general principle of law by the Nuremberg Tribunal, that 'act of state' cannot protect individuals indicted for offences against the law of nations.

Experience has shown that States cannot in all circumstances be trusted to respect any standard of rights within their own territories. Barbarities against minorities have in recent years shocked the conscience of mankind. If human rights are to be respected, the United Nations must be armed with competence and with means of enforcement which will modify past conceptions of the sovereignty of the State in the world community. Clearly the law of the Charter of the United Nations which seeks to define the relation of States to the world community must develop appropriate compromises between the domestic jurisdiction of the States and the competence of the United Nations to maintain human rights. The responsibility of the State and the power of the United Nations must be so interpreted as to give assurance that every individual will enjoy human rights.

The considerations set forth in this memorandum suggest that in the drafting of an International Bill of Human Rights, absolutistic concepts of the individual, of the State, and of the world community must be abandoned. The individual and the State, though distinct, are related to one another and this relationship varies with conditions. Among these conditions is the relation of the State to other States and to the world community.

Human rights can only be defined if due consideration is given both to the original nature of man and to the contemporary standards of world civilisation. Any definition of human rights can, however, be implemented as law only if the relationship of each right to the requirements of the State and to the authority of the United Nations is recognised. The functions of the State in protecting the values of the national culture, in organising social experiments, and in maintaining national solidarity must be recognised. The functions of the United Nations in co-ordinating national cultures within the world culture, in organising international co-operation for human welfare and progress, and in maintaining international and world law can develop only gradually. Human rights must be stated in terms which recognise their relativity, and the implementation of each right must develop independently and gradually as the world community develops in solidarity and organisation.

Comparison of Soviet and Western Democratic Principles, with special reference to Human Rights
John Somerville

THE differences between the Soviet and western democratic conceptions are not of principle, but rather of problem-area and method of implementation. On both sides the basic philosophic writings and constitutional documents stress the principle of human rights; that is, that people have inalienable rights in virtue of the fact that they are human beings, irrespective of differences of race, colour, sex or social background. On both sides this stress derives in large part from a common historical source; the general idea of the brotherhood of man, which is, of course, quite old, and the special philosophic and political developments in seventeenth century British and eighteenth century American and French society which produced concrete manifestations of such great historical importance in the area of human rights.

The contrast between the western democratic tradition, and the younger Soviet conception, as it has developed so far, can be traced along the two lines mentioned: area and method. Put briefly, this contrast might be formulated as follows. As to area, the primary emphasis of the western democratic tradition has so far been on political rights, while the primary Soviet emphasis so far has been on social rights, that is, on factors connected with race, colour and sex in relation to such areas as employment, health care and education. As to method of implementation, the primary emphasis of the western democratic tradition has been on giving individuals freedom from government interference, while the primary Soviet emphasis has been on government planning.

Two important points should here be noted. First, these different emphases are not necessarily contradictory, but may be viewed as supplementary. They may well be regarded as different phases or stages in the growth of the democratic principle. Men and women the world over have for centuries needed freedom from arbitrary governmental action in the sphere of political rights. But they have also needed freedom from arbitrary personal or group action on account of race, colour or sex in the sphere of social rights. Moreover, history has amply demonstrated that a given culture or society may have a strong tradition of individual political rights functioning for generations or even centuries, without this tradition, important and valuable as it is in itself, resulting in the attainment of widespread social rights in respect to differences of race, colour, sex, or social background. The hope of mankind really lies in reaching that condition wherein people everywhere will possess both political freedom from arbitrary government action and social freedom in relation to the means of physical and mental development. Put in other terms, our hope should be that Soviet society, as it grows, will extend its conception of human rights more and more to the political sphere, and that western society will extend its conception of human rights more and more to the social sphere. Philosophic analysis lends strength to this hope by pointing out that there is nothing intrinsic to either conception which would prevent this further growth. The two conceptions may be regarded as emphasising different aspects of the same principle.

A second point, connected with the preceding, and likewise important to note, is that the choice of emphasis in each case was hardly accidental. Historical analysis shows that it was dictated largely by the concrete, pressing problems of time and place. When the Soviet régime came to power, it was confronted by these basic problems, among others: mass illiteracy (around 75 per cent), totally inadequate health care, semi-starvation of millions, chronic widespread economic insecurity, and a system of aggravated race discrimination inherited from the Tsarist régime, not to speak of the ravages and tensions of protracted Civil War and armed foreign intervention.

In terms of calm historical reflection, it is perhaps not surprising that this régime, in the thirty years it has so far existed, should have concentrated on the area of social problems. In the language of human rights, as expressed in the Soviet Constitution, this concentration resulted in an emphasis on such conceptions as the right to continuous employment, implemented by State planning and collective ownership of the means of production, the right to education at all levels free from financial, race, colour, and sex barriers, the right to health protection, implemented by a government budgeted national health service, and protection of the newly extended rights of women and of ethnic minorities by strict legal enforcement. Whatever the political sins of the Soviet régime, it should be said to its credit that it has made more progress in the area of these social problems in the course of one generation than the preceding Tsarist régime made in centuries. Instead of about 25 per cent literacy, there is now about 81 per cent. Health care, economic security, the position of women and of ethnic minorities have improved concomitantly.

Historical analysis will also show that the choice of emphasis of the western nations in the area of human rights was far from accidental. While it is impossible to present any adequate historical survey within the limits of this brief report, we can, in a broad view, recognise that the key problem of the western peoples was largely political in the sense that they were historically prepared to take great progressive steps, and to solve their basic problems in new and more fruitful ways if they could but free themselves from the restrictive interference of governments which were largely feudal in orientation. This they succeeded in doing, and one of the priceless results has been the western tradition of political rights and liberties. In other words, the western situation was one in which, if the people were let alone, they could advance, and in which government activity presented itself largely as a hindrance. On the other hand, the Russian situation was incomparably worse. Government action, nationally co-ordinated, presented itself largely as a necessity. While there were certainly other factors operative in the whole historical situation, this pragmatic factor, arising out of the concrete needs in each case, should perhaps be given emphasis.

On our side, I think we might best utilise and strengthen the existing basis of co-operation by concentrating on the area of agreement rather than on the differences. (This should also be done on the other side.) To bear fruit, this process must not confine itself to abstract intellectual recognition at the higher administrative levels. It must find a congenial place in the general educational effort. The predominant pattern of effort in most western nations so far has unfortunately been to emphasise differences rather than agreements, and to concentrate upon what we might recognise as sins and mistakes rather than upon what we might recognise as virtues and achievements. Frequently, in contrasting the western democracies with the Soviet system, what we really contrast is our ideals with their shortcomings, forgetting that they also have ideals and we also have short-comings. Thus, many of us refuse to recognise, let alone emphasise that, in their view, their social principles represent a development of the democratic idea, that they look upon their system as a type of democracy, with differences from contemporary western patterns, but organically connected with the same source, and dedicated to the same ends.

There is, of course, one social system which is explicitly excluded from membership in the U.N.—Fascism, or its German version, Nazism. We cannot help but see sound philosophic reasons for this exclusion: the Fascist and Nazi philosophies emphatically reject, in principle itself, and not simply by any partial deficiency of practice, the very conceptions we have been discussing: the whole idea of the brotherhood of man, the proposition that human beings have equal and inalienable rights irrespective of race, colour or sex, the philosophical and historical developments of the seventeenth and eighteenth century democratic enlightenment. Thus they proudly teach, not only doctrines of racial superiority, but the doctrine that the values of war are superior to those of peace, that aggressive warfare represents the highest form of personal and national conduct. There is an obvious barrier in principle to co-operation with such a system for the purpose of maintaining peace and promoting democratic values. Fortunately, there is no such barrier in the case of the Soviet Union. In spite of these facts, there is still a widespread tendency to couple the Soviet and Nazi-Fascist systems, as if they were built upon an identical set of values, and were dedicated in their philosophies to the same ends. If this tendency is not overcome through proper educational effort, the road to co-operation will remain blocked in the public mind, and the possibility of utilising the actual basis of co-operation will go by default.

Reflections on Human Rights

Kurt Riezler

THE natural law, in its original conception, was intended to include both rights and duties. The exclusive emphasis on the rights of man belongs to the eighteenth century. In our own time, a considerable change of feeling has occurred. Modern man seems to be willing to admit that rights are conditional on duties.

This change of feeling is obvious with respect to property rights. A natural right of doing with one's property whatever one pleases can no longer be claimed. Social legislation interfering in the ways a man runs his factory is supported by public feeling everywhere. The rights of property imply duties.

Hence it seems that any modern formulation of a bill of natural rights should be supplemented by a bill of duties. Any formulation, however, of these obligations of man encounters difficulties far greater than the formulation of a bill of rights. If we assume that the principle of natural law should be respected by, or find an expression in, positive law, any formulation of such obligations will provide the actual power-holder not only with the moral excuses and the intellectual tools but also with the legal instruments to disregard the rights of man. It is he who decides whether the obligations have been respected.

There is only one such obligation, the legal recognition of which may do no harm (though perhaps not much good either). It is everybody's duty to recognise the human rights of his fellow citizen. This would mean, in practice, that whoever advocates the disregarding or abolishing of these rights loses the moral claim to, and the legal protection of, his own human rights.

If, however, these duties of man should be duties towards the 'public welfare' the 'Society' and the State, and rights are made conditional on the fulfilment of these duties, the duties will uproot the rights. The rights will wither away. Whoever is in a position to interpret the *salus publica* or to act in the name of Society or State can use the allegedly unfulfilled duties to shove aside the rights.

A bill of duties of the citizens towards the State would require as its counterpart a formulation of the duties of the 'sovereign' State towards the citizen. However, though the State can compel the citizen, the citizen cannot compel the State to respect these duties.

Hence the possibility that a government transgresses the rights or fails in its duties would logically require not only a right, but a duty, of rebellion or revolution on the side of the citizen—a thing completely empty under modern technological conditions. As this right and duty of revolution can be misused, the State will again have a right and the duty to suppress such revolutions. That means the theoretical justification of civil war by natural law.

Conclusion

Any bill of rights that makes the rights conditional on duties towards society or the State, however strong its emphasis on human dignity, freedom, God, or whatever else, can be accepted by any kind of totalitarian leader. He will enforce the duties while disregarding the rights.

Hence a bill of rights would better be restricted to rights, *i.e.* to those rights which as minimum conditions, however insufficient, of human freedom, any State or society can respect and protect—these are the old civil liberties. Any addition, be it of economic rights, be it of duties, means in practice weakening the civil rights and their hold on the human mind.

The Conception of the Rights of Man in the U.S.S.R. based on Official Documents

Boris Tchechko

Introduction

THE Memorandum on the Rights of Man produced by the Philosophy Section of UNESCO gives, in succinct form, a general survey which is extremely fertile in analytical and constructive ideas; it is most satisfactory to have available such a valuable work of guidance, giving an adequate treatment of one of the greatest problems of contemporary civilisation.

As a preliminary to the endeavour to arrive at a higher synthesis by the comparison of certain guiding ideas or even different conceptions of life, it is advisable that the premises of the problem should be stated as precisely as possible. In this connection, it seems to us that the true starting-point of Marxist-Leninist philosophy has not been made sufficiently evident. In particular, it seems to us inaccurate, both historically and ideologically, to present Marxism as a sort of light coming from the East and to consider the West, on the other hand, almost as the natural guardian of the so-called 'Western' spiritual and ethical values.

The links which attach Marx and Engels to the great English intellectuals, such as Francis Bacon, Hobbes and Locke, with his theory of experience, and to the French Encyclopedists, are so well-known that it is unnecessary to dwell on them. The contributions of Kant and Hegel, often in conflict with one another, must also be mentioned; last but not least, the system of dialectical materialism could scarcely have been conceived without the ancient foundations laid in Aristotle's *Universalia in Re* and Plato's *Dialogues*.

The right way to reach the higher synthesis we are seeking to establish in the light of ideas and facts which can be verified in history, is perhaps to realise the full and entire inter-dependence of the ideas of East and West—even from the ill-defined and debatable standpoint of geographical demarcation—instead of accepting the rather rough and ready contrast between East and West, based on the once-famous phrase of Rudyard Kipling 'East is East and West is West.'

The country of the Incas should properly be considered as the original home of State Socialism, as is proved in an extremely interesting work, not yet published, written by a professor at the Catholic University in Paris, M. Jean Pouzyna (following the parallels drawn between Campanella's *City of the Sun* and Thomas More's *Utopia*).

Furthermore, at one time, both Egypt and China experienced a fully developed system of State control. In short, it seems to us difficult, if not actually misleading, to try to contrast Marxism with Liberal Capitalism as the concepts of East and West respectively. In view of the close inter-relationship of the ideas and concepts of every continent and every race, we have to regard those ideas and concepts as stages in the general development of the world as an economic entity.

The 1936 Constitution of the U.S.S.R.

On such a view of the relentless stages in the economic evolution of mankind and the associated rights of man, the 1936 Constitution of the U.S.S.R., rightly called the 'Stalin' Constitution, not only constitutes one of the most decisive stages in the advance of the ideas of the democratic emancipation of man, but also—and this is of vital importance—sets man as a worker in ideal political, social and economic conditions, and gives him facilities for work and intellectual life.

Following the decision of the Seventh Congress of the Soviets of the U.S.S.R., the Commission on the Constitution, under the chairmanship of Stalin, submitted its report to the Eighth Extraordinary Congress, after investigation among the people lasting five and a half months.

General Characteristics

In particular M. Stalin said on that occasion: 'it will be a short clear historical document, almost a record of the celebrations of the victory of Socialism in the U.S.S.R., the liberation of the workers of the U.S.S.R. from capitalist slavery, the victory of fully-developed democracy carried to the logical conclusion, in the U.S.S.R.'[1] Ten years later, M. Chvernik, the President of the Council of the Supreme Soviet of the U.S.S.R., wrote: 'the new Constitution is a document describing simply and succinctly an historical victory of importance to the whole world, the victory of Socialism in the U.S.S.R., the liberation of the workers from capitalist slavery, the abolition of private ownership of the instruments and means of production.'[2]

The fact that the Constitution was unanimously adopted by the Congress should never be regarded as the result of pressure brought to bear upon the free choice of the delegates; on the contrary, each one of them gave his approval, with a full knowledge of the facts, to the proposals submitted to him by M. Stalin and M. Molotov, on behalf of the Commission on the Constitution, which had been working for years on the preparation of the texts. Thus, each article had been hammered out by a team, in accordance with the system generally adopted in the U.S.S.R., so that, by its content, form and repercussions for the future, it was linked to the deepest aspirations of the workers as a whole.

Intellectuals in the U.S.S.R.

First of all, we should like to clear up once more any possible misunderstanding about so-called 'forbidden territory' for intellectuals in the U.S.S.R. Intellectuals are looked on with favour in every field. Articles 2, 3 and 123 of the Constitution, which proclaim and guarantee the equality of all citizens without restriction and which have the force of an indefeasible law, are quite explicit on that point. There is no conflict between *Homo economicus* and *Homo sapiens*. In this connection it seems appropriate to quote an extract from an article in *Pravda* of June 18th, 1936: 'The drafts of the Stalin Constitution reflect an exceptionally important fact—that intellectuals have equal

---

[1] *Pravda*, February 26th, 1947.

[2] N. Chvernik—*Stalinskaia Konstituzia Sozialistitcheskago Obtschestva Cospolitisdat 1946.*

rights and freedom in a Soviet country, on exactly the same footing as the working classes and the peasants: the Soviet intellectual is a member of society with the same rights as all other citizens in a country which has abolished the classes which used to exploit the others and in which the working classes, peasants on the collective farms and intellectuals enjoy equal rights and property.'

Guiding Principles of the Constitution

An analysis of the guiding principles[1] enshrined in the Constitution involves a type of classification which, in view of the close relationship between the ideas and forms of words used, is somewhat artificial.

The Right to Work. The first principle is contained in Article 118 of the 1936 Constitution, the text of which is given below;[2] it is the right to live, not in the abstract, but the right to live in conditions suitable for the healthy functioning of any human organism, with its need to breathe, to drink, to eat and to create, leading to the right to regular employment paid according to the quantity and quality of labour. Article 118 can (and indeed must) be regarded as the king-pin of the whole Soviet system, since the right to work is ensured by the *Socialist organisation of the national economy* with its Five-Year Plans.

Individual Liberty. The second guiding principle is that of individual liberty within the social and economic machine, the whole mechanism of which is designed to achieve a

---

[1] Bergson gives a purely philosophical definition of them, whereas Marx wrote: 'a theory becomes a practical force when it is absorbed by the masses.' (*Œuvres Philosophiques*, Paris, 1927, vol. 1, page 96)

[2] 'Citizens of the U.S.S.R. have the right to work, *i.e.* they have the right to secure employment, remunerated according to the quantity and quality of their work.

The right to work is guaranteed by the socialist organisation of the national economy, the continual development of the productive forces of Soviet society, the removal of the risk of economic crises and the abolition of unemployment.'

Connected and derivative problems are dealt with elsewhere, such as the right to leisure and the right to education, which are treated in Articles 119 (1946) and 120, respectively.

single purpose: to give man, in his creative aspect, the opportunity to express himself in every field of human activity (Articles 124 to 128).

Equality. The third principle—that of equality in all branches of economic, political, cultural, social and public life is included in Article 123 which has the force of an indefeasible law.

Returning to that cornerstone of the Constitution, Article 118 read in conjunction with Article 119, 120 and 121, which are dependent on it, we quote an article from the newspaper *Pravda* of October 16th, 1936, which gives an admirable statement of the feelings of all citizens of the U.S.S.R.: 'The right to work! the right to education! the right to leisure! the vast majority of men living in the world look upon these words as the expression of a cherished dream, not yet to be realised; for Soviet citizens, however, these are natural self-evident rights.'

In the endeavour to achieve a higher synthesis, legal authorities have proposed to confer an additional personal guarantee on all Soviet citizens by proposed legislation under the general provisions of Article 118—the right to institute judicial proceedings against any Soviet organisation which, with vacant posts, refuses without sufficient reason to engage the individual concerned.[1]

The Ideological Foundation of Socialism in the U.S.S.R.

The socialist organisation of the national economy, on which the above-mentioned articles of the Constitution are founded, has its roots far back in the history of the U.S.S.R. Russia did not in its development undergo the stages of feudalism and capitalism and therefore never had that respect for private property which was enshrined by the French Revolution in the famous Preamble to the Constitution of 1789—the Declaration of the Rights of Man and the Citizen (Article 17).

Count Witte,[2] one of the greatest statesmen of the older

---

[1] Dogadov, *Sovietskaya Justizia*, 1939, Nos 19-20
[2] Summary of the speeches made before H.I. the Grand Duke Michael Alexandrovitch in 1900 to 1902 (Russian, *St. Petersburg, 1912*, page 137)

Russia, remarked that Russia had entered the stage of industrial development much later than other States and that the capital invested in industry amounted to no more than two milliard rubles, representing eight rubles per head of the population, as compared with 300 in England and 90 in Germany. On the other hand, the *Mir* (a type of association of peasants bound to the land) had civic rights throughout Russian history until the agrarian reforms of Stolipine in 1906.

As early as 1820, the Revolutionary movement known as the Decembrists[1] in which the best of the nobility took part, provided in its programme, under the title of 'Russian Truth,' for the establishment of a Republic and the inalienability of land—and even more of the riches of the earth—which the movement declared belonged to the nation as a whole. It is interesting to see that the State collective farms (*Sovkhozes*) and the private collective farms (*Kolkhozes*) had their glorious fore-runners as far back as 1820. The *Intelligentzia* (the most progressive elements among the intellectuals), who originated various movements for political liberation, boasted, almost to excess, of the material disinterestedness of their personal life and of their reformatory zeal.

The Slavophiles (1830 to 1940), who preached the orthodox faith, obstinately defended the peasant communities as being the economic and spiritual units of Russia.

The ideas of the *Narodniki* (socialist popularists) and the Nihilists (from the Latin word *nihil*—nothing) were closely related to anarchy, but there was no system in them, and true anarchists such as Prince Kropotkin and others repudiated them. The Westerners, including Herzen, Granovsky and Belinsky, advocated individualism and legal formalism on the so-called Western model, but, as they had very close links with international socialism, they were obviously by no means defenders of property rights in any form. In short, all ideological movements in Russia during

---

[1] Among them were Prince Trubetskoy, Prince Volkonsky, Prince Oblonsky, Muraviev, Rilciev, Pestel, nearly all officers of the Imperial Guard.

the eighteenth century were definitely hostile to Western ideas of the right to property, even as expressed in the Declaration of the Rights of Man of 1789, with all the provisos included therein.[1]

A galaxy of famous names such as Bakounin, Prince Kropotkin and Herzen, spread their ideas throughout Europe, thus strengthening the foundations of international socialism.

Lastly, the greatest Russian poets and thinkers, with that deep sense of truth and individual and social justice which is, generally speaking, characteristic of the Slav mind, men like Tolstoy and Dostoievski, have given us living and moving embodiments of those ideas—the Christian philosophy of Platen Karatayev in all its naïvety, Pierre Bezukhov's irresistible impulse towards spiritual perfection (*War and Peace*), Levine's *Sehnsucht* (*Anna Karenina*). Is it possible to forget the conversations in *The Brothers Karamazov*? Needless to say, they could never support the age-old slogan: *Beati Possidentes*. It is characteristic of Tolstoy's life, whose existence on his little estate of Yasnaya Polyana was simple enough, that towards the end of his life he should leave his home, fleeing from the pleasant comfort which was no longer consonant with his intense longing for complete liberation from the so-called bourgeoisie.

The Commission on the Constitution, under the leadership of Stalin and Molotov, certainly assimilated the ideological stock-in-trade of the *Intelligentzia* and put it to the best possible use, as they did the ideas furnished by the Declaration of Independence (July 4th, 1776) and the Declaration of the Rights of Man (1789); but its work would have been impossible but for the clear and precise contribution drawn from the guiding principles of Marxism.

Declaration of Independence

It would be interesting to compare the Constitution of 1936 with the work of Thomas Jefferson, helped by Adams, Franklin and Sherman, which is considered by the *Encyclopedia*

---

[1] N. de Basily, *La Russie sous les Soviets*, Paris, Plon, 1938, pages 479 *et seq*

Britannica (volume 7, page 125) as 'the best known and the noblest of American state papers.'

This opinion was confirmed recently by a prominent statesman, Mr Winston Churchill, who, in an article in the *Figaro* of April 15th, 1947, under the title of '*Si j'étais américain*' ('If I were an American'), wrote: 'that declaration is complete in itself; nothing can be omitted; nothing can be added; nothing can be repudiated.' Mr Marshall, the United States Secretary of State, did not share that opinion when, on March 14th, 1947, at Moscow, he expounded to the Conference of Foreign Ministers the theory of the five freedoms (*New York Herald Tribune*, March 18th, 1947, 'Demonstrating Democracy'), the rights of the individual, the rights of political association, the right of publication, the right of movement, the right of trade. Incidentally, the five rights mentioned above are by no means the same as the four freedoms proclaimed by his former chief, the late President Roosevelt. Obviously, such enthusiastic approval of a document which, though valuable, dates from the end of the eighteenth century, could not, in the circumstances, be shared by the Commission on the Constitution.

Although the American document[1] was indeed the masterly work of Thomas Jefferson, a man of high moral authority, it was composed by people whose reasoning was attuned to the atmosphere and circumstances of the time. The document was inspired by the very vague theories of the indefeasible rights to life, liberty and the pursuit of happiness, and met the needs of the struggle for the economic and political emancipation of the American continent, on which British control weighed heavily and which was waiting, with its vast untapped wealth, for pioneers. In fact private enterprise was called upon to supply the lack of means of production and social organisation.

On the other hand, if the same tenets were applied in the modern world, they might degenerate into an unenforceable law, for the lack of economic and social safeguards. One idea, however, dependent on the general idea of liberty, is still as potent as ever; that is the right to 'change or abolish any form of government and to set up a new government

---

[1] Jefferson's works, vol. 7, page 305

based on such principles and such organisation of power as the people may consider most appropriate to achieve its ends of security and happiness.' (*op. cit*)

The Commission on the Constitution could do no more than note the Declaration of Independence as an historical fact of great importance, whose practical value was nevertheless relative in view of the fundamental change in economic life and, particularly in methods of production, distribution and consumption.

The Declaration of the Rights of Man, derived from the Declaration of Independence,[1] influenced by the 'Social Contract' and Calvinism with its doctrine of individual liberty in relation to any earthly authority, and foreshadowed by the philosophical movement of the Encyclopedists and the Masonic Lodges, has been established as the historical monument of political thought in the eighteenth century and the first part of the nineteenth. The logic and lucidity of the ideas and passions which inspired it still exercise their attraction in our day, in spite of some contradictory anachronisms, such as Article 13, which demands that all citizens should contribute *equally* to the community's finances, on the basis of their taxable capacity. It is a well known fact, however, that indirect taxation affects most hardly the least wealthy members of the community and indeed that in the country which gave birth to the Declaration of the Rights of Man the major portion of the national expenditure has always been covered by indirect taxes and dues (State monopoly of tobacco, matches, etc). The political emancipation of the French bourgeoisie was completed and Article 17 of the Declaration confirms the supremacy of the Third Estate and centres power in the hands of its leaders.

Dialectical and Historical Materialism—the Scientific Instrument in the U.S.S.R.

The Commission on the Constitution certainly drew inspiration for its own work from the glorious past but, in the light of the great changes which had come about—the

---

[1] According to Prof. M. Jellinck's famous work *Die Erklärung der Menschen-und Bürgerrechte.*

industrialisation of Europe and the beginning of Marxist philosophy—political thought was compelled to take account of other hypotheses, those of the formulæ of that dialectical materialism which is the foundation of the U.S.S.R. Diamat —an abbreviation for dialectical materialism—has so preponderant a place in the scientific, political and social life of the peoples of the U.S.S.R. that, in order to understand the full significance of a particular idea or formula or to find its place in the system, it is necessary to call into service the basic ideas of dialectical materialism.

From the philosophical point of view, the materialist proposition takes the familiar form: '*non est in intellectu quod non est in sensu*'; uncompromising idealists used to find a means of evasion by adding '*nisi intellectus ipso.*'

As a method of analysing and evaluating ideas, men and things, Diamat differs appreciably from all other systems, because the determining factors are based on the data supplied by historical materialism, which regards the system of obtaining and producing material goods as the chief force in the construction of society and its various phases of development.

The instruments of production, men with their experience of production and their working habits, constitute the productive forces of society, while the relationships between men in production determine ultimately what type of social organisation is to be adopted, based on one of the five fundamental types: the primitive community, slavery, the feudal system, the capitalist system and the socialist system. 'Historical materialism brings the principles of dialectical materialism to the study of social life; it applies those principles to the phenomena of social life, to the study of society and to the history of society.'[1]

According to the Marxian dialectic nature is considered not as a fortuitous conglomeration of objects and phenomena, but as a unified and coherent whole; that whole is in a

[1] History of the (Bolshevic) Communist Party in the U.S.S.R. Summary prepared by the Commission of the Central Committee of the Communist Party (B) of the U.S.S.R. and approved by the Central Committee, Moscow 1939, pages 98 *et seq.* It is common knowledge that Chapter IV of the work in question was largely written by M. Stalin (p 99)

state of constant movement and change. In this connection Engels wrote: 'The whole of nature, from the tiniest particles to the largest bodies, from the grain of sand to the sun, from the unicellular organism to man, is, as it were, part of an eternal process of appearance and disappearance, a state of continual flux, perpetual movement and change. . . . Nature is the touchstone of dialectic and it must be admitted that modern natural sciences have furnished an ever-increasing wealth of material for such experiment.'[1] The Marxian dialectic reaches the following conclusion with regard to the nature of things: 'any change is a transition from quantity to quality.'

Constants, as they are called in physics, are most frequently only the nodal points at which the addition or subtraction of movement (a quantitative change) gives rise to a qualitative change in a body, in which, as a result, quantity becomes quality (*op. cit*). Lenin for his part says[2] that 'dialectic, in the proper sense of the term, is the study of contradictions in the essence of things.' Engels adds that the materialist conception of the world simply means the conception of nature as it is, without extraneous additions.[3] There is no doubt that, in the light of Diamat applied to history, the rights of man lose their immutable character and become malleable material, for the handling of which a profound understanding of the real facts of politics, *i.e.* those which are founded on the economic conditions of the period, is necessary.

The essential substance of the ideas of liberty—whether political, social or individual—varies from century to century; the Declaration of Independence conceives liberty from the standpoint of the exploitation of the natural wealth of the country; the extreme and almost anarchic form of individualism is at its height. There is justification for every form of freedom and no arguments against; it is the time of clearing the ground in the economic sphere. The Declaration

[1] Karl Marx and F. R. Engels, *Complete Works*, Moscow 1935 (German edition, page 491)
[2] *Philosophical Notebooks* (in Russian) page 263
[3] Marx and Engels, *Complete Works*, volume 14, page 651 (Russian edition)

of the Rights of Man is founded on the assumption that the main purpose of liberty is to serve the ends of the bourgeoisie, which had thrown off the yoke of the royal power and the nobility of Sword and Robe. Habeus corpus came into being in order to provide a safeguard, in judicial procedure, for man's physical body. Its underlying purpose was to help the future 'Ironsides' of commerce and industry. The 1936 Constitution of the U.S.S.R., which is founded on the principles of dialectical materialism, aims at nothing but ensuring the true liberty of the individual by safeguarding his right to work within the socialist organisation of the national economy. The economic and philosophical standards of Marxism are not the same as those of capitalism.

With regard to political liberty, for instance, entailing liberty of conscience, publication, association, and, ultimately, of the formation of political parties,[1] constructive thought in the U.S.S.R. has reached a quite different conclusion.

At the Eighth Congress of Soviets, M. Stalin stated that 'several parties and, by deduction, party freedom, can only exist in a society in which there are antagonistic classes, with mutually conflicting interests, side by side. In the U.S.S.R., however, there are no such classes.'[2] What seems high treason to democracy, leaves Soviet citizens unmoved, as they are citizens of a classless society, and therefore without conflicting interests. In the U.S.S.R., political liberty is regarded chiefly as the right to break free from a capitalist State, because, in socialist society, the individual; has no desire for liberation from the State.[3] Individual liberty—individualism in all its forms—looks quite different when it is considered from the point of view of the enslavement of the individual in a capitalist State. The famous Russian writer and philosopher, Maxim Gorki,[4] defines individualism as a fruitless attempt by man to protect himself from the violence and oppression of the capitalist

---

[1] Articles 125 and 126 of the Constitution of 1936.
[2] *Pravda*, November 26th, 1936
[3] John Somerville, *Soviet Philosophy*, New York, 1946, p 74
[4] *Culture and the People*, pp 117 *et seq*

State. Gorki rejects the animal individualism of the bourgeoisie in the name of the individual, who can regard himself free only in a socialist society.

The concept of liberty as determined by the socialist form of society completely upsets the definition of the rights of man.

In his most important work,[1] Mr Sidney Webb, discussing the burning question whether the Government of the U.S.S.R. is a democracy (and not a dictatorship), draws attention to the fact that the question should not be put 'in terms of the old classifications or previous definitions, which are sources of sociological error.' The reply he gave was in the affirmative, in spite of the official opinion by M. Stalin that 'in the Soviet Union, where the dictatorship of the proletariat is an accomplished fact, not a single problem of policy or organisation is decided by our Soviets and other mass organisations without directives from our Party.'[2]

This principle of government is in accordance with the system of teamwork to which we have already referred. In his 'Interview with a German writer'[3] M. Stalin said: 'From experience of three revolutions, we know that out of every hundred decisions taken by a single person, without being supervised and tested by the community, ninety or so are not sufficiently objective.'

The New Democratic Civilisation

The fact that the U.S.S.R. is ruled by all its adult citizens, without any form of discrimination, so that all its inhabitants are included in a vast network of collective organisations in accordance with the principles of the new political economy as embodied in practice in the Five-Year Plans; the fact that a systematic philosophy and a new code of behaviour based on a fresh ethical conception of the relations of man to the universe and his duties towards his fellows has been created—all these factors led Mr Sidney Webb to the conclusion that: 'we seem to be concerned with something

---

[1] *Soviet Communism*, London 1944, p 347
[2] *Leninism*, 1928, vol. 1, p 33
[3] *Moscow*, 1932, pp 5 *et seq*

more important than a Constitution—with a new civilisation'[1]; that, in fact, is the subsidiary title of his work mentioned above.

Mr Somerville,[2] a sagacious observer, remarks that the conception of democratic government, as understood in the U.S.S.R., is not restricted to the normal institutions of government, but, on the contrary, gives rise to higher bodies formed by all the economic and social institutions.

It is no longer a question of the form, but rather of the underlying principle of government; true democracy is shown not only by the fact that property rights have been transferred to the State (by nationalisation) but also, and chiefly, by the fact that there is an active democratic administration at every level of the processes of production (through socialisation). The Soviet system, in practice, has discovered a rapid means of making democratic the large economic organisations, such as combines and trusts, in which the management of affairs had to be concentrated in the hands of a few highly qualified people, besides the familiar forms of direct administration in collective farms, factories, etc. That means is 'self-criticism'—the critical examination by all the workers at every level of production or administration, an ordered and regimented criticism, admittedly, which has produced most satisfactory results. Such a periodical examination brings to light all the faults of the administration, on the one hand, and, on the other, provides a channel and direction for all constructive suggestions for improving labour.

From all these general considerations related to the application of dialectical materialism, firstly to history, and secondly to the organisation of government and society, from the strenuous efforts of all the peoples of the Soviet Union during the last few decades and particularly during the great sufferings of the patriotic war which, as Stalin said in a speech to the electoral meeting held on February 9th, 1946,[3] was: 'a kind of test of our Soviet order, our State, our Government, our Communist Party'—from all the foregoing, and many other factors which have been merely

---

[4] *Op. cit*, pp 347 *et seq*
[2] *Op. cit*, p 47
[1] N. Chvernik, *Op. cit*, p 11

touched on in this paper, the shape of a new civilisation begins to appear, with a rather different type of man, with a conception of ethics which he considers to be the most democratic in the world.

Soviet Ethics

Soviet man is convinced that 'in a classless society, everyone leads a higher life from the moral standpoint, because the existing social and economic institutions do not compel men to exploit one another.'[1] A Soviet philosopher[2] has written: 'What is important to society becomes important to the individual, without thereby losing its social importance —this is demonstrated in the vigour of individual aspirations and energy.'

There is but a step from such a concept to the acceptance of the principle of socialism—from each according to his means, to each according to his labour.

Soviet man is convinced of the superiority of socialist economy, because that economy necessarily excludes the possibility of war and economic crises.[3] The figures which are quoted as representing the direct and indirect losses due to the two world wars, have not been prepared and checked with the requisite care, and the approximate estimates drawn from various sources should be considered subject to reserve; for various reasons, a total figure of 600 milliard dollars (200 for the first world war, and 400 for the second) is, in our opinion, the most nearly accurate.

It is impossible to estimate, even approximately, the cost of periodical economic crises; the origins of such crises are as debatable as they are ill-defined, ranging from the effect of the sun's radiation on the weather, and consequently upon the crops, through the psychological explanation of crisis cycles, involving the forces of production, distribution and consumption, properly so-called, to the explanation provided by M. Stalin[4]: 'Economic crises in capitalist countries

---

[1] Somerville, *Op. cit*, pp 90 *et seq*
[2] An article by M. Rubinstein in the Russian newspaper *Under the Banner of Marxism*, Moscow 1943, No 9-10
[3] Articles 1-12 of 1936 Constitution
[4] *History of the Communist Party in the U.S.S.R.*, Moscow 1930, p 115

—where capitalist private ownership of the means of production is in direct conflict with the social character of the productive process and the nature of the productive forces— are an illustration of the clash between relationships in production and the nature of the productive forces, and of the conflict in which they are engaged. . . . The socialist economy of the U.S.S.R.—where communal ownership of the means of production is perfectly suited to the social character of the productive process, and where there are, consequently, no economic crises or wastage of the forces of production—is an example of the perfect adjustment of relationships in production to the nature of the productive forces.'

Soviet man realises that, under a capitalist system, the 'normal reserve of unemployed workers' is inevitable, as Marx said; this opinion is strengthened by the admission of the late Lord Keynes, an authority on financial matters recognised throughout the world, that some degree of unemployment, called cyclical unemployment, is an inevitable consequence of technical development.

The Soviet system of ethics not merely proclaims the equal rights of men and women, but endeavours to protect women, mothers and children, so that woman's natural function shall not be to her disadvantage. In the U.S.S.R., a woman does not have to choose between her desire to have a home or a career; the two are perfectly complementary (Article 122).

The Soviet system of ethics recognises full freedom of conscience by the separation of the Church from State and School, and by putting on the same level religious observance and anti-religious propaganda (Article 124).

The Technical Development of the 1936 Constitution

In the light of the principles mentioned above, the changes made in various articles of the 1936 Constitution —changes which are, so to speak, technical—are understood, on examination, more readily and appear more logical.

Reverting to the most crucial of all the rights of man in the twentieth century—the right to economic existence— we see that once the general idea of emancipation had been conceived by the builders of socialism, it was tirelessly and systematically pursued.

In the earlier Constitutions of 1918 and 1924, for instance, the expression of the right to work (Article 118) could not be included, because unemployment was not finally abolished until 1931, andt he right to leisure was included only in 1936 (Article 119). The earlier Constitutions provided only for an 8-hour working day, holidays with pay and health insurance. The patriotic war and the demands of reconstruction made changes necessary in Article 119.

At its meeting held in February, 1947, the Supreme Soviet of the U.S.S.R. approved the new form of Article 119, which was more suited to the bitter reality of that moment in history. Under Article 119 'the citizens of the U.S.S.R. have a right to leisure. This is guaranteed by the reduction in the length of the working day to 8 hours for manual workers and clerks, to 7 or 6 hours for a class of occupations in which working conditions are arduous, and to 4 hours in workshops in which conditions are exceptionally arduous; by the establishment of annual holidays, with pay, for manual workers and clerks; and by the provision of a vast network of sanatoria, rest-houses and clubs for workers.'

In 1918, free universal education was provided only for manual workers and poor peasants, whereas the Stalin Constitution (Article 121) extends it to all citizens of the Soviet Union.

Freedom of publication and of assembly was proclaimed in 1918, but practical safeguards were provided for the working-class and the peasants because there were still classes at that time.

In 1936—under Article 125—everything was provided for all workers and their organisations: printing facilities, paper, public buildings, streets, postal and telegraph facilities, etc.

Personal inviolability naturally did not exist in the civil war years, or even during those of the N.E.P.; in 1936 it was recognised by Articles 127 and 128 of the Constitution.

In 1918, for similar reasons, certain classes of citizens—the clergy and former government officials—were deprived of the right to vote. In 1936, Articles 134 and 135 recognised the right of all Soviet citizens to vote. The fundamental rights and duties of the citizen appeared for the first time in 1936 (Chapter 10 of the Constitution).

The development of Soviet views on the question of the sovereign rights of the constituent republics of the Union, is extremely instructive; as far as possible, the State withdraws, and allows the national aspirations of the federate or republics full play. At its meeting in February, 1947, the Supreme Soviet approved the changes and amendments to Articles 14, 18, 13, 22, 23 and 48, by which the constituent republics of the Union were given the right to establish diplomatic relations with foreign States and to conclude with those States agreements for the exchange of diplomatic and consular representatives; furthermore, the republics were given the right to have their own national armies. As M. Molotov, the Soviet Foreign Minister, said in his report to the Supreme Council on February 1st, 1944, this 'constitutes a great development in the scope of the activities of the federated republics.'[1]

At the same time, at the same meeting of the Supreme Soviet of the U.S.S.R., in February, 1947, M. Vishinsky, the Vice-Minister of Foreign Affairs, stated:[2] 'The epoch-making decisions taken by the Supreme Soviet of the U.S.S.R. represent an important advance in the development of the national question in the U.S.S.R., by consolidating and extending the sovereign rights of the federated republics.'

Conclusion

The United Nations Commission on Human Rights is shortly to begin drawing up a theoretical code of rights for all human beings throughout the world.

This work may have a very important influence, by providing a basis on which national legislative assemblies may work, and may perhaps help towards the development of a law of habeas corpus, not only in the legal field with regard to individual liberty, but, even more, with regard to the observance of the legitimate material requirements of man in international life.

It may be hoped that ideas, theses and suggestions will come from various sources, covering all contemporary philosophical movements. The work will necessarily be eclectic, and will, so to speak, serve as a catalytic agent for

---

[1] and [2] *Pravda*, February 26th, 1947

all the constructive forces of society, by creating an atmosphere and conditions more propitious for the discovery of a general body of principles, which can only be a 'golden mean.'

On the threshold of the atomic age, and pending application of nuclear energy to technical development, humanity finds itself compelled to seek a *modus vivendi* for the nations at the international level, as well as for individuals. It is probable that the present ideas of social life will have to undergo profound changes in order to adapt themselves to the dazzling prospect before us in the material field; it will therefore be essential to give the rights of man that practical foundation which has been lacking in past centuries.

On the Draft Convention and Universal Declaration of the Rights of Man

Levi Carneiro

THE first declarations of the rights of man, proclaimed by several nations, go back to the eighteenth, or even the seventeenth century. At first, they were characteristic of the democratic régime, but are today inscribed in nearly all, if not all, modern constitutions, where they form a long and detailed section which tends to become increasingly long and detailed.

Originally, they were limited to civil and political rights; they were then extended to other, economic rights, which have also been described, rather vaguely, as social rights. In addition to rights, these declarations set forth the guarantees without which the rights cannot become effective.

It is by the extent of these guarantees that we can judge the value of the political régime of each nation. Not infrequently nationalist prejudices deprive foreigners of what are called social rights. Nor is it rare for vicissitudes of internal politics to destroy all these rights and guarantees. We also see the existence and survival of oppression, with the aid of modern automatic weapons and the resources of the public treasury, which the dictators of today always know how to exploit. Thus national declarations have proved inadequate.

The joint proclamation of these individual rights, made by the civilised nations, will constitute not only a perfect guarantee for man, the full expansion of his personality, in every corner of the globe; it will also be a proof of the political identity of nations, of the realisation of democracy throughout the world, of the universal spread of culture. All national declarations will have a common denominator.

We must not imagine that all nations have now reached the same degree of perfection in the recognition and guarantee of the rights of man. But the joint declaration will serve as a guide to the legislators of the different countries; it will encourage the expansion and improvement, along the same lines, of national declarations, which are still incomplete or inadequate, raising them to the level which all should attain. It is necessary not merely to make good the omissions in the declaration of each country, but also to try, as far as possible, to eliminate discrepancies due to different, sometimes diametrically opposed, concepts.

Relations between States are based on the assumption that the internal politics of each nation are the concern of all nations. The international declaration will thus be a factor for democratisation and international peace.

The international declaration of rights will also be a factor for peace, because it will be able to reconcile the two divergent, if not antagonistic, political concepts confronting each other in the world today. Although reconciliation on a world scale is quite impossible, the declaration of rights will be made by the nations sharing the same ideal. In this connection, we should stress the declarations of the Pan-American Conferences of Rio de Janeiro and Bogota, and the report of the Inter-American Legal Commission. In any case, the international declaration can no longer be delayed.

For the same reason, the international declaration must be even more far-reaching and complete than any of the national declarations at present in force.

Some will think that the international declaration should contain only rights that are uniformly recognised by all nations. If drawn up according to this criterion, the declaration would be too laconic. Moreover, it would be useless; it would be superfluous to make a joint declaration of rights which every country already recognises and guarantees. The elementary, fundamental rights, recognised by all nations, do not need an international declaration to command respect.

When, in the middle of the war, President Roosevelt proclaimed the four fundamental rights: freedom from want and fear, freedom of speech and worship, he was thought to be going too far. Today, no one can be satisfied with the affirmation of these elementary rights. The simple rights, granted by the Charter of the United Nations, to the Economic and Social Council, of making 'recommendations' in order to 'promote respect for the human rights and fundamental liberties of all peoples, and to make these rights and liberties effective,' no longer satisfies the demands of our contemporary legal conscience. These rights and liberties must be given a real and effective guarantee.

It seems to be generally admitted that a declaration of rights should be made at the same time as the Convention, the former being wider in scope, the latter containing only those rights which are recognised and guaranteed by all the nations party to the Convention. I am sorry not to share this view. A simultaneous declaration and Convention reduce each other's value. The declaration will be ineffective and, accordingly, complete; the Convention will be imperfect, and for this reason, operative. I prefer the declaration in the form of a convention, complete and operative.

Moreover, the declaration and the Convention, in their present draft form, have important technical defects. In some points, the Convention is more detailed, and in others, the declaration. I am certain that the same procedure should not be adopted as is usually followed by international conventions. What should be made is a declaration of rights, but a declaration inserted in a convention and completely binding in all its legal effects—a single document, therefore.

Of course, each State, when signing the Convention, will have the right to make reservations concerning clauses or declarations to which it does not immediately subscribe, and which it does not pledge itself to respect. These reservations will gradually disappear. Little by little each State will recognise the rights which it did not recognise at the outset. It is only in this way that the Convention can become a factor of democratic progress in the world.

The recognition of certain fundamental rights can be demanded immediately. The existence of a democratic government can be made to depend on this recognition. It will be a requisite minimum for admission into the international community, more significant than the vague expression 'nations united for peace,' adopted in the United Nations Charter.

This minimum will consist of the rights concerning life,

liberty, work, education, equality and participation in the government of one's own country. It is on this basis that we must establish the other, increasingly numerous and more clearly defined rights, by which progress towards democracy is made.

Each of the fundamental rights involves sub-divisions, applications and consequences which form a complete table of rights. Some of them, in particular cases, give rise to other rights, by reason of special circumstances, such as age. The right of living implies the right to a minimum subsistence, to health, by medical and hospital treatment, the fight against disease, the free constitution and defence of the family; the right to State protection, nationality and naturalisation.

Freedom implies a great number of other rights, including some of the fundamental rights mentioned above, such as the right to work and the right to participate in government. The latter becomes the right to a government chosen by universal suffrage. Freedom includes not only the four freedoms mentioned by Roosevelt; there is also liberty of conscience, thought, opinion, worship, association, residence and change of residence, freedom of information, the dissemination of information and scientific research. From the right to work, we have the right of ownership, the right to leisure, the right to share in economic advantages, and the right to fair remuneration.

All these rights demand and presuppose the right to justice and the right to resist oppression. The right to justice becomes continually more complex; it includes the right to be tried under a previous law, to trial in public, to the assistance of freely chosen counsel, to be free from all pressure; the right to hear one's judges and to be heard by them; the right to swift, sure and effective protection of all threatened or unrecognised rights. In addition to all the rights listed and defined, it is necessary to safeguard implicit rights, all those which are necessary for the exercise of each of the explicit rights, or which follow from the explicit rights or constitutional government. This is provided for in the Brazilian and the American Constitutions.

The Convention will go far towards codification, if we may

use the expression, of international relations, by attempting to subordinate these relations to infallible, clearly-defined legal rules. This work is complex and difficult, and is being achieved gradually along the lines defined above.

However, the Convention will immediately necessitate a central body analogous to the International Labour Office to co-ordinate and supervise its execution. Later, it will involve a jurisdictional body, which might be the International Court of Justice. Finally, it will need a specific, autonomous tribunal, before which individuals may plead against States, in order to safeguard their rights. This will be the last stage in a laborious evolution, which cannot be achieved straight away. The course of this evolution is inevitably bound up with world political conditions, and particularly with the realisation of collective security. But nothing must be done to prevent or hinder it.

Towards a Bill of Rights for the United Nations

F. S. C. Northrop

A BILL of rights for all the nations cannot be based solely upon the traditional values and ideological assumptions of any one of the nations. If it is to capture the aspirations and ideals of all the peoples of the world, it must be rooted in at least some of the accepted institutions and social doctrines of each and every people.

The usual approach to the bill of rights or to the establishment of any other cultural value ignores the foregoing principle. It is usual, for example, to assume that the traditional modern French and Anglo-American concept of freedom and its attendant bill of rights exhausts the meaning of the concept. Precisely this assumption operates when anyone proposes to extend the governmental forms of the United States of America to a United States of Europe or a United States of the World. Such proposals have always left their recipients cold.

Yet the reason for such a reaction is surely not far to seek. The classical French and Anglo-American concept of freedom, which its bill of rights is designed to achieve, is conceived for the most part in, or after the analogy of, purely political terms. Freedom consists both politically, economically and even religiously in being left alone. Although this is perhaps somewhat of an exaggeration, Emerson's dictum that the best government is the minimum government tends, according to this conception, to hold. Furthermore, the economic freedom to have the work necessary to maintain even a minimum livelihood tends to be left to chance, as a mere by-product of the individual actions of men or groups who operate independently. Similarly, psychological freedom of the sentiments, the emotions and the passions, which the Spanish and Latin Americans cherish, is hardly even recognised as existing. And often in the religious field, because of a freedom to believe any faith, there tends to arise a culture in which people have no deep-going convictions about anything.

In short, the price of a society rooted in the traditional modern bill of rights, has tended to be a culture of *laissez-faire* businessmen's values, with all the other values and aspirations of mankind left anæmic and spiritually and ideologically unsustained.

A bill of rights written in terms of the contemporary Russians' values and ideology would have virtues and demerits different in content but similar in its neglect of the values of other cultures. The same would be true of a bill of rights grounded in Spanish or Latin-American values. For the latter bill of rights, the price which others would have to pay would tend to be a social system which escapes social anarchy at the cost either of monarchy or military dictatorship. A bill of rights formulated in terms of Oriental values would illustrate the same general thesis, as the difficulties of the contemporary Orient clearly indicate.

But to become aware thus of the inadequacies of a bill of rights defined in terms of the traditional values and ideology of any one of the nations or cultures of the world is to find the clue to the construction of an adequate bill of rights for a United Nations. The values and ideology of each nation or culture throughout the world must be determined and brought out into the open in terms of their basic assumptions. The existence of these different values and ideals must be frankly and honestly faced and admitted. In fact, the basic premise of this new bill of rights must be the right of any people to a world so organised socially that at least some of their values and ideals can have expression. A true bill of rights must guarantee a world in which there can be many ideologies, not merely one ideology. In short, the foundation of an adequate bill of rights must be conceived not solely in terms of political freedom but in terms of a plurality of cultural values.

More, however, is necessary. A designation of the diverse ideologies of the peoples of the world shows not merely that they differ but also that certain of them contradict one another. The latter is the case with respect to the ideologies of the present Western democracies and communistic Russia. Here we reach the real heart of the difficulty: an adequate bill of rights must guarantee the type of world in which there can be many ideologies; yet not even a catholic bill of rights can support a contradiction. For contradictories cannot be embraced. This means that an adequate bill of rights must both guarantee a world with a plurality of differing values and guarantee also a procedure by means of which peoples and nations can and must pass beyond their present ideologies when these ideologies are so mutually contradictory as to threaten the peace of the world.

Unless this second guarantee is provided, a recognition and fostering of the existent ideological pluralism of our world will generate war rather than peace and destroy rather than create a united world. This follows because contradictories anywhere, if not transcended, destroy one another.

The prescription for guaranteeing a transcendence of the contradictory and conflicting valuations and social ideals of certain existent peoples and cultures of the world should be clear: obviously one must go beneath the traditional ideologies to the considerations and methods which lead people anywhere to an ideology.

No conception of human values, no economic, political or religious ideology, as the history of human civilisation clearly shows, comes *a priori*, perfect in every detail, God-given from heaven. Even the founding fathers of the United States and even Karl Marx were mortal men and not a perfect God. And being mortal men, they envisaged Utopia as the lessons of history and the finite empirical knowledge at their disposal at the time permitted them to envisage it. Thus at best they got facets of the truth, but not every facet.

Analysis shows that the basic assumptions of the political and economic Utopia of classical modern French and Anglo-American democracy are those for the most part of pre-Kantian British empirical modern philosophy. It is equally well known that the philosophical assumptions of contemporary communistic Russia are those of Karl Marx. Nor did the latter philosophical assumptions spring, with complete originality, into the mind of Karl Marx directly from the perfect omniscience of God. The philosophy of Karl Marx is a composite of contributions of his human historical predecessors, namely, Hegel, Feuerbach and the French socialists.

Nor were the contributions of the British empirical philosophers to the modern French and Anglo-American conception of human values and its bill of rights, or the contributions of Hegel, Feuerbach, the French socialists and Marx to the communistic Russian conception of a bill of rights as expressed in the Russian Constitution of 1936, mere philosophical speculations. Both sets of philosophical premises brought forward empirical, scientifically verifiable information in their support. This means that the philosophical premises at the basis of the diverse human values and ideologies of the peoples of the world are in part at last scientifically testable premises. Consequently, ideological conflicts are issues which can be discussed in the light of empirical and scientific evidence and treated by means of the methods of scientific inquiry. It follows, therefore, that any bill of rights which will guarantee effectively the processes for transcending the inescapable contradictory and conflicting ideologies of the contemporary world must prescribe freedom of scientific inquiry and of philosophical investigation of the underlying problem to which the existent diverse, and in some cases contradictory, ideologies are different answers.

An adequate bill of rights, therefore, must possess two basic guarantees: (1) The guarantee of a world in which all the differing ideologies of the world gain expression, each one in part at least; (2) The guarantee of the freedom for, and the establishment of the scientific and philosophical inquiry into the basic premises of human and social ideologies necessary to provide the means for transcending and resolving the ideological conflicts of the contemporary world. The minimum foundation for a bill of rights is a political philosophy which is both a philosophy of all the world's cultures and a philosophy of science.

Human Rights in the Chinese Tradition
Chung-Sho Lo

BEFORE considering the general principles, I would like
to point out that the problem of human rights was
seldom discussed by Chinese thinkers of the past, at least
in the same way as it was in the West. There was no open
declaration of human rights in China, either by individual
thinkers or by political constitutions, until this conception
was introduced from the West. In fact, the early translators
of Western political philosophy found it difficult to arrive
at a Chinese equivalent for the term 'rights.' The term we
use to translate 'rights' now is two words 'Chuan Li,' which
literally means 'power and interest' and which, I believe,
was first coined by a Japanese writer on Western Public
Law in 1868, and later adopted by Chinese writers. This of
course does not mean that the Chinese never claimed
human rights or enjoyed the basic rights of man. In fact,
the idea of human rights developed very early in China,
and the right of the people to revolt against oppressive
rulers was very early established. 'Revolution' is not
regarded as a dangerous word to use, but as a word to
which high ideals are attached, and it was constantly
used to indicate a justifiable claim by the people to overthrow
bad rulers; the will of the people is even considered to be the
will of heaven. In the *Book of History*, an old Chinese classic,
it is stated: 'Heaven sees as our people see; Heaven hears
as our people hear. Heaven is compassionate towards the
people. What the people desire, Heaven will be found to
bring about.' A ruler has a duty to heaven to take care of
the interests of his people. In loving his people, the ruler
follows the will of Heaven. So it says in the same book:
'Heaven loves the people; and the Sovereign must obey
Heaven.' When the ruler no longer rules for the welfare of
the people, it is the right of the people to revolt against
him and dethrone him. When the last ruler Chieh (1818-
1766 B.C.) of the Hsia Dynasty (2205-1766 B.C.) was cruel
and oppressive to his people, and became a tyrant, 'Tang'

started a revolution and overthrew the Hsia Dynasty. He felt it was his duty to follow the call of heaven, which meant obeying exactly the will of the people to dethrone the bad ruler and to establish the new dynasty of Shang (1766-1122 B.C.). When the last ruler of this dynasty, Tsou (1154-1122 B.C.) became a tyrant and even exceeded in wickedness the last ruler Chieh of the former dynasty, he was executed in a revolution led by King Wu (1122 B.C.) who founded the Chou Dynasty, which in turn lasted over 800 years (1122-296 B.C.). The right to revolt was repeatedly expressed in Chinese history, which consisted of a sequence of setting up and overthrowing dynasties. A great Confucianist, Mencius (372-289 B.C.), strongly maintained that a government should work for the will of the people. He said: 'People are of primary importance. The State is of less importance. The sovereign is of least importance.'

The basic ethical concept of Chinese social political relations is the fulfilment of the duty to one's neighbour, rather than the claiming of rights. The idea of mutual obligations is regarded as the fundamental teaching of Confucianism. The five basic social relations described by Confucius and his followers are the relations between (1) ruler and subjects, (2) parents and children, (3) husband and wife, (4) elder and younger brother and (5) friend and friend.

Instead of claiming rights, Chinese ethical teaching emphasised the sympathetic attitude of regarding all one's fellow men as having the same desires, and therefore the same rights, as one would like to enjoy oneself. By the fulfilment of mutual obligations the infringement of the rights of the individual should be prevented. So far as the relation between the individual and state is concerned, the moral code is stated thus: 'The people are the root of the country. When the root is firm, the country will be at peace.' In the old days, only the ruling class, or people who would be expected to become part of the ruling class, got the classical education; the mass of the people were not taught to claim their rights. It was the ruling class or would-be ruling class who were constantly taught to look upon the interest of the people as the primary responsibility of the government. The sovereign as well as the officials were taught to regard themselves as the parents or guardians of the people, and to protect their people as they would their own children. If it was not always the practice of actual politics, it was at least the basic principle of Chinese political thought. The weakness of this doctrine is that the welfare of the people depends so much on the good-will of the ruling class, who are much inclined to fail in their duties and to exploit the people. This explains the constant revolutions in Chinese history. It is, however, interesting to compare the different approach to the problem of human rights by the Chinese with the theories of human rights developed in the West by thinkers of the seventeenth and eighteenth centuries.

Let me state now what I regard to be the basic claims, the principles from which all human rights may be derived for all the people of the modern world. A declaration on the rights of man for the entire world should be brief yet clear, broad yet concise, fundamental yet elastic, so that it may be interpreted to suit the needs of peoples in different circumstances. For this reason, I lay down here only three basic claims, valid for every person in the world, namely: (1) the right to live, (2) the right to self-expression and (3) the right to enjoyment.

(1) The right to live

The right to live seems to be such a natural thing, yet it is neither properly recognised nor universally enjoyed by all the people. The world is big enough for everybody to live in, yet many are deprived of a proper dwelling place. The natural resources of the earth, used according to the scientific knowledge at our disposal, should provide plentifully for all the people to live comfortably, yet natural resources are wasted in many ways and are not made accessible to all those who need them. Each individual should be allowed to have his proper share in society as well as to make his proper contribution to it, and no individual should be allowed to have more than his share or to live idly at the expense of others.

(2) The right to self-expression

We want not only to live, but also to live with the sense of dignity and self-reliance. We are social beings. Each individual naturally considers that he has a proper place in society. In order to contribute fully to the society, each individual should have the fullest degree of self-expression. Social progress depends on each individual's freedom of expression. The right of national groups to self-determination is also a form of self-expression.

(3) The right to enjoyment

By 'enjoyment,' I refer to the inner aspect of the life of the individual. Our life should be not only materially adequate and socially free but also inwardly enjoyable. That there is an inner aspect of life is undeniable. 'Enjoyments' are of different kinds, but they are all connected with the inner life of the individual. The mental satisfaction of the inner life leads to peace of mind, and the peace of mind of the individual is a necessary condition of the peace of the world. The elementary right to enjoyment is to a life free from drudgery; it means that each should have an adequate amount of leisure and also be able to make good use of that leisure. No one should be constantly overweighed either by work or by social activities. He should have the opportunity to refresh himself and enjoy life. Other forms of enjoyment are æsthetic, intellectual, cultural and religious. Although not everyone can find enjoyment in the mystical experiences of religion, religion is a form of enjoyment for the inner life of many, which should not be repudiated by alleging it to be mere superstition. There should be religious toleration not only for all religions but also for atheism. Each should enjoy the right of giving the greatest satisfaction to his emotion and intellect without interfering with what others treasure most in their inner life.

The three basic claims of human rights stated above, namely, the right to live, the right to self-expression and the right to enjoyment, can, I believe, cover all the fundamental rights that a modern man should enjoy. The right to live is on the biological and economic level. The right to self-expression is on the social and political level. The right to enjoyment is on the æsthetic and spiritual level. When man can enjoy the rights at all levels, he attains a full life. It is time for all the nations and each individual in the world to be conscious of the following conditions, namely: (1) that the world is an organic whole, so we should work in co-operation to improve the individual lives of people as a whole; (2) that each individual is an end in himself, and all social institutions are the means to develop each individual as fully as possible; (3) that each individual or national group should respect the rights of others to the same degree as we treasure our own; and (4) that each, by making the most of himself, can at the same time contribute best to the world at large.

Human Rights: the Islamic Tradition and the Problems of the World Today

Humayun Kabir

THE first and most significant consideration in framing any charter of human rights today is that it must be on a global scale. In the past, there have been many civilisations but never one world civilisation. Two different conceptions of human rights could and sometimes did subsist side by side and because of lack of communication, could even be unaware of one another. Today such a state of affairs is unimaginable. Whatever happens in one corner of the globe has an almost immediate repercussion on other parts. Days of closed systems of divergent civilisations and, therefore, of divergent conceptions of human rights are gone for good.

The second consideration is that not only must there be uniformity between countries but also uniformity within countries. In the past, civilisation and culture were often the concern of a section or a class within the country. It was only those classes who had any rights. As the systems of civilisation were more or less self-contained and closed, the dispossessed classes within the country reconciled themselves to their fate. In many cases they were unaware that any system other than that to which they had been born was at all possible. There were, no doubt, revolutionary changes in human affairs from time to time. More often than not, these changes occurred when two divergent cultures or world outlooks met. Today the situation is entirely different. The continuous condensation of space and time is bringing different regions of the world more and more into contact and compelling, through comparison of conditions in different areas, a movement towards uniformity within the country itself. A charter of human rights today must therefore be based on the recognition of the equal claims of all individuals within one common world.

It is necessary to emphasise this because of one fundamental flaw in the Western conception of human rights. Whatever be the theory, in practice they often applied only to

Europeans and sometimes to only some among the Europeans. In fact, the Western conception has to a large extent receded from the theory and practice of democracy set up by early Islam, which did succeed in overcoming the distinction of race and colour to an extent experienced neither before nor since. It is against the background of a compelling movement towards uniformity that we have to examine the different existing conceptions of human rights.

The problem of the twentieth century is to reconcile the conflicting claims of liberty and security. A new charter of human rights must secure to each individual, irrespective of race, creed, colour or sex, the minimum requirements for a bare human existence, viz:

(a) the food and clothing necessary for maintaining the individual in complete health and effectiveness
(b) the housing necessary not only from the point of view of protection against the weather but also from that of allowing him space for relaxation and enjoyment of leisure
(c) the education necessary for developing the latent faculties and enabling the individual to function as an effective member of society
(d) the medical and sanitary services necessary for checking and curing disease and for ensuring the health of the individual and the community.

These are the four basic rights on the enjoyment of which all other rights depend. It will be noticed that they appertain to the security rather than the liberty of the individual. This is only a recognition of the fact that liberty is essentially a social concept and has no significance outside society. On the other hand, society itself is based on the need for security and therefore the demands of security must take precedence over the demands of liberty in respect of the minimum human needs.

The totalitarian systems have enriched our conception of human rights to the extent that they have compelled recognition of this fact. Their error seems to be that they have drawn no limit to the precedence of security over liberty for the individual. Both theory and experience, however, indicate that, once the basic minimum of security is reached, human beings place greater value on the rights and claims associated with the concept of liberty. Freedom of conscience or worship may be meaningless for a person whose mental faculties are restricted to the existing superstitions of his environment, but the moment he has attained some intellectual consciousness, he attaches the greatest value to the right of freedom of thought. Similarly, once the basic requirements of food, clothing and housing have been met, the individual is willing *to forego the claims to their extension* and even accept some diminution in them for the sake of rights like freedom of speech or assembly.

To sum up. The modern charter of human rights must secure to all individuals in all communities and countries a basic minimum of human requirements in respect of food, clothing, housing, education and sanitary services. Since this cannot be done without planning and control, the rights of the individual must be subordinated to the community to the extent required for securing these claims. Once, however, the basic minimum has been assured, the individual must be at liberty to press for other claims without check or interference from State or society.

The crux of the problem is, however, to determine (a) what constitutes the minimum human requirements in respect of security and (b) the degree of control and interference by the State necessary to secure these basic standards. On both these points there is room for wide divergence of opinion, and any formulation of human rights would be wrecked unless the difference can be overcome or methods found to resolve them without conflict or violence. From this is derived the decisive importance of political democracy. The community as a whole must decide both what constitutes the minimum human requirements and what degree of control and authority may vest in the State to secure them. It is true that political democracy loses much of its significance without economic and social freedom. A residue of liberty even then exists and there are hopes for its further expansion. Without political democracy the very possibility of social and economic democracy is destroyed. Political democracy is therefore the basis on which alone the structure of full human rights can be raised.

Similarly in the relation between the group and the world as a whole, it must be the world which determines both the content of the four fundamental requirements and the method necessary to secure them. In all other matters and subject to the over-riding ,authority of the world as a unit to preserve the fundamental rights, each group or community should be free to pursue such policy as it may desire for realising the values it considers highest.

The implication of this is the creation of a world authority —democratically based on the will of all groups and individuals of the world—to ensure the achievement of the fundamental human rights. The lessons of history also point the same way. As already stated, right is itself a social concept and requires the creation of some authority within whose orbit individuals may enjoy it. Science is making the world into one through constant improvements in methods of contact and communication. This is breaking down the barriers of separate authority and of separate systems of rights. The corollary to a world charter of human rights is therefore the creation of some world authority.

Unfortunately, there seems no immediate prospect for the setting up of such a world authority. The demand for uniformity of rights cannot however wait, for within the same system there is no room for different standards. What can be done is to define the minimum human requirements in respect of the four basic rights mentioned above and ask for an agreement of all States to accept and enforce them. There must also be a similar agreement as to the degree of interference with individual liberty permissible for the purpose of securing those ends. Thus, the rights to food and clothing involve the obligation to work, but there must obviously be some limit to the hours of such work, or to the class of persons called upon to perform such work. A world charter should therefore confine itself to the definition of the content of the four fundamental human rights and the degree of control and interference permitted to the State for securing them.

The Hindu Concept of Human Rights

S. V. Puntambekar

THE proper study of mankind is man. There is something more in man than is apparent in his ordinary consciousness and behaviour under a given system of environment, something which frames ideals and values of life. There is in him a finer spiritual presence which makes him dissatisfied with merely earthly pursuits. The ordinary condition of man is not his ultimate being. He has in him a deeper self, call it soul or spirit. In each being dwells a light and inspiration which no power can extinguish, which is benign and tolerant, and which is the real man. It is our business to discover him, protect him and see that he is utilised for his own and humanity's welfare. It is the nature of this man to search for the true, the good and the beautiful in life, to esteem them properly and to strive for them continuously.

Then we must note that there is also an incalculable element in the human will and an endless complexity of human nature. No system, no order, no law can satisfy the deep and potential demands of a great personality, be they religious, political, social or educational. Men are often endowed with great potential energy and creative power which cannot be encased within the bounds of old formulæ and doctrines. No fixed discipline can suit the developing possibilities of new human manifestations in the psychological, ethical or spiritual fields. No system can satisfy the growing needs of a dynamic personality. There always remains something unthought of and unrealised in the system. Hence we want freedom for man in the shape of human freedoms.

There is always a tendency for new values and new ideals to arise in human life. No ready formulas and systems can satisfy the needs and visions of great thinkers and of all peoples and periods. Freedom is necessary because authority is not creative. Freedom gives full scope to developing personality and creates conditions for its growth. No uniformity or conformity or comprehension of all aspects of life will be helpful. The present centralisation of all authority, its bureaucracy and party dictatorship, its complexity and standardisation, leave little scope for independent thought and development, for initiative and choice.

Can we be aware of a call for national freedom and for human freedom, when we are so rigid, inflexible, fanatic and exclusive in our political, religious, cultural and socio-economic outlook? Not having succeeded in imposing onr rules and systems on all countries and continents, some of us still harbour feelings of superiority and hatred, coercion and dominance against our neighbours.

Therefore first let us 'be men,' and then lay down the contents, qualities and inter-relations of human freedoms. We must respect humanity and personality, tolerate our differences and others' ways of internal and external group behaviour, and combine to serve one another in calamities and in great undertakings.

To talk of human rights in India is no doubt very necessary and desirable, but hardly possible in view of the socio-cultural and religio-political complexes which are so predominant today. There are no human beings in the world of today, but only religious men, racial men, caste men or group men. Our intelligentsia and masses are mad after racial privileges, religious bigotry and social exclusiveness. In short we are engaged in a silent war of extermination of opposite groups. Our classes and communities think in terms of conquest and subjugation, not of common association and citizenship. There is at present a continuous war of groups and communities, of rulers and ruled, in our body politic and body social, from which all conception of humanity and tolerance, all notion of humility and respect, have disappeared. Bigotry, intolerance and exclusiveness sit enthroned in their stead.

The world is mad today. It runs after destruction and despotism, world conquest and world order, world loot and world dispossession. The enormous hatred generated against human life and achievements has left no sense of humanity or human love in the world politics of today. But shall we renounce 'being men' first and always? What we want is freedom from want and war, from fear and frustration in life. We also want freedom from an

196

all-absorbing conception of the State, the community and the church coercing individuals to particular and ordered ways of life. Along with this we desire freedom of thought and expression, of movement and association, of education and of expansion in the mental and moral spheres. In any defined and ordered plan for living, we must have the right of non-violent resistance and autonomy, in order to develop our idea of the good human life.

For this purpose we shall have to give up some of the superstitions of material science and limited reason, which make man too much this-worldly, and introduce higher spiritual aims and values for mankind. Then on that basis we shall have to organise our social life in all its aspects. We want not only the material conditions of a happy life but also the spiritual virtues of a good life. Man's freedom is being destroyed by the demands of economic technocracy, political bureaucracy and religious idiosyncracy.

Great thinkers like Manu and Buddha have laid emphasis on what should be the *assurances* necessary for man and what should be the *virtues* possessed by man. They have propounded a code as it were of ten essential human freedoms and controls or virtues necessary for good life. They are not only basic, but more comprehensive in their scope than those mentioned by any other modern thinker. They emphasise five freedoms or social assurances and five individual possessions or virtues. The five social freedoms are (1) freedom from violence (*Ahimsa*), (2) freedom from want (*Asteya*), (3) freedom from exploitation (*Aparigraha*), (4) freedom from violation or dishonour (*Avyabhichara*) and (5) freedom from early death and disease (*Armitatva* and *Aregya*). The five individual possessions or virtues are (1) absence of intolerance (*Akrodha*), (2) Compassion or fellow feeling (*Bhutadaya, Adreha*), (3) Knowledge (*Jnana, Vidya*), (4) freedom of thought and conscience (*Satya, Sunrta*) and (5) freedom from fear and frustration or despair (*Pravrtti, Abhaya, Dhrti*).

Human freedoms require as counterparts human virtues or controls. To think in terms of freedoms without corresponding virtues would lead to a lopsided view of life and a stagnation or even a deterioration of personality, and also to chaos and conflict in society. This two-sideness of human life, its freedoms and virtues or controls, its assurances and possessions must be understood and established in any scheme for the welfare of man, society and humanity. Alone, the right of life, liberty and property or pursuit of happiness is not sufficient; neither, alone, is the assurance of liberty, equality and fraternity. Human freedoms and virtues must be more definite and more comprehensive if they are to help the physical, mental and spiritual development of man and humanity.

In order to prevent this open and latent warfare of mutual extermination, national and international, we must create and develop a new man or citizen assured and possessed of these tenfold freedoms and virtues which are the fundamental values of human life and conduct. Otherwise our freedoms will fail in their objects and in their mission to save man and his mental and moral culture from the impending disaster with which the whole human civilisation is now threatened by the lethal weapons of science and the inhuman robots of despotic and coercive powers and their ideologies and creeds.

We in India also want freedom from foreign rule and civil warfare. Foreign rule is a damnable thing. This land has suffered from it for hundreds of years. We must condemn it, whether old or new. We must have self-rule in our country under one representative, responsible and centralised system. Then alone we shall survive.

I know that men who are devoted to and dominated by rigid ideas of cultures and religions cannot feel the call of national or human freedom. But we cannot give up higher objectives and aspirations for their sake and their prejudices.

The Rights of Man and the Facts of the Human Situation

Aldous Huxley

THE increasing pressure of population upon resources and the waging, threat of, and unremitting preparation for total war—these are, at the present time, the most formidable enemies to liberty.

About three-quarters of the 2.2 billion inhabitants of our planet do not have enough to eat. By the end of the present century world population will have increased (if we manage to avoid catastrophe in the interval) to about 3.3 billions. Meanwhile, over vast areas of the earth's surface, soil erosion is rapidly diminishing the fertility of mankind's four billion acres of productive land. Moreover, in those countries where industrialism is most highly developed, mineral resources are running low, or have been completely exhausted—and this at a time when a rising population demands an ever increasing quantity of consumer goods and when improved technology is in a position to supply that demand.

Heavy pressure of population upon resources threatens liberty in several ways. Individuals have to work harder and longer to earn a poorer living. At the same time the economic situation of the community as a whole is so precarious that small mishaps, such as untoward weather conditions, may result in serious breakdowns. There can be little or no personal liberty in the midst of social chaos; and where social chaos is reduced to order by the intervention of a powerful centralised executive, there is a grave risk of totalitarianism. Because of the mounting pressure of population upon resources, the twentieth century has become the golden age of centralised government and dictatorship, and has witnessed the wholesale revival of slavery, which has been imposed upon political heretics, conquered populations and prisoners of war. Throughout the nineteenth century the New World provided cheap food for the teeming masses of the Old World and free land for the victims of oppression. Today the New World holds a large and growing population, there is no free land and over the vast areas, the much abused soil is losing its fertility. The New World still produces a large exportable surplus. Whether, fifty years from now, it will still have a surplus, with which to feed the three billions inhabiting the Old World, seems doubtful.

It should be added, at this point, that while the population of the planet as a whole is rapidly increasing, the population of certain extremely overpopulated areas in Western Europe is stationary and will shortly start to decline. The fact that, by 1970, France and Great Britain will each have lost about four million inhabitants, while Russia will have added about seventy-five millions to its present population, is bound to raise political problems, which it will require consummate statesmanship to resolve. But political problems are not the only ones that will arise. In Western Europe the reduction in the quantity of population is destined, it would seem, to be accompanied by a deterioration (owing to the infertility of the more gifted members of the community) of its quality. In the light of existing trends, Sir Cyril Burt foresees that, by the end of the present century, the average intelligence of the British population will have declined by five IQ points. How far personal liberty, group co-operation and local and professional self-government—the three factors which constitute the essence of any genuine democracy— are compatible with the qualitative deterioration of the population remains to be seen.

By destroying accumulated wealth and the sources of future production, total war has sharply increased the pressure of existing populations upon their resources and has thereby sharply curtailed the liberties of vast numbers of men and women, belonging not only to the vanquished nations, but also to those which were supposed to be victorious. At the same time the fear of, and busy preparation for, another total war in the near future is everywhere resulting in an ever greater concentration of political and economic power. Bitter experience has proved that no individual or group of individuals is fit to be entrusted with great powers for long periods of time. The socialist rulers of welfare states

may imagine that they and their successors will be immune
to the corrupting influence of the enormous powers which
total war and mounting population pressure have forced
upon them; but there is, unfortunately, no reason to suppose
that they will prove to be exceptions to the general rule.
The abuse of power can be avoided only by limiting the
amount and duration of the authority entrusted to any
person, group or class. But so long as we are menaced by
total war and mounting population pressures, it seems very
unlikely that we shall get anything but a steadily increasing
concentration of power in the hands of the ruling political
bosses and their bureaucratic managers. Meanwhile conscription, or military servitude, is almost everywhere
imposed upon the masses. This means in practice that, at
any moment, a man may be deprived of his constitutional
liberties and subjected to martial law. Recent history has
shown that even socialist rulers are ready to resort to this
device for coercing persons engaged in inconvenient strikes.
It is virtually certain that, at the present time, no government actually desires war. But it is also probable that many
governments would be reluctant to give up all preparations
for war; for such preparations justify them in maintaining
conscription as an instrument of control and coercion. And
we may add that universal disarmament, if it should ever
be achieved, would not necessarily mean the end of conscription. Compulsory service to the States will probably
persist in some other than military form—as a scheme for
the 'training of youth,' for example, or as a 'labour draft.'
To a highly centralised government the advantages arising
from the power to regiment and coerce its subjects are
too great to be lightly sacrificed.

A constitutional bill of rights, whose principles are applied
in specific legislation, can certainly do something to protect
the masses of ordinary, unprivileged men and women
against the few who, through wealth or hierarchical position,
effectively wield power over the majority. But prevention
is always better than cure. Mere paper restrictions, designed
to curb the abuse of a power already concentrated in a few
hands, are but the mitigations of an existing evil. Personal
liberty can be made secure only by abolishing the evil

altogether. UNESCO is engaged at present in facilitating the task of mitigation; but it is in the fortunate position of being able to proceed, if it so desires, to the incomparably more important task of prevention, of the radical removal of the present impediments to liberty. This is primarily an affair for the scientific section of the Organisation. For the problem of relieving the pressure of population upon resources is primarily a problem in pure and applied science, while the problem of total war is (among other things, of course) a problem in ethics for scientific workers as individuals and as members of professional organisations.

To provide all of the 2.2 billion persons at present inhabiting the planet with a nutritionally adequate diet, it would be necessary to double the existing food supply. It will take years, by conventional methods, to achieve this goal and by that time the population will be, not two billions, but more than three—and malnutrition will be very nearly as serious and as widespread as it is today.

Every industrial nation spends huge sums on research into the techniques of mass destruction. Thus, two billion dollars went into the production of the atomic bomb and many hundreds of millions more are at present being spent upon research into rockets, jet planes, the dissemination of pneumonic plague and the wholesale destruction of food plants. If comparable amounts of money and scientific ability could be devoted to the problem of producing food-stuffs artificially, it seems likely enough that methods would quickly be found for providing the half-starved millions of Europe and Asia with an adequate diet. The synthesis of chlorophyll, for example, might be, for the later twentieth century, the equivalent of what the exploitation of the empty lands of the New World was for the nineteenth. It would reduce the pressure of population upon resources and thereby remove one of the principal reasons for highly centralised, totalitarian control of individual lives.

The prosperity of an industrialised society is proportionate to the rapidity with which it squanders its irreplaceable natural capital. Over large areas of the earth's surface, easily available deposits of useful minerals have already been exhausted, or are running low; with the increase in population and the progressive improvement in industrial techniques, the drain upon the planet's remaining resources is bound to be accelerated.

Useful minerals are very unevenly distributed. Some countries are exceedingly rich in these natural resources, others lack them completely. When a powerful nation possesses a natural monopoly in some indispensable mineral, it is thereby enabled to increase its already formidable influence over its less fortunate neighbours. Where a weak nation finds itself blessed, or cursed, with a natural monopoly, its stronger neighbours are tempted to acts of aggression or 'peaceful penetration.' Scientific workers have it in their power to postpone the day of planetary bankruptcy and to mitigate the political dangers inherent in the existence of natural monopolies. What is needed is a new Manhattan Project, under international auspices, for the development of universally available surrogates for the unevenly distributed and soon-to-be-exhausted minerals, on which our industrial civilisation depends for its very existence—*e.g.* wind power and sun power to take the place of power produced by coal, petroleum and that most dangerous of all fuels, uranium; glass and plastics as substitutes, wherever possible, for such metals as copper, tin, nickel and zinc. A project of this kind would be valuable in several ways. It would shift our industrial civilisation on to a foundation more permanent than that accelerating exploitation of wasting assets, on which it rests at present; it would break those natural monopolies which are a standing temptation to war; and finally it would make possible an extension of personal liberty and a reduction of the powers wielded by the ruling minority.

We now come to the ethical problems confronting scientific workers as individuals and as members of professional organisations. Whatever may have been the wishes of the inventors and technicians involved, applied science has in fact resulted in the creation of monopolistic industries, controlled by private capitalists or centralised national governments. It has led to the concentration of economic power, strengthened the hands of the few against the many and increased the destructiveness of war. Applied science in the service, first, of big business and then of government has made possible the modern totalitarian state. And applied science in the service of war departments and foreign offices has begotten the flame thrower, the rocket, saturation bombing and the gas chamber, and is now in process of perfecting methods for roasting whole populations by atomic explosions and for killing the survivors by means of man-made leukemia and artificially disseminated plague. The time has surely come when scientific workers must consider, individually and collectively, the ethical problem of 'right livelihood.' How far is a man justified in following a course of professional action which, though involving no immediate wrong-doing, results in social consequences which are manifestly undesirable or downright evil? Specifically, how far is it right for the scientist or technologist to participate in work, the outcome of which will be to increase the concentration of power in the hands of the ruling minority and to provide soldiers with the means for the wholesale extermination of civilians? Up to the present applied science has been, to a great extent, at the service of monopoly, oligarchy and nationalism. But there is nothing in the nature of science or technology which makes it inevitable that this should be so. Professionally speaking, it would be just as easy for the scientific worker to serve the cause of peace as of war, of personal liberty, voluntary co-operation and self-government, as of monopolistic statism or capitalism, universal regimentation and dictatorship. The difficulties are not technical; they lie in the realms of philosophy and morals, of value judgments and the will that acts upon those judgments.

The Rights of Man: a Biological Approach

R. W. Gerard

SCIENCE and Technology have revolutionised the material existence of man and are revolutionising his mental existence. Scientists are the autocatalysts of social evolution, acting on and reacted upon by the society so as to produce accelerating change. Science has created the present milieu *in* which men must live and interact and it is creating new viewpoints as to *how* men must live and interact. Biology, especially, dealing with organisms—with systems composed of individual units integrated into a community which is an effective whole—has much to say of the forces operating in such communities of individuals, of the freedoms, duties, controls that must be present, and of regular trends in these over the enormous span of organic evolution. Its findings seem equally valid for the community of cell entities in the individual complex animal or the community of animal entities in the individual complex society. And they seem equally valid (if less complete) for the human as for the sub-human animal. Science views man primarily in his natural setting—discarding the supernatural as a source of knowledge—and would approach the problem of human rights and duties as a special case of the problem of part and whole, as best exemplified by living organisms.

The central problem of man in society is that of outlining the territory of the individual within the larger territory of the group. Were society simply a mosaic of the completely separate territories of its members or, conversely, were men equal and random occupants of a homogeneous group territory, this problem would not exist. It must, however, remain true, from the very nature of an organism, that the individual man, an entity in his own right, and the communal man, a part of the community, exist simultaneously. This is the inescapable dichotomy: each man (and his neighbour) is a complete whole, dedicated to self-survival and in basic competition with other men; but each man (with his neighbour) is a component unit of a larger whole, the society, and dedicated to group-survival by basic co-operation with other men in the group. Of course, this duality is repeated with varying emphasis at many levels—individual and family, family and community, member and minority group, political party and political unit, state and nation, nation and world state. And, of course, territory is not a spatial unit nor a single entity; it is the surrounding in which the individual (unit) exercises dominant control of his environment, and its extent is different for different aspects—physical, biological, psychological, sociological, legal.

Man, immersed in a group culture and largely served by his fellows, is enabled to differentiate and to fulfil latent capacities. He becomes more than anthropoid; but also less, for he would survive poorly on his own. As organisms surrendered immortality, but gained more effective living—perhaps even self-consciousness—when single cells banded into multicellular units, so man must lose and gain freedoms as he forms a society. He must accept group restrictions in gratifying his primitive urges, he is not free to take what he can by force; but he receives from the group new urges and means of gratifying them; he comes to possess language and is free to think with its aid.

Man's rights and duties, then, cannot be absolute but remain always relative to his milieu. As some privileges are attained, others must be surrendered. Whether particular exchange is desirable depends on the value assigned to each freedom, and this is again largely determined by the culture. Indeed, in an important sense, the most complete freedom is enjoyed by the person (or group) most completely moulded to the prevailing culture. A 'free-falling' object is fulfilling its 'destiny' without hindrance by conflicting forces. A man is free to the extent that he is permitted to satisfy, or attempt to satisfy, felt needs; and his rights are therefore a composite of the desires stimulated in a society and the restrictions placed upon gratifying them. Until chickens were domesticated and pots turned, no right to a chicken in every pot could come into question. Before language developed sufficiently to stimulate and communicate abstract thought, freedom of speech was no problem; it was neither present nor desired.

To the extent that man's social environment expands,

so can the many individual territories do so without undue pressure. But compression as well as expansion occurs and boundary problems are inevitable. The 'rights of man' are attempts to define the territory of the individual (or the small group) *vis-à-vis* his neighbours and the larger group. They can never be absolute and they must not too long remain fixed by any codification. For man in society evolves and territories are not merely relative but are also varying. The acute problems arise in each period only in regard to the growing points. The right of every man to breathe is not now in question, because it is universally assumed to exist. The right of every man to a plot on Mars is not now in question, because it is universally assumed not to exist. But what would happen if invention enabled some entrepreneur to meter air (as toilet facilities have become metered) or to import Martian uranium? Indeed, in the pre-atomic-fission era uranium was more a nuisance than a prize; as was petroleum before the internal combustion engine. Changes in the society altered the values of these materials and so created a new set of problems as to rights. As newspapers, radio and other mass media have developed, so have arisen problems of freedom of communication; as men have cohered, on the basis of specialisation, into groups with special interests or beliefs, so have arisen problems of the right to a job or to strike, the right to worship or to scoff, the right to conform or to revolt. This may all be pointed up in the field of health. . . . Health is not only individual, it is also public; and public health measures are accepted with relatively little demur by individuals. (When a considerable interest group is involved, however, as with farm butter as against vegetable oleomargarine, this is not so.)

A final word from biology on the problem of enforcement and of power. Man as an individual has certain urges, which insensibly pass into desires, habits, customary privileges, recognised interests, legal rights. Man as a member of a group accepts certain controls, habits, customary responsibilities, recognised obligations, legal duties. Rights and duties become codified in laws, which is useful, and crystallised in them, which is disastrous. For change continues and codes must yield or break. The continuous growth of vertebrates seems to be a better device than the spasmodic moultings of insects. When tensions become great enough, the weakest element gives. With rigid social systems, this usually mean revolution and brute mechanical force. With less rigidity, multiple small changes occur and the power is exerted by 'persuasion' via communication. It is striking that in biological evolution certain general trends are evident. Cells in organisms and organisms in groups tend to greater cohesiveness and interdependence. Co-operation increases relative to conflict. The influence of the whole on the unit is enhanced relative to that of the unit on the whole. And the integrating forces shift from an emphasis on mechanical control to ever greater use of communicative control, via nerve and hormone. A rigid unadaptable species remains stagnant and is superseded in evolution; a highly specialised one is most easily wiped out by a change in conditions. Evolutionary mechanisms operate on the group even more than on the individual. It is a violence to demonstrable truth to say that the organism exists for the cell or the group for the individual, just as it is to say that the cell exists for the organism or the individual for the group.

Society is a form of epi-organism, and social evolution cannot violate general laws of biological evolution, however unique it may be in particulars. The biologist cannot supply details of what present human rights should be. He can say:

1. Rights are relative to the society. Minimal ones will be universal, others valid only in very special cultures.

2. Some rights must be abrogated as new ones are demanded. Which will be valued more in each case depends on the group culture.

3. Greater dependence of the individual on the group is in the line of evolution. Altruism is growing relative to selfishness, and control is being exercised relatively ever more by suasion, as compared to force.

4. Any doctrine which regards man only as an individual or only as a unit in a group is necessarily false. The duality of man, as an individual whole *and* as a social unit, is inescapable. The extremes of eudemonism and utilitarianism, individualism and collectivism, anarchism and totalitarianism, *laissez-faire* and absolute economic socialism are

untenable. The rights of man involve rights of the individual (or small group) as against other individuals (or groups) or the whole society—which implies duties of them to him—and rights of the whole (or small group) as against the individual (or group)—which implies duties of him to it.

5. The particular codification of rights at any time will be imperfect and rapidly become less good. With any formulation should be included provisions for mandatory re-examination and reformulation at appropriate intervals.

Rights and Duties concerning creative expression, in particular in Science

J. M. Burgers

THERE shall be freedom of creative expression, except in so far as harm thereby may be done to other people, or irresponsible or weak people may be seduced to acts which are harmful to themselves or to others. Restrictions for this purpose can be made only by constitutional authorites in consultation with and under the guidance of representative scientific and educational opinion, and must be subjected to periodic revision.

2. The community has the duty of setting aside from its funds means for developing the creative abilities of its gifted members.

3. The part played by science in modern society makes possible and at the same time puts upon us the obligation of international co-operation, as well as of looking into the future in the interest of coming generations.

The community has the duty of setting aside from its funds means for elaborate scientific research, as a means for alleviating wants of mankind, for the development of mankind, and for the pursuit of truth.

The community at the same time has the duty of providing men and women with education and information preparing them for co-operation and citizenship in a society largely influenced by science.

4. When scientific work leads to the possibility of technical applications or of other measures of importance for, or affecting in any way, large sections or the whole of mankind, such applications or measures should come under the sponsorship of international bodies, deriving their status and power from international authority. Such sponsorship may include supervision, control, direction or exploitation (*e.g.* atomic energy).

5. There shall be freedom of scientific intercourse and publication, and free access to all published material, independently of the way in which scientific work is financed.

No secrecy restrictions may be put upon scientific research

or its publication for competitive purposes, either by private companies or by nations. Secrecy deemed necessary for purposes of protection against social evils can be enforced only by international authority, in consultation with and under the guidance of representative scientific and educational opinion, and must be subjected to periodic revision.

6. Every scientific worker is responsible for what he publishes and for the form in which he publishes it.

Every scientific worker has the duty to contribute towards the understanding of the implications of science and the possibilities afforded by it.

7. Every scientific worker has the duty to insist upon the necessity of considering the social and moral implications of science; and to exert his influence against the misuse of science.

Scientific workers must have the right to consider and investigate the way in which applications of their work are brought into society and affect the people concerned (or mankind as a whole); and to make known the results and conclusions to which their researches in this respect have led.

8. Scientific organisations may bring forward claims for the protection of nature, which must be taken in full consideration by international and national authorities and can obtain priority over proposals for exploitation.

Comments

A number of points in the Memorandum submitted by UNESCO[1] under '*Problèmes particuliers*' referred to the possibilities of creative work. The most important are: '8. Freedom of expression (including freedom of the writer and the artist).' '12. Freedom of scientific and philosophic enquiry and publication.' Points 5, 6, 21 and several others more or less touch upon closely related matters.

Admitting the principle that the ultimate object of human life is to aim at truth in as full a sense as possible, and in view of the fact that that conception requires personal freedom as well as stimulation and criticism derived from intercourse with other free minds, social organisation must guarantee

---

[1] See Appendix I

the freedoms mentioned in 8 and 12. Every curtailment of these freedoms can develop into obstructions of the road towards truth.

Nevertheless the following points require attention:

(a) Every expression of what a man or a woman or a group of people believes to be true, is subject to the limitations of the mind which framed the expression, and to misunderstanding, to unexpected reactions and even to misuse by other people.

(b) The realisation of an artistic conception or the pursuit of scientific work may require means far surpassing the possibilities of individuals and of small groups of interested persons, so that it must be decided whether material support can be granted out of the general fund of richness which the community has at its disposal.

(c) Creative work, in particular in science, gives power; hence the central problem of modern society: who shall decide about the application of this power?

Certain rules must be framed to cope with these matters.

The greatest difficulties are involved in the problem of power. They are particularly enhanced by the fact that human society has a tendency to develop into competing organisations. Technical advances, leading to extremely efficient means of communication, as well as influencing opinions and instinctive tendencies in men and women, have led to an enormous rise in power and size of such organisations, at the same time reducing their number. The consequence is that the struggles between the remaining bodies take on an increasingly fierce character and menace the whole world with destruction; while inside each group the freedom for individual play of mind and individual choice in action becomes less and less.

A consequence of this development is that scientific workers become bound to machinery set up for competition or for fighting and lose the power over the results of their work. The situation can make it impossible for them to discontinue this work, even when it takes a direction they would feel strongly opposed to. The further consequence is the growing enforcement of secrecy on scientific research and its results, which has now even been laid down in legislative form in some countries.

The impetus of political development is extremely strong at present. At the same time the interconnection of all social relations and the extreme complication of present day human affairs make it extremely difficult to obtain a proper view of one's obligations, the more so as scientific workers are accustomed to analyse a situation, and to focus their attention mainly on some detail they can treat with exactness. This makes them less apt to come to synthesising pictures; whenever they try they are conscious of their limitations.

The only way to work against the outbreak of a life-and-death struggle between the now existing (or developing) centres of power, must be found in openness and fearlessness of mind, and in strengthening the urge for attaining and expressing truth existing in individuals and in independent groups. Only by the free and open contest of opinions formed in as many minds and in as diverse minds as possible, can the danger be evaded that our society will run into directions which will bring an end to all creativeness, either by ruining the world or by curtailing the free operation of personal responsibility and moral consciousness.

The introduction of legal secrecy restrictions into science brings extreme dangers:

> to our personal attitude of mind;
> to the development of science as pursuit of truth;
> to adequate and ethically justified application of science;
> as a legal principle which will have destructive and far-reaching consequences for our civic rights;
> and as a cause of distrust and suspicion between groups and nations which ought to come to co-operation.

These dangers are so imminent at present that any dangers involved in free communication of discoveries in what is now the forefront of scientific advance, must be risked, rather than that 'secrets' should be guarded for fear of misuse, by competing groups. Similarly there should be no restrictions upon the discussion of political and religious questions and theories. The world apparently stands before great changes, the outcome of which cannot be seen; we must accept our part in it with the firm faith that honesty

and intelligence have a value in themselves. In view of what
is coming it is unwise to make reciprocity in this respect a
matter of principle; one party at least must start in the right
direction.

The freedom of publicly communicating their discoveries
for all scientific workers entails the duty to give attention
to what comes out of the application of their work and to
the conditions of the world in which they are working.
They must devote part of their time to help the public
to understand the meaning and importance of scientific
findings; they must give advice in those cases where their
work influences social relations or where new applications
become possible; they must make investigations concerning
these matters and make known their results and views.
The positions in which they are working must afford them
the necessary freedom for this.

Science and the Rights of Man

W. A. Noyes

I F the advent of gunpowder to Western Europe had much
to do with the disappearance of the feudal system, and the
French Revolution which culminated in the Napoleonic
Wars showed the way for the inclusion of science in making
war felt by whole populations, it is evident that recent
scientific advances may prove to be one of the chief factors
in the enslavement of mankind. Because of his importance
in warfare the scientist can no longer be considered as a
free and independent individual and whether he likes it or
not, he is tied to the military destinies of the various countries.
The rights of man and the rights of the scientist have become,
therefore, inextricably entangled. The struggle of the
scientist to maintain his freedom of action has an important
bearing on the struggle of mankind for prosperity and
happiness.

Modern means of transportation have caused an inter-
relationship between the various nations of the world which
formerly did not exist. No longer is it possible to look
disinterestedly upon diseases in the far corners of the world.
For the same reason that centres of poverty and of social
disturbance have been potential sources of trouble within
one country, these phenomena anywhere in the world
constitute threats for those portions of humanity which now
enjoy high standards of living. It may even be that extrava-
gance in the use of natural resources by one nation would
be of such vital concern to other nations that threats to
world peace would be involved. We have hardly made a
beginning in conserving our natural resources for the national
good. We are a long way from looking on natural resources
as assets which must be conserved for the good of the world.
The implied threat to certain rights of man considered
heretofore as fundamental in a society made of individualists
is so obvious as not to need detailed comment.

The foregoing paragraphs present humanity in general
and scientists in particular with a very real dilemma.

The conflict between nationalistic aspirations and the real need for a broader outlook is not one which can be resolved in a few months or years. It is evident, however, that certain rights of scientists and consequently certain rights of man will necessarily be curtailed for the common good. The really important question is whether this curtailment will lead to such a decrease in happiness and to such an invasion of privacy that life would cease to have any real meaning. Freedom to travel, to impart information, and even to engage in certain forms of livelihood will be so intertwined with the political sphere that the greatest caution must be exercised in plotting a course for the future.

The first duty of the scientist is to ensure that the black spots in the world, where poverty and disease are all too common, are eradicated. This necessarily implies more universal scientific education together with the imposition of certain laws restricting freedom of personal action as regards matters pertaining to health and the use of natural resources. It is difficult but possible to carry these steps forward without at the same time invading the most important rights of man as understood in the enlightened countries of western Europe and the Western Hemisphere, but inevitably material progress will run counter to certain deep-seated prejudices, arising partly from religion, in large fractions of the earth's population. The social and political implications of what we usually term progress are so vast that it is difficult at this time to make any sweeping generalisations concerning the future. There are differences of religion and of political ideologies which will always exist. Such differences should be encouraged, for each culture can contribute its bit to the happiness of mankind. The question arises mainly as to whether these differences can be prevented from leading to war, because war is the main instrument in the destruction of the rights of man.

Scientific training is supposed to lead to the cultivation of an objective attitude, one which permits judgement of matters on their merits without the incorporation of prejudice. Scientists by no means always carry this objective attitude into their discussions of political matters, but the scientific type of mind should be adaptable to social problems. Perhaps the greatest contribution the scientist can make in preserving the rights of man is to educate the world into a free discussion of all matters without personal animosity. Such an ideal cannot be reached overnight. The intolerance of the true scientist toward errors in fact and errors in logic must be tempered by a real tolerance toward varying basic postulates in the social sphere. Ultimate truth is difficult to reach in the physical sciences. It may never be attained in the science of human relationships.

It is vital for the future of the world that intense animosities and hatreds be allayed. This cannot be done solely by social and psychological studies. Good nourishment and congenial surroundings are essential if persons are to divorce their inner feelings from immediate problems. The immediate objective of the politician should be to avoid war at all costs, and the immediate objective of the scientist should be to ensure that all levels of society in all nations are freed from economic anxiety. If this is done, then given a long enough period of peace, the rights of man can gradually be worked out, and a code of ethics evolved which will fit the human race into a scientific world. The rights of man will have to be redefined, but we are confident that they can be redefined in such a way that the elements essential to human happiness are preserved.

The Right to Information and the Right to the Expression of Opinion

René Maheu

IT is an error to continue to regard freedom of information as an extension of freedom of expression, the latter itself proceeding from freedom of thought. The individualist concept implicit in this classical sequence, contemporaneous with a press organised on more or less artisan lines, not merely lags behind the concepts of modern political sociology; the economic and technical realities of today clearly involve the adoption of an entirely different viewpoint.

Whether it be the press, news agencies, the cinema or broadcasting, information today is only to a limited degree an expression of opinion. Essentially it is the pre-conditioning (or the satisfying) of opinion. It either precedes or follows opinion. Moreover that opinion is the opinion of the public and not of news operators, whose task it is in most cases to suppress their personal views. It is a question of mass opinion, and mass behaviour; the techniques of modern news belong to the field of mass psycho-sociology, and not of individual psychology.

The conditioning or exploitation of mass opinion and mass behaviour is today a major industry, whose operation is only to a minor degree affected by the individual views and reactions of its producers and even consumers: that is the social fact which we must take as our starting point.

Neither ethics nor politics can disregard this formidable mechanism. The task is to humanise it. I believe that is one of the major problems of this age.

If we are to prevent what too often occurs, the large-scale alienation of the masses, the same revolution must be achieved as regards information in this century as took place in education in the last century. Information must be a right (hence, too, a duty) and that right must belong to those whose thought is at stake.

The inclusion of the right to information among the rights

of man means more than seeking a mere increase or improvement in the knowledge available to the public. It involves radical reconsideration of the function of information. It means that the products, the methods and even the organisation of the news industry must be reassessed from the point of view not of the interests or prejudices of those who control its production, but of the human dignity of those who henceforth are justified in expecting of it the means of free thought.

From the moment that information comes to be regarded as one of the rights of man, the structures and practices which make of it an instrument for the exploitation, by alienation, of the minds of the masses, for money or for power, can no longer be tolerated; information becomes, for those who impart it, a social function in the service of intellectual emancipation.

The right to information is a natural extension of the right to education, and that very fact makes it possible to define its concrete content.

That content is sometimes defined as 'facts' or raw news, *i.e.* news not interpreted. There should be no illusion about the practical value of the traditional distinction between fact and opinion. What is a fact? A piece of evidence. And the selection of a fact is an implicit expression of opinion. There is nothing more misleading than the chimera of mechanical objectivity. Nor can human liberty look for salvation to the impersonal.

A better definition of information would probably be a detached presentation of materials capable of use by anybody in the formation of an opinion. Whereas an expression of opinion—whether persuasive or challenging—is always militant, the characteristic of information, unlike propaganda or publicity, which proceeds by observation, is availability.

This being so, it will be asked whether a corollary of the recognition of man's right to information is not admission of the right of all to access to all sources of knowledge in all circumstances. Leaving out of account questions of physical impossibility, this straightway suggests to the mind the many restrictions imposed for the protection of the most legitimate political, economic or personal interests: secrets of State, manufacturing secrets, domestic privacy.

But the proclamation of the right to education does not

ipso facto mean that the child has a right to learn anything, at any age, and anyhow. It only means that it is the duty of adults to give the child the knowledge necessary for his development in the light of his needs (and capabilities) at his age. A right is no more than an instrument—an instrument for building up man in man's mind. And an instrument is only an instrument if it is related to needs.

The same is true of the right to information as of all other rights: its legitimate content must be defined in terms of real needs. Conditionally, of course, on the word 'needs' being understood to mean the needs of human development, and not of self-interest or passion.

Of their very nature those needs involve a large measure of recourse to human fraternity and to exchanges between men, an appeal that will always extend far beyond mere egotism. It is true, however, that, as there are great variations in living conditions and modes of development, the needs of human groups are not identical at all points in time and space. These groups do not all need the same information.

There must be no fear of introducing into a consideration of the rights of man this element of historical and sociological relativity. So far from putting in peril the effective achievement of those rights, only a realistic appreciation in the light of that relativity can give them concrete meaning for the men who must fight to make them triumph.

The right to the expression of opinion is much more closely geared to historic relativity. While the right to information must be numbered among the conditions of democracy and thus has the force of a principle, the right to the expression of opinion is part of the exercise of democracy and, as such, shares the relativity of all political realities or practice. A régime blessed with stable institutions and with a body of citizens apathetic or tolerant or whose critical faculties are highly trained, can give the freest rein to the expression of individual views. Indeed it must do so, in the sense that, more than any other, it needs that indispensable stimulus to maintain progress.

Against this a democratic order in peril in a State torn by passion or possessed of the devils of credulity or, again, a democracy fully committed to a revolutionary or systematic process of reconstruction, is justified in imposing considerable limitation on the freedom of individual expression, the exercise of which is necessarily hostile to complete unity.

Recognition that the right to the expression of opinion must be conditioned by the historical perspective of a particular democracy, is not sacrificing a human right to reason of State. On the contrary, that right is thus given its full meaning by refusal to sacrifice to an abstract concept the merits and chances of success of a concrete undertaking.

Nor is it a question of limitation from outside, as when human liberty is assailed by Fascism or any other tyranny, whether forcibly or by fraud. What is meant is the self-imposed restraint inherent in liberty, which is known as the sense of responsibility.

Just as it is derived from liberty through a twofold internal relationship, so that responsibility is itself twofold.

Firstly, all liberty exists in relation to a certain situation and consequently assumes that situation wherefrom it emerges, at the very moment when by its operating it affirms its power to repudiate it. Thus any expression of free opinion, to be valid, to be its true self, must have regard to the historical and sociological background against which it stands.

Secondly, any expression of free opinion is an attempt to affect the liberty of others. That expression is in essence far more an appeal directed to other free men than the mere exteriorisation of an inner conviction. If I express my thought, I do so partly, no doubt, to clarify or demonstrate my own views, but mainly to convince others. But I cannot, without danger of self-contradiction, use my liberty to appeal to the liberty of others without treating their liberty as liberty, *i.e.* without respecting it.

Thus recognition of the perspective of the historical moment of society and respect for the liberty of others impose on every citizen in the expression of his views a twofold set of imperatives, whereby he must judge the possibles; these are summed up in the single word responsibility. Responsibility decides the extent to which the right to the expression of opinion is valid. And hence that extent is relative like responsibility itself.

In strict ethics only the subject can and may assess his

responsibility, and consequently put a term to the exercise of his liberty in the act of expression of opinion.

But politics replace the disintegrated particles of absolute individual subjects by an ideal collective subject modelled on the framework of the State. Democracy is the reign of the 'general will' of the individual citizens. Whether that 'general will' is a real force in a living being or a regulating fiction, is a matter of philosophic theory. In practice it is enough that in normal conditions that 'general will' be identified by hypothesis, with the majority vote, though capable—in extraordinary periods, *e.g.* during a revolution —of being embodied in a minority. Thus in a democracy there is a recognised judge of the individual's responsibility in the expression of his views. To be a democrat is to acknowledge that judge.

Admittedly, as no one can be fully a democrat save in a democracy already achieved, and as there are only imperfect potential democracies, it is at all times the citizen's right— and even his duty—to judge his judge. It is the fear of that ultimate appeal which holds back the steps of majorities along the path of tyranny. And similarly it is always ultimately the citizen who decides freely in his own mind whether this is the time for law or for revolution.

That is where politics finally yield to ethics and are absorbed in them. Doubtless in such an appeal *ad infinitum*, where rules and safeguards successively pass away, there are growing risks of errors. But is there any liberty without risk? Risk abides in the heart of man, for man exists only by inventing himself.

Education and Human Rights

I. L. Kandel

A STUDY of recent statements on human rights reveals the curious paradox that the one condition which is essential to their realisation and proper use is hardly ever mentioned. Perhaps the omission of any reference to education can be explained on the assumption that it is taken for granted as a human right and as the essential foundation for the enjoyment of human rights. The history of education, however, provides ample evidence that education has not been regarded as a human right nor has it been used as an instrument for developing an appreciation of the importance of human rights for the fullest development of each individual as a human being. Historically two motives have dominated the provision of education. The first and the earliest motive was directed to indoctrinating the younger generation in the religious beliefs of their particular denominations. The second motive, which came with the use of the national state, was to develop a sense of loyalty to the political group or nation. In both cases the ends that were sought emphasised acquiescent discipline rather than education for freedom as a human being.

Because education has not yet been recognised universally as a human right, it is essential that it be included in any declaration of human rights that may be drawn up. The right to education needs greater emphasis than it is given in the rights of man, prepared by UNESCO.[1] One of the tragic results of the traditional organisation of education into two systems—one for the masses and the other for a select group—is that, even when equality of educational opportunity is provided, certain social and economic classes feel that the opportunities are not intended for them. The provision of equality of educational opportunity demands in some countries measures to change the psychological attitudes produced by the traditional organisation.

[1] *Cf* Appendix I

Thus M. Henri Laugier in discussing plans for the reconstruction of education in France, wrote:

'So many generations in France have lived in an atmosphere of theoretical equality and actual inequality that the situation has in practice met with fairly general acceptance, induced by the normally pleasant conditions of French life. Of course, the immediate victims of the inequality are barely conscious of it or do not suffer from it in any way. It does not occur to the son of a worker or an agricultural labourer that he might become the governor of a colony, director in a ministry, an ambassador, an admiral, or an inspector of finance. He may know that such positions exist, but for him they exist in a higher world which is not open to him. Most frequently this situation neither inspires nor embitters him, nor does it arouse in him a desire to claim a right or to demand a definite change!'[1]

The recognition of education as a human right is, however, only one aspect of the problem as it concerns the rights of man. Free access to education at all levels may be provided without affecting either the content or the methods of instruction. Traditionally, the quality of elementary education differed from the quality of secondary education; the former was directed to imparting a certain quantum of knowledge, most generally to be acquired by rote and resulting in what the French call *l'esprit primaire*; the latter was intended to impart a liberal or general cultural education. In neither case was there, except by indirection, any deep-rooted training for the use and enjoyment of those freedoms which are included in the list of human rights. The emphasis, particularly, since most types of education were dominated by exigencies of examinations, was rather on the acceptance of the authority either of the printed word or of the teacher.

When the pendulum began to shift from an emphasis on discipline, indoctrination, and authoritarianism to an emphasis on freedom, it was too often forgotten that freedom is a conquest and that education for freedom of any kind

[1] In *Educational Yearbook*, 1944, of the International Institute, Teachers College, Columbia University, p 136 *f*, edited by I. L. Kandel, New York, 1944

demands a type of discipline in learning to appreciate the moral consequences of one's actions. Education for freedom does not mean, as it has frequently been thought to mean, a *laisser-faire* programme of content or of methods of instruction, but the intelligent recognition of responsibility and duty. If this principle is sound, it also means a change in the status of the teacher and of teaching. If the teacher is to be more than a purveyor of knowledge to be tested by examinations, then the traditional limitations placed upon him by courses of study prescribed in detail, by prescribed methods of instruction, and by control through inspection and examinations must be replaced by a different concept of the preparation that is desirable for the teacher. That preparation must be raised to the same level as preparation for any other liberal profession. If the efforts of the teacher are to be directed to the development of free personalities and to education for freedom of speech, expression, communication, information and inquiry, the teacher through his preparation should become professionally free and recognise that freedom without a sense of responsibility easily degenerates into licence.

Before the rights of man can be incorporated into programmes of education, another change is essential. In the past, education has been used as an instrument of nationalistic policy, which too frequently meant indoctrination in either national or racial separatism and superiority. And even where the humanities formed the core of the curriculum, so much attention was devoted to the scaffolding that the essential meaning of humanism was lost. The common goals inherent in the ideal of the rights of man can only be attained as programmes of education and instruction are based on the realisation that there is no national culture which does not owe far more than is usually admitted to the influence of the cultural heritage of man of all races and of all ages. It is upon this foundation that the freedoms included in the rights of man can be laid; it is only in this way that the true concept of humanism as an end in education can be developed. Their attainment, finally, depends upon training in the methods of free inquiry. Education for the various freedoms demands discipline. To paraphrase Rousseau, man must be disciplined to enjoy the freedoms which are his rights.

The Rights of Man in Primitive Society
A. P. Elkin

I

Introduction

IN this contribution, I confine myself to man in primitive society, drawing in particular on my knowledge of, and work amongst and for, non-self-governing peoples, usually referred to as primitive peoples, in Australia and the adjacent islands of the South-West and South Pacific.

To say that the principles of the Atlantic Charter can and must be applied to such peoples, does not mean, however, that governing and mandatory powers should at once divest themselves of all responsibility for, or interest in, their colonial or mandated native peoples and leave them to themselves. To do so, after having interfered in, controlled, and allowed interference with, the latter's indigenous way of life, would make their 'last state worse than the first.' What is meant is (1) that such sovereign powers will administer native peoples only until such times as the latter become self-dependent economically and politically, and (2) that the policy of such administrations will include such educational, health, economic, cultural, legal and political measures, that this aim of self-dependence and self-direction in relation to the peoples of the world, will be reached in the shortest possible time.

This time-condition is required lest representatives of the administering power—officials, employers or missionaries —should rationalise the *status quo* of subjection on political, economic and educational aspects of life, as a necessary stage which must be retained for an indefinitely long period, until the native peoples are ready, *in the opinion of the governing power, to take even one step out of tutelage.* In actual fact, this present, or pre-war, condition suits the 'invaders' or 'intruders' economic interests. To keep a people as permanent apprentices or wards, and therefore as cheap labour, and to justify this compulsory employment as necessary training for civilisation and citizenship, constitute a convenient situation, especially if the implication be overlooked that the particular trainees will never realise that citizenship and are not expected to do so. Perhaps a later generation will, so it may be argued, but unless radical changes are made in the systems of employment, government and education, this will never occur.

Those immediately concerned are seldom perturbed by this poor prospect. Even well-intentioned missionaries still echo glibly the fallacy that Papuans or other ethnic groups are child races, who must be treated as such and who may grow up intellectually and emotionally, but not yet.

In both these cases, native peoples are deprived of their rights as human beings, simply on the grounds of belonging to a culture different from ours and less complicated industrially and financially. They must, however, adapt themselves to this new situation, for it is backed by force— the administration. And this they do by consciously assuming the rôle of an inferior, by being perpetual apprentices in our occupations, and by being childlike to satisfy our vanity. In themselves, and with reference to their own cultures and societies, as anthropologists can testify, they are not stupid, inferior or childish.

Another argument advanced for keeping primitive peoples in tutelage from generation to generation, is that a stone-age people cannot advance to the steel-age in a generation, for it took Europe so many centuries. The fallacy is obvious; peoples of primitive cultures have not to invent the many steps between the two ages. Their task is to adapt themselves to the present age, that is, to the twentieth-century environment as it is in, and spreads from, Europe, Asia and America. This they have the intelligence to do, and to do quickly. But they need now the education which will enable them to understand their problem and task. Given education and literacy, and experience gained by their own representatives visiting and observing the conditions of life in those countries from which ideas and practices are brought to their own country, their grasp of the situation will deepen, their intelligence will advance, and they will build up a working adaptation.

They have, moreover, a right as human beings to be

allowed to do this. But that is not all. 'Civilised' powers and peoples have disturbed and confused native peoples' ways of life, upset their adjustment to their environments, and indeed, changed the very environments. Therefore, primitive peoples have a right to receive from the civilised world assistance in understanding, and making new adjustments to, the changes in their environment, changes resulting from civilisation and its bearers.

II

Rights of Primitive Man

(1) Primitive and Civilised Man, alike Human Beings

A basic right of primitive man today is the right to be considered a human being in the same manner and degree as civilised man. He is part of the same international complex of relationships, possesses the same fundamental needs, and has the same potentialities of intelligence. The differences are those of history and of cultural environment and heritage.

(2) The Right to his own Pattern of Civilisation and Personality

A second basic right of primitive man, which can be recognised today, is the right to be civilised according to the pattern which he will develop—to each separate people its own pattern—but fitting into the general pattern of human values and rights on the world-scale, with its economic and cultural relationships. This is, of course, the right to freedom of self-determination in the cultural and religious spheres and in the sphere of personality development.

(3) The Right to Education in Civilisation

If the basic right of free personality development within a people's own pattern of civilisation is to be respected, the institutions and methods of education introduced and used amongst a primitive people must not be instruments of imposed propaganda, but must possess two fundamental aims. These are: first, the development of an appreciation by a people of its own cultural background and of the individual's relation to it, and an understanding or, at least, an awareness of the cultural changes resulting from contact with civilisation; and, second, the opening of the door, on approved educational principles, to world thought, science, technical achievement, literature and religion, to be used and built into their own changing culture as they find possible.

That is, *in the third place, primitive peoples have a right to benefit from the civilised world's advances in both the method and content of education, conceived of in the widest sense.* This right derives from, and must be subservient to, their second basic right.

(4) *The Right to Community Land*

Deprivation of land or external interference with the use of it, has religious, moral and psychological as well as economic effects. It undermines communal life and its sanctions, leaves the individual adrift, and leads to unbalanced personality development.

It is clear, therefore, that a *basic right of primitive man, as a human being, both as an individual and as a community, is the right to retain his land with its many-sided associations and meanings.* That is, all administering powers should guarantee their primitive peoples the permanent use of their land. As the First Point of the Atlantic Charter reads: The powers concerned 'seek no aggrandisement, territorial or other.'

(5) *The Right to Economic Development*

To use the words of the Fourth Point of the Atlantic Charter, the products of their lands and labour should ensure them 'access, on equal terms, to the trade and to the raw materials of the world which are needed for their economic prosperity.'

Therefore, *primitive man, though his community be non-self-governing, has today a right to the full use of the products of his land and labour and to take his place in the exchange of world products.*

(6) *The Right to the Disposal of one's own Labour*

Seeing the effects of the conditions which have arisen in Aboriginal Australia, and under the Indenture labour system in the South-west Pacific, and admitting that native peoples are human beings with a right to their own way of life and to the use of the lands to which they are bound in the several ways mentioned in the preamble to the Fifth Right, it follows that: *primitive man has a right, as a human being and a social personality, to the free control and disposal of his own labour power, and should not be deprived of this by invasion, by force, by deceit, or by abuse of his unavoidable ignorance of the terms and conditions of employment which he is asked or persuaded to accept.*

(7) *Primitive Woman's Right to a Secure Sexual and Related Social and Economic Position*

In the frontier or marginal regions of intrusive settlement and administration, the 'invaders' or immigrants consist for the greater part of males. It is only after many years, when conditions have become safe and more comfortable that, apart from a very few brave and devoted women, wives and families of their own ethnic group settle with them. In the meantime, however, the male settlers have not all remained continent. Through force, prestige, payment, economic pressure, or the attraction of the novel, they have obtained sexual partners, either in prostitution or concubinage. Such cohabitation is seldom sanctioned by any contract, or even ritual, which they or their kith and kin would acknowledge, or which they themselves would regard as binding, if they left the country or decided later to marry one of their own 'colour.'

From their point of view the position seems simple, but it is very different as far as the native women are concerned. Very few of these are recognised in their own society as prostitutes to be hired or sold. They have their place as potential wives and mothers in the native system of reciprocal bonds between clans, families and other social groups. They are important links, and their betrothal and marriage set in operation series of mutual gifts and services and other forms of behaviour, on which the maintenance of social and economic activity and of social cohesion depends. But the 'permanent' and even temporary liaisons of women with white men disturb and partly disrupt the normal working of the social system. As a result, some betrothals cannot be fulfilled, and apart from the resulting dissatisfaction and sense of deprivation, the several social, economic and ceremonial bonds which should have been forged between the groups concerned, fail to materialise. In this way damage is done to the community—damage which is not repaired by the gifts which the women may be able to obtain and distribute to their relations. In these liaisons, the woman and, of course, the non-native man with whom she cohabits, remain outside the native social structure, and the gifts do not require an exchange of effort or gifts on the part of her relations, as would occur in native marriages.

The woman also runs the risk of finding no place, psychological or marital, in the structure if she is discarded by her non-native *de facto* husband, or is no longer wanted as a prostitute by non-natives. She may, indeed, have to become a prostitute in the village to which she returns, or else seek a haven on a Mission. The degree of social insecurity or ostracism which such a woman incurs varies from society to society. The non-native man, however, can drop her, and she has no redress. In other words, she has legally no rights in this matter.

Thus, through the woman, an attack is made, though not designed, on the spirit, and on the very existence, of the tribe. Her position as a social or tribal personality is not considered; she is just thoughtlessly regarded as an individual of sexual possibilities, with no need for social security for her life. The disposal or use of her person, her body, is not considered in relation either to her society's rights or to her own as a human being and a woman.

Finally, we see inherent in these conditions of contact in marginal regions that *primitive woman has a right to a secure sex position with its related social and economic rôle in her own society, that this rôle is essential to the latter's existence, and that neither she nor her society should be deprived of her rôle by prostitution, concubinage or any temporary and non-legalised form of sexual liaison with men of the dominant and intruding group.*

(8) The Mixed-Blood Minority Group's Right to the Rights of the Society of which it Forms Part

The real difficulty is that in this Pacific and Australian region, the mixed-blood is culturally and socially a 'half-caste.' When brought up, as is common, in some degree of association with non-natives, he finds it difficult to fit in satisfactorily to the natives' way of life; but he also realises that he is not acceptable to the non-native society. To members of the latter, he is just a native, and any attempt

on his part to rise in social and cultural life is met with
strong prejudice. Consequently, he is a misfit, and lacks
a social personality. It is only as the mixed-bloods in a
region increase in numbers to such an extent that they
intermarry and form 'in-groups' of their own, that some
degree of personal integration can be attained. In relation,
however, to the dominant community, the mixed-bloods'
attitudes and patterns of behaviour—partly native and
partly European—can be irritating, the result of their
realising their outcast position.

The obvious fact in Australia and in the Islands is the
growth of the mixed-blood group, struggling for economic,
social and cultural rights, and in time demanding to be
freed from discrimination. To prevent or to tide over this
stage, mixed-blood minority groups must be given the
content, not merely the formal pronouncement, of political,
legal, economic, social, cultural and religious rights as part
of the total community.

In other words, *mixed-blood minority groups are entitled to,
and should be accorded, a right to the rights acknowledged in the
society of which they form a part, and to be freed from 'race' discrimination.*

(9) *The Right of Justice*

In the relations of the representatives of an administering
or possessing people with a non-literate indigenous people
the maintenance of justice is likely to be supplanted by what
is considered good for the latter, and, at best, by a considerate
and sincere paternalism. This is usually considered unavoidable, especially when, as in Melanesia, there is no strong
centralised native political system, through which 'indirect
rule' can be instituted. It means, however, the *imposition*
of rules of behaviour in social, economic, and even religious
spheres. But regulations governing community behaviour
are not likely to be considered just unless both they, and the
sanctions enforcing them, are self-imposed either on the
basis of established custom or of legislative measures, or at
least are understood and accepted as fair in the circumstances.
What usually happens in the contact situation, however, is
that the orders are obeyed and the sanctions accepted

because they are the fiat of the Administration or Government, which has the physical force to back its fiats. Alternatively, they may be accepted and followed because the local administrative officers are respected.

Such administration may be for the good of the native people, but this is not necessarily an acknowledgement that the latter possess fundamental human rights.

This process of 'conquering rule' under forms of justice requires constant watchful examination, and replacement by forms germane to native ways of maintaining equitable relations between individuals, and between individuals and the total community. There are such forms. In addition, a new content must be given to the forms to meet the problems arising from contact and the process of civilising. By education, by showing respect to primitive man as a human being of intelligence, who possesses rights of the same order as civilised man, and by willingness to co-operate with him, a solution of the problem of justice will be obtained.

To put the matter briefly: *primitive man in the contact situation and in non-self-governing conditions has a right to contribute to the constitution, content and working of the forms through which justice is sought and administered.*

(10) The Right to Political Self-Determination

It is often overlooked that there are always some members of a native people who are quite unaware of their subordinate position, resent it, and occasionally become vocal about it. This comes as a shock to well-intentioned administrators, but is taken as proof by many employers and caste-conscious settlers of the natives' treacherous or ungrateful character. Moreover, if a limited but subordinate share in the policy making and administration be given to educated natives, they are apt to be irritated by this limitation, and to resent openly the policy and its implementation, just because it is, at least in the last resort, imposed.

On grounds of expediency, therefore, the problem of political self-determination and self-government of native peoples needs to be tackled quickly. Moreover, this time-condition is important and even fundamental. To withhold a right from a people because they are not considered ready for it by the governing power, or because the time is not considered convenient for granting it, is an infringement of the right. Steps therefore should be taken to prepare both parties for association in government and administration, and to make this effective on a basis of equality and self-determination in the shortest possible time.

This is, *primitive peoples have a fundamental community right to political self-determination. Where this has been taken from them, it should be returned in a form, worked out with their co-operation, to meet the present circumstances of contact with the civilised world.*

(11) *The Community's Right to Freedom of Religious Beliefs and Practices*

The religious beliefs and practices of any people are part of its equipment for providing moral and social sanctions, for dealing with the contingent and for furnishing grounds of certainty and hope in the face of apparently unsolved problems of life and death. In other words, religion is a mechanism of adaptation to the total environment—social and geographical, past, present and future, seen and unseen, known and unknown. Since, however, this total environment varies for each particular people, its means of adaptation, including religion, must be its own, worked out in its own history. Thus, in spite of its universal aspects, religion appears only in 'national' or 'tribal' forms, interrelated with the other institutions and with the total way of life of each particular nation or tribe. This fact underlies the conflicts of religions in the past. Those conflicts have not been simply concerned with different dogmas or rituals, but also with political, economic and social differences and ambitions. The religious dogma provided the inspiring symbol on which the various interrelated motives and urges were centred. This is true also of the religious conflicts within Christendom; and even in the cases of denominational conflicts within one national boundary, motives besides those connected with doctrinal or ritual differences operate, for example, the struggle for political or administrative power, and the carry-over from earlier national and territorial divisions.

In other words, religion is not an independent cultural trait, with only incidental influence on, or relation to, other cultural traits. Likewise, it is not wholly a matter of individual relationship between the believer and the supernatural object of his belief. Indeed, except in an age of sophistication and cultural breakdown, religion is very much more a matter of cultural heritage than individual decision, for what is at stake is not simply individual salvation, but national or tribal continuity.

Amongst a primitive people, however, the part played by religious and magical beliefs and institutions in the functioning of society is so vital and complex, that hastily to undermine the former, as by conversion of individuals, is to jeopardise the whole social structure. Moreover, the individuals, so converted by, and attracted to, the new and foreign religion, are not aware of the social effects of the change in their beliefs and in their attitudes to accepted customs. It is also doubtful whether the adults of the community as a whole realise these consequences, though they may be puzzled by the conversions and may resent them. The implication is that in much 'successful' missionary activity, the right of a primitive people to determine the content and course of its culture is not respected. Indeed, comparatively few Christian missionaries in the past have been concerned with the principle of freedom in religion. Urged on by the injunction 'to preach the Gospel to every creature,' to baptise, and so save them from eternal damnation, they have paid little or no respect to the cults of the people whom they sought to convert. In particular, they have shown little appreciation of the functional rôle of those cults in community life. Moreover, they have urged on individuals a creed derived from a western cultural and social context, without advising them that only after a long period could this creed, with its implications for social relationships, and the native way of life be adjusted to each other. In short, the native adherents were not aware of the social effects of accepting the introduced creed. Generally speaking, too, the missionaries were also unaware of this, although they did deliberately attack some social and moral customs. They also took pride in the convert who remained steadfast, in spite of a conflict of loyalties, to the missionary and to the new creed on the one hand, and to the traditional beliefs and social practices on the other hand.

In addition, too, the missionaries in most primitive regions had behind them the prestige, authority and force of the

European administration. It is, therefore, doubtful whether the natives' conversion was based on freedom of choice amongst alternatives, seeing that they were ignorant of the implications of their decision, and that they could not be unmindful of the authority attached to the missionaries.

On the other hand, it must be remembered that missionaries have seldom been the only, or the first, contacts which the natives had with western civilisation. Traders, planters, recruiters and administrative officers were, and are, also its representatives. And if the economic and administrative interference has been, and will be, allowed, it is difficult to argue against the presence and work of missionaries in the South and South-west Pacific. In the first place, Christianity is an integral and historic element in western civilisation, and as native peoples are to be brought into closer relationship with that civilisation, they should see it as a whole, and understand its sanctions and ideals. In the second place, about half of the native peoples are adherents of various Missions, and many of them are keen Christian missionaries, who will in time work out an adjustment of Christianity and native life. Moreover, the contact situation as a whole has resulted in much disintegration of native moral and social sanctions and loss of spiritual beliefs. It is, therefore, reasonable to present other religious sanctions and beliefs, especially those which are part and parcel of the invading culture and of the civilisation to which, in the modern world, they must become adjusted.

To sum up: in the contact position of civilised administering peoples and primitive peoples, the right to freedom of religious belief and practice is inherent in a people's right to cultural self-determination, provided that the individual's right to life and health is not infringed. With regard to this proviso, no Administration will permit any rites, even though associated with religion, which are repugnant to the enlightened conscience of mankind, such as head-hunting, cannibalism, human sacrifice, exposure of the dead in villages and prostitution. The right of the community or people as a whole to self-determination and existence must be weighed against the right of the individual to freedom of choice in what he regards as his personal benefit or salvation.

In the contact position, the right to freedom of religious belief and practice is a communal as well as an individual right, and attacking the former through the latter may lead to disintegration of the community, and not to religious progress.

In the contact position as it is, the native peoples have a right to understand the religious element in western civilisation, but to have it presented to them without any suggestion of compulsion or material inducement, and without implied or associated condemnation of their indigenous beliefs and sanctions. With education and understanding of the differences, they will make their decision. Whether this be to modify or to condemn the latter or to blend the old and new, or to reject the new, its value will depend on the understanding of the individual and community implications with which it is made, for religion is a social institution and not merely an individual satisfaction.

Therefore, in the present-day contact situation, a *primitive man both as a community and as an individual, has a right, inherent in that of cultural self-determination, to freedom of religious belief and practice. This involves both respect for indigenous beliefs and sanctions, and the 'free' presentation of the religion of the dominant and invading culture.*

(*12*) *The Right to Health of Body, Mind and Spirit*

The contact of Europeans with peoples of primitive culture in the South and South-west Pacific and in Australia, has had several disastrous effects. New diseases have been introduced against which no immunity existed. The taking of natives from their own environment to work in another quite different one, has taken its toll. The decrease of the village food-producing and reproductive powers through over-recruitment has had debilitating and depopulating effects in some regions, which are only very slowly, if ever, overcome by closing the latter to recruiting. The diet-scale and health on some plantations and stations have been far from satisfactory. And finally, many natives in the islands died during the early and desperate stages of the Japanese War from dietary deficiencies and disregard of other health measures.

In spite, therefore, of the devoted work of missionaries during the past fifty years, and of a limited amount of health services conducted by the Administrations, the native peoples' health has not, speaking generally, gained from the coming of the European.

This does not mean that their health was perfect in pre-white days; for example, malaria and deficiency diseases took their toll. But it is only in recent years that civilised man has begun to admit that *primitive man has a right to physical health*. This admission, however, implies a heavy responsibility, namely, expensive surveys of diseases and of diet and the gathering of vital statistics amongst primitive peoples, especially amongst those to whom civilisation owes much by way of reparation for the damage to health and population wrought since contact began.

The illness developed by primitive man out of the contact-situation, has not only been physical in nature. It has also affected his mental and spiritual adjustment. The success of Government officers, of missionaries and of employers in attracting the younger generation away from traditional sanctions and ways of life and even from the villages and camps to live in foreign ways, has caused much mental distress and conflict in the elders. Often, too, the 'younger' become disillusioned after they reach middle-age and realise that they have not been, and are not likely to be, admitted to the Europeans' way of life, except in an inferior degree and in a separate caste. They see that they are used, and at best, patronised. The resulting so-called inferiority complexes are manifested in attitudes which are described as cheeky or dangerous, and which did result, in the war in the Islands, in a few cases of betrayal. Actually they are symptoms of contact-illness, psychological in nature. Moreover, as seen in the introduction, primitive peoples are too often compelled by circumstances to play an inferior or child-like and subservient rôle, which they despise. Unfortunately, this can become an accepted habit and prevent that progress in arts and crafts of which they are capable. In other words, they become mentally dull. In the long run, of course, this does not pay the invading and employing group.

No group, however, whether dominant or not, has a right to cause psychological illness or mental backwardness in another group, any more than one individual would be granted a right so to afflict another. On the contrary, every people has a *right to mental health and development.* The corollary to this is that the administering power must remove the causes of such mental illness and retardation, and provide such educational and economic opportunity that primitive man's ability will be fully developed.

Thus, as we see him in the contact-situation, *primitive man has a right to physical, mental and spiritual health: in short, to a fit and good life. While admitting this as a fundamental human right for the members of a society within that society, we see that in the contact-situation, it takes on the aspect of just reparation, which it is the duty of the administering power to pay.*

III

Conclusion and Summary

The question of human rights is one of the relationship of the individual to his fellows within a community, and of community to community. Fundamentally, the individual is a social personality, and his rights are an integral part of his place and rôle in his society and in its external relationships. Apart from the society he would have no rights. But, because his personality is socially conditioned, his rights are not co-terminous with his desires, but can only exist in so far as they do not impinge upon the rights of the rest of the community. The basic necessity is the living together. Consequently, the community must have rights as against the individual, but in the interest of all its members. In the larger world of contact, too, it must have rights admitted by other communities or powers, so that its members will have a social and cultural continuum; for without this, they could not become social personalities.

The form and content, however, of both communal and individual rights vary in the different situations and conditions of a community's history, including its contacts with other peoples. Human rights therefore have to be reviewed from time to time both as to form and content, lest they become so abstract and generalised as to be meaningless in actual human relations. Thus the propositions that an individual, as a human being, has a right to his life, to the free disposal of his physical and intellectual powers, and to as much food as he needs, especially if he has earned the means for obtaining this—may seem fundamental and enduring rights. But when a community is in jeopardy, through war or food shortage, these rights give place to the right of the community to persist, even at the expense of the individual.

And this aspect of relativity applies to all human rights, for they arise out of, and are conditioned by, the necessity of communal life, the mould and nurturer of personality. But this communal living implies mutual respect, which in turn demands a *modus vivendi*—a complex of rights and duties arising from a common source, the former mutually accepted, and the latter generally acknowledged, and socially enforced. This *modus vivendi*, however, must change as the generations change, as knowledge and contact increase, and as aspirations become more complex.

Human rights, therefore, have no content unless they are related intimately and causally to the actual community situation. For example, the change of a country's basic economy from agriculture to manufacture deprives the farmers of their previous rights and security, for these can no longer be guaranteed, while decades may pass before fresh content and, indeed, form can be given to the 'rights' of the individual, now a factory hand, for many issues are involved. So too, the Melanesian had his *modus vivendi*, with its rights and duties, in his village—gardening—fishing—clan-organised social organisations. But contact with the bearers of civilisation has disrupted this system, and a modified complex of rights and duties has to be evolved, which accepts the intrusion of western civilisation, non-natives, central and regional administration as distinct from village and clan systems, new ideas of law, of morality and of religion, employment, trade, 'half-castes' and so on.

It is in the light of this context in the South and Southwest Pacific and in Australia, that this series of twelve rights, each preceded by a preamble, suggesting its causal context, is here presented.

These, like all rights, can be guaranteed only by the communities and administrations concerned—and that in three ways: (1) By positive legislative or administrative action designed to ensure some or all of them. (2) By legislative or administrative action of a negative or protective kind, prohibiting under penalty interference with the individual in certain spheres of activity. (3) By officially doing nothing, except being a latent court of appeal, and leaving the individuals free to determine their own behaviour within the limits set by the positive and negative action mentioned, that is, without damaging the rights of others. The effectiveness of these methods however, in the contact position, depends on the development of supporting public opinion amongst both the native and non-native elements in the population. The existence of the legislation, regulations and courts help in this regard, provided that the natives are encouraged and educated to use their rights and to perform the correlated duties. Otherwise rights, policies and regulations remain a dead letter, interred quietly by those non-natives who desire the *status quo*. Fortunately, the moral pressure of an informed and enlightened world-conscience, through international groups and organisations, or administering powers, can do much to make these rights effective in the culture-contact situation and amongst non-self-governing peoples.

Only a careful analysis of the position in each region could determine whether the twelve rights suggested here, are of wider application. Possibly they contain principles which could be applied in most contact and minority-group situations, though their content and application might need to be considerably varied.

The Rights of Dependent Peoples

Leonard J. Barnes

THE general picture of a colony, is of a territory where economic subordination entails political disability; where political disability may bring with it severe restrictions upon civil liberty and an exceptional widening of the legal meaning at the word 'sedition' (such restrictions being at their most severe when the metropolitan authorities regard the native culture as backward or inferior); and where official anxiety about sedition and allied offences leads to judicial and police practices which in the metropolitan country would be regarded as unusually harsh.

The consequence is that the subject peoples as a whole, and particularly their more cultivated and better educated representatives, exhibit to a marked degree the frustrations and the corruptions of impotence. For it should not be forgotten that, true as it may be that absolute power corrupts absolutely, the psychological effects of absolute powerlessness are no less damaging. .

Formulations of human rights naturally tend to reflect the major frustrations of those who make them. If a right, declared and claimed, is to be more than an empty aspiration, if it is to serve as 'a working conception and effective instrument,' it will express the natural demands of dissatisfied groups and of the have-nots of the social order. Liberty is the cry of the bond, equality the cry of the victim of discrimination, fraternity the cry of the outcast, progress and humanity are the cry of those whom their fellows use as means instead of respecting as ends, full employment is the cry of the worker whose daily job or lack of job stunts his soul and mocks his capabilities, social planning is the cry of those who are trampled underfoot when privilege and power strive to make the world safe for themselves. That is why declarations of the rights of man are strong allies of social progress, at least when they are first promulgated. For social progress *is* reorganisation in the interests of the unprivileged.

Hence it might be predicted that when colonial peoples set about drafting a bill of rights their claims will tally generally with those of depressed and disabled groups everywhere, but will also show a special distribution of emphasis corresponding to the special character of colonial disabilities. And in fact, wherever colonial discontent achieves articulate form, it shows a keen awareness both of the fundamental significance of an equity-less economy, with its necessary corollary of political subordination, and of the organic connection between these and the denials of civil liberty common in colonial territories. It is, further, ready enough to subscribe to the traditional democratic slogans of liberty, equality and fraternity, partly because colonial peoples have wide experience of being used as means to other people's ends, and partly because such slogans are handy for embarrassing the metropolitan authorities.

But all these diverse sentiments and attitudes are given a particular colouring, they wear a particular livery, distinctive of colonial experience. This colour, this livery, is the claim to equal rights with citizens of the metropolis, the protest against a discrimination that appears, to those on whom it falls, to be as arbitrary as it is comprehensive.

For this reason progressive movements among colonial peoples tend to assume a nationalist and liberationist form. They are liberationist because their awakening political consciousness sees the established constitutional ties with the metropolis as emblems of foreign domination. They are nationalist because separate nationhood is the repository of state power, and without state power at their disposal the liberationists can neither sever their political and economic dependence on the metropolis nor take over the administrative functions of the metropolis after the severance has been made.

We should, therefore, see the colonial peoples both as aggregations of individuals repressed and thwarted by specific forms of disprivilege, and as emergent nations struggling to attain equal status with the so-called independent countries in point of sovereignty and international recognition. The claim—we emphasise this—is to formal equality of status. It is not to material equality of function.

Nor is it necessarily to full national sovereignty in the classical signification of the term. Colonial peoples object to limitations of sovereignty when they are fastened on them from without, and appear as badges of inferiority. They might well accept limitations, provided they could do so of their own choice in the interests of effective international organisation, and provided they were assured that the majority of other free countries were genuinely making the same acceptance.

Such is the position of the dependent peoples, and such are their needs or rights. The needs cannot be satisfied by legislative enactment, nor can the rights be guaranteed by constitutional charter. Attempts to give the force of unalterable law to the claims of particular groups or communities have often been made. But since no legislators can bind their successors for ever, the attempts prove in the end either fruitless or superfluous.

For the hope of seeing their claims acknowledged in practice the colonial peoples must rely on the establishment and maintenance of certain broad politico-economic conditions inside and outside their own countries. Of such conditions perhaps the most indispensable are:

(a) an international system of co-operative peace and defence, without which the security and integrity of small countries tend to be merely nominal;

(b) social planning of the lend-lease type, under which the colonies could draw on the richer countries for capital needed for colonial development, without surrendering the equity in that development, and without creating such vested interests in the colonies themselves as may impede the growth of popular responsibility in either the economic or the political field;

(c) a working system of political and economic organisation both in the metropolitan countries and in the colonies, such that social power and responsibility may be given the widest possible distribution; as education in the colonies widens the compass of popular responsibility, so political advances should extend the opportunities for its exercise;

(d) full employment both in the metropolitan countries

and in the colonies; and this not merely in the sense of a productive job of some kind for every man and woman able and willing to take it, but also in the ampler sense of work offering scope for the highest skill that each individual, in the given social conditions, is capable of developing.

Human Rights and the Law Breaker

Margery Fry

IN considering the rights of the individual in relation to the State in which he lives, the limiting case is, in peace time, that of the person accused or convicted of breaking the law of that State. From very early times, long before the formation of organised Governments, the community has assumed the right to protect itself against these enemies within its borders, by the corporate action of law, as it does in war against exterior foes. And, though in very primitive times, it is largely ritual offences, transgressions of taboos and customs of the tribe which are thus punished, still the private injuries, which at first were the subject of individual revenge, very early came to be considered as equally the concern of the whole community.

It has often been pointed out that the individual in a primitive society has an extremely small range of free action, and perhaps the growth of early law should be regarded rather as a definition and consequently a limitation of the power of the community over the individual than a limitation of the freedom of the individual in the interests of the community.

The history of this definition and limitation is the history of criminal law. The formulation of that law, the definition of the actions which justify the State in interference with the citizen has, in all civilised epochs, engaged some of the best minds; very much less attention has been paid to the question of what limits should be set to the forfeiture of his rights by the lawbreaker. Far too often this forfeiture has been regarded as complete, involving life itself. Where life is spared, to what length is the State entitled to go in stripping an offender, permanently or temporarily, of his other freedoms? Has a human being some rights which the community has no moral sanction in mulcting him of?

Such questions have been fully recognised only during the last 200 years, and to Beccaria belongs the credit of being the first writer to bring them prominently before the notice of the civilised world. Himself stimulated by the French philosophers of the eighteenth century, he, in turn, greatly influenced them.

Beccaria had proclaimed the measure of crime to be the injury done to society. Offences against God which do not endanger public security should be left to divine justice, and the object of punishment should not be the infliction of pain, but simply to deter the offender and others from future crimes. Thus he disclaimed—as did his followers—a semi-theocratic duty laid upon the State to punish moral depravity as such. The doctrines of these penologists of the period at the end of the eighteenth and beginning of the nineteenth centuries have never been either refuted or put into practice in their entirety. It is impossible to consider without horror the immensity of the needless human suffering which could have been saved if their views had really prevailed. 'Wherever the laws suffer a man, in certain cases, to cease to be a *person* and to become a *thing*, there is no liberty,' wrote Beccaria. The history of the last twenty years in Europe has illustrated this only too vividly. It has, moreover, shown that where no limit is set to the power of the State over those who break its laws, where no rights at all are acknowledged to be universal, a definite international tension is likely to be set up. The minority of one country is often attached by racial or political links with the majority of another, and inhumanity in the treatment of such a minority convicted of breaking laws intended for the benefit of the majority has aroused, again and again, extremely bitter international hatreds.

It was perhaps partly this aspect of the case, though it was not oblivious of its humanitarian side also, which determined the League of Nations to place the question of Penal Administration upon its agenda in 1929, and to request the co-operation of the International Penal and Penitentiary Commission in framing a set of Minimum Rules for the Treatment of Prisoners. These, after circulation to States (members and non-members of the League) were finally approved by the League as constituting a minimum below which no State's penitentiary system should fall (1934). The International Penal and Penitentiary Commission thus called into consultation by the League of Nations is itself an expression of the common interest of States in the proper administration of penal sanctions, *i.e.* of the ultimate relation of the State to the individual law-breaker. It had been in existence since 1872 as a standing body of penal experts appointed by various Governments, and had organised ten International Conferences on penal questions. The minimum rules which the Commission proposed for the treatment of convicted prisoners were thus the result of long and wide study of legal punishment over the greater part of the civilised world.

Though not framed in the form of a statement of 'rights,' these rules would, if carried out in their entirety, ensure that the man in prison should not 'become a thing' but should retain at least some of the conditions without which life becomes intolerable, even though the exercise of most of his cherished liberties were denied him. In fact, taking the list in UNESCO's Memorandum on Human Rights,[1] even if the Rules were scrupulously observed, the only freedoms reserved to the prisoner (during his incarceration) are numbers 1 and 14—unless it be urged that 'the good life' can be pursued even in a gaol.

It is to be observed that the right to decent treatment as a prisoner is not identical with (18) the right to justice, since the offender who has been justly condemned should not thereby forfeit all claims to a tolerable existence.

Actually, so far from these rules being completely observed, with all their recommendations, it is doubtful whether any country has even attained these so-called 'minimum' standards. The degree of attainment varies immensely from country to country, and in all countries which have directly suffered from the effects of the war conditions have, in general, gravely deteriorated in spite of a few notable exceptions. Some of these exceptional modern experiments tend to show that the limitation of normal freedoms, the suffering (though not as a rule physical suffering) deliberately inflicted by States for the prevention of crime is usually in excess of what, upon a utilitarian calculation, is justifiable, since milder methods can be found as efficacious for maintaining observance of the law.

---

[1] *Cf* Appendix I

The 'Minimum Rules' dealt mainly with the treatment of convicted persons, but abundant evidence was forthcoming that the treatment of untried or unconvicted people in custody was, in many countries, at least as gravely in contradiction with elementary human rights. The League of Nations was engaged in collecting, from the technical organisations with which it was in communication, proposals for regulations 'to protect witnesses and persons awaiting trial against the use of violence, and any other forms of physical or mental constraint.' These proposed rules were actually discussed at a meeting of the same organisations in June, 1939. This piece of work remained unfinished (but more than ever necessary) at the outbreak of war.

Both the practical extent and the guarantees of the minimum rights of the prisoner vary very greatly from country to country. In many the continued existence of capital punishment is an assertion that in the last resort the individual may forfeit every right.

The question of guarantees is peculiarly difficult in the case of prisoners. Their voice, as against that of those in authority over them, cannot make itself heard through the prison walls; their statements are often suspect. Safeguards through the admission of qualified persons to the prisons are most important. The surest guarantee against abuses lies in an alert and well-informed public opinion. Such an opinion U.N.O. is eminently qualified to guide. The acceptance by the League of Nations of definite standards for the treatment of those who are deprived of their liberty was a step in the right direction. Unfortunately the absence of any system of international inspection and reporting allowed this acceptance to be, in too many cases, a purely verbal one. But even so it will be an irreparable loss to the world if the foundations already laid are allowed to disintegrate before a new and lasting structure for the defence of the rights of a peculiarly defenceless part of the human race is erected upon them.

APPENDIX I

THE classical formulations of human rights which have been influential in Western culture were first stated in the eighteenth century. They were drawn up on the basis of a conception of individual human rights as absolute and inherent. They thus followed out for the individual the conception which had inspired the idea of the divine right of kings and· the imprescriptible rights divinely conferred on the Church, although they attempted to set up against the notion of divine right an equally absolute but non-theological formulation of inherent natural rights.

Two historical events had been mainly responsible for preparing the way for this formulation of human rights— first, the Reformation with its appeal to the absolute authority of the individual conscience, and secondly the rise of early capitalism with its emphasis on freedom of individual enterprise from the shackles of Church or State authority.

The eighteenth century formulation of human rights was truly revolutionary, as shown by its importance in the American and French revolutions and its subsequent effects on political thought in the early nineteenth century; and the subsequent 150 years have been devoted to attempts towards the realisation of the ideals therein embodied. Great progress has been made in this effort, despite temporary setbacks and obscurations. Thus, after the first half of the nineteenth century, the principle of religious freedom has been scarcely questioned in the Western democracies, and the right of the individual to the franchise has been progressively rendered more general. Similarly, the principle of the right of national groups to self-determination was much extended.

On the other hand, the passage of time also revealed various unexpected shortcomings and difficulties. Thus it soon became apparent that political freedom by no means guaranteed economic or social freedom. The industrial workers of the mid-nineteenth century were certainly no better off than those of earlier ages, and the freedom to choose one's employment appeared a dubious privilege when the alternative was not to be employed at all. Again, the freedom of individual enterprise became profoundly modified through the rise of even larger business and financial combinations, culminating in the enormous trusts and cartels, often international in their operation, of the twentieth century. Freedom of the press was similarly, though to a less extent, curtailed by the twentieth century developments which so largely converted the press into an affair of big business, of State policy or of party politics, and led to the formation of newspaper chains and syndicated news.

Meanwhile, there were developments in thought which profoundly affected men's general outlook. Among these, two of the most important were the promulgation and general acceptance of the theory of evolution, and the rise of Marxism. The chief effect of both of these on the question of human rights was to provide a dynamic and relativistic frame of reference for their consideration. It was realised that all the manifestations of life, including human societies, evolve and change, and accordingly that human rights, whether of individuals or of groups, can be properly considered only in relation to the conditions of time and place.

In addition, Marxist theory laid especial stress on material and economic conditions, thus re-emphasising the need to analyse the effects of technological advance and of changes in socio-economic structure on human rights, as ideals, as working conceptions and as effective instruments. One of the most important effects of technological advance on our problem was the increased power of military weapons, which made rebellion against authority far more difficult and dangerous.

In the international field, the end of the first world war saw an early attempt at a general formulation of the rights of groups, in the shape of the principle of national self-determination; but its incompleteness and vagueness were speedily realised when the results of efforts to put it into practical operation were appraised. To the last few decades also belong the attempts to formulate the rights of nations and similar groups in relation to the rights of international or supra-national groupings—attempts which are still continuing.

Finally, the widespread unemployment of the inter-war period, with its acute financial depression, spelled a crisis for the development of the eighteenth century formulation of the rights of man: among other things, it led to a rapid development of schemes of social security, which ran counter to many of their traditional individualist conceptions.

Meanwhile, these conceptions had been challenged in another way—by the development of the U.S.S.R. after the revolution of 1917. Historically, Russia had never passed through a period comparable to that which had marked the Reformation and the early rise of capitalism in the west, when the emphasis had been on the individual, in regard both to conscience and opinion, and on economic enterprise, as against organised authority whether of Church or State. Furthermore, events soon drove it to adopt the principle of over-all planning and of one-party Government.

However, one new individual right of freedom was incorporated into Soviet constitutional theory and practice—namely freedom from exploitation for private profit. Further, the principles of racial non-discrimination and of cultural self-determination for the so-called nationalities of the U.S.S.R. have been thoroughly implemented in practice.

Under these circumstances, a quite different working conception of human rights grew up in the Soviet sphere, as is witnessed by the present frequent opposition of the western and the communist usage of the word 'democracy.'

In addition, the revolutionary situation, which was accompanied by both external and internal threats to the stability of the régime, made it inexpedient to allow full freedom of opinion and conscience, of expression, of press, or information.

In this connection, it is to be recalled that all nations restrict some or all of these freedoms in situations of emergency such as war or revolution; and further that, as a matter of historical fact, political and other conditions have often affected the degree of freedom allowed in particular spheres (for instance, in the case of the Roman Catholic minority in Britain).

We must also note that the twentieth century has witnessed a trend towards organised economic and social planning in a number of countries other than the U.S.S.R., including some of the western democracies. Since organised planning automatically restricts certain traditional individual freedoms, this has led to renewed interest in a consideration of their theoretical basis.

Thus from one angle the present state of the subject may be regarded as a confrontation of two different working conceptions of human rights, which have arisen from different historical formulations and have developed in relation to different sets of social circumstances. The one started from the premise of inherent individual rights, and with a bias against a strong central authority and against government interference, while the other was based upon Marxist principles and the premise of a powerful central government, and early wedded to total planning (which automatically magnifies the central power) and to one-party Government (which inevitably restricts certain political freedoms). Each has become modified in the course of its history, and in both cases many of the modifications have been in the direction of the other system.

These two working conceptions are in some ways complementary, in others opposed. One of the major tasks immediately ahead of us is thus clearly to find some common measure for the future development of the two tendencies, or in the terms of the Marxist dialectic to effect a reconciliation of the two opposites in a higher synthesis.

In this connection it is worth remarking that the ideal held up by both tendencies is far from dissimilar. The western formulation presupposed that liberty would be followed by equality and fraternity, in economic and social as well as political opportunity, while Marx expressly laid down that the dictatorship of the proletariat, once it has been successfully implemented, will be followed by a 'withering away of the State.' Again, many western social philosophers incline to the view that truly free enterprise in an age of abundance made possible by the application of science will be able to dispense with all kinds of restrictions on individual freedom and opportunity, while conversely Marxist theory maintains that collectivism properly applied will eventually permit the fullest degree of individual development and variety.

We must not, however, neglect the fact that in other parts of the world other theories of human rights have emerged, are emerging, or are destined to emerge. Fascism is one such. Most thinkers agree that it can be shown to be untenable on theoretical grounds, and in any case it has been discredited and defeated in practice.

Then a quite new formulation of human rights would be required to embody the views of a man like Mahatma Gandhi, or of those numerous Indian thinkers who believe in the social importance and individual value of meditation and mystical experience. And we can be reasonably sure that the ferment of thought now apparent in the peoples of black and brown and yellow skin-colour, from Africa to the Far East, is destined to result in still other formulations.

Meanwhile the immediate issue is clear. The world of man is at a critical stage in its political, social and economic evolution. If it is to proceed further on the path towards unity, it must develop a common set of ideas and principles. One of those is a common formulation of the rights of man. This common formulation must by some means reconcile the various divergent or opposing formulations now in existence. It must further be sufficiently definite to have real significance both as an inspiration and as a guide to practice, but also sufficiently general and flexible to apply to all men, and to be capable of modification to suit peoples at different stages of social and political development while yet retaining significance for them and their aspirations.

These considerations point to several lines of enquiry, both general and special.

(a) General

1. What are the relations between the political, the social and the economic rights of individuals (of different sexes and ages) and of groups, in societies of different types and in different historical circumstances?

2. How far are the differences between the divergent formulations of ideal human rights and freedoms in different societies accurate indications of the material differences in economic and social conditions in the regions concerned?

3. How far have the personal relations and group relations (*e.g.* class, national and international) of man been altered in the main advanced regions of the world during the last hundred years:
   (a) by intellectual and cultural developments in the fields of the sciences, the arts and philosophy.
   (b) by material and social developments in the field of applied science and technology, social and economic structure and national and international organisation?

4. In particular:
   (a) how far have the traditional human rights of the eighteenth century declarations been affected by the industrial revolution and its consequences before the first world war?
   (b) to what extent have the rights of individuals and groups been modified, in theory and in practice, by developments since that time?

5. What are the relations between rights and duties? (a) for individuals, (b) for groups? And what are the relations of individual freedoms to corporate or social responsibilities?

6. What emergencies justify the restriction or abrogation of normal rights and freedoms?

(b) Special

What, in the world today, are the theoretical grounds, the practical extent, and the efficient guarantees of specific rights or freedoms, such as:

1. Freedom of conscience or worship (a) for individuals (b) for organised religious groups;
2. Freedom of speech (the right to free speech) and freedom of opinion;
3. Freedom of assembly;
4. Freedom of association and freedom for consequent action (the right to strike);
5. Freedom of movement (a) within (b) across national boundaries (c) freedom to leave one nation for another;
6. Freedom of communications and the right to accurate information (a) within (b) across national boundaries (freedom of the press, etc.);

7. Political freedom and equality (a) for organised political parties (b) for individuals in the exercise of the franchise (the right to vote);
8. Freedom of expression (including freedom of the writer and the artist);
9. Freedom and equality of economic, social and educational opportunity;
10. Freedom of opportunity for pursuit of the good life;
11. Freedom of teaching;
12. Freedom of scientific and philosophic enquiry and publication;
13. The right to work or not to work; the right of leisure;
14. Freedom and equality of access to the means of subsistence (a) for individuals (b) for nations;
15. Freedom from fear (the right to protection);
16. Freedom from want (economic rights: the right to economic security and to a basic level of material well-being);
17. Freedom from exploitation and oppression (social rights);
18. The right to justice;
19. Freedom from preventible disease (the right to health);
20. The right to property;
21. The rights and freedoms of minorities (a) racial (b) political (c) religious (d) cultural or linguistic, including the right to self-determination;
22. The rights and freedoms of politically dependent (non-self-governing) peoples;
23. The rights of nations in relation (a) to each other (b) to existing or possible international or supranational organisations;
24. The rights of women, of children, of the disabled and of the aged;
25. Any other rights and freedoms?

Paris, March 1947

*THE GROUNDS OF AN INTERNATIONAL
DECLARATION OF HUMAN RIGHTS*

A N international declaration of human rights must be
the expression of a faith to be maintained no less than
a programme of actions to be carried out. It is a foundation
for convictions universally shared by men however great
the differences of their circumstances and their manner of
formulating human rights: it is an essential element in the
constitutional structure of the United Nations. In order that
all peoples and all governments shall be made aware that the
authority and goodwill of the United Nations will be exercised with ever increasing power to apply these means for
the advancement of human happiness in the great society,
it is fitting that its members solemnly proclaim a declaration
of rights to the civilised world. Such a declaration depends,
however, not only on the authority by which rights are
safeguarded and advanced, but also on the common understanding which makes the proclamation feasible and the
faith practicable.

The preparation of a Declaration of Human Rights faces
fundamental problems concerning principles and interpretations as well as political and diplomatic problems
concerning agreement and drafting. For this reason the
UNESCO Committee on the Philosophic Principles of the
Rights of Man has undertaken, on the basis of a survey
of the opinion of scholars in the various parts of the world,
an examination of the intellectual bases of a modern bill of
rights, in the hope that such a study may prove useful to the
Commission on Human Rights of the Economic and Social
Council both in suggesting common grounds for agreement
and in explaining possible sources of differences. The UNESCO
Committee is convinced that the members of the United
Nations share common convictions on which human rights
depend, but it is further convinced that those common
convictions are stated in terms of different philosophic

---

[1] Final result of the UNESCO enquiry on the theoretical bases of
human rights, drafted by the committee of experts on the basis
of the various contributions to the enquiry.

principles and on the background,of divergent political and
economic systems. An examination of the grounds of a bill
of rights should therefore serve to reveal, on the one hand,
the common principles on which the declaration rests and
to anticipate, on the other hand, some of the difficulties and
differences of interpretation which might otherwise delay
or impede agreement concerning the fundamental rights
which enter into the declaration.

The United Nations stands as the symbol to all of victory
over those who sought to achieve tyranny through aggressive
war. Since it was created to maintain the peace of mankind
and, as it maintains peace, to make ever more full the lives
of men and women everywhere, it is fitting that it should
record its faith in freedom and democracy and its determination to safeguard their power to expand. That faith in freedom and democracy is founded on the faith in the inherent
dignity of men and women. The United Nations cannot
succeed in the great purposes to which it is committed
unless it so acts that this dignity is given increasing recognition, and unless steps are taken to create the conditions
under which this dignity may be achieved more fully and
at constantly higher levels. Varied in cultures and built
upon different institutions, the members of the United
Nations have, nevertheless, certain great principles in
common. They believe that men and women, all over the
world, have the right to live a life that is free from the
haunting fear of poverty and insecurity. They believe that
they should have a more complete access to the heritage,
in all its aspects and dimensions, of the civilisation so painfully built by human effort. They believe that science and
the arts should combine to serve alike peace and the well-
being, spiritual as well as material, of all men and women
without discrimination of any kind. They believe that,
given goodwill between nations, the power is in their hands
to advance the achievement of this well-being more swiftly
than in any previous age.

It is this faith, in the opinion of the UNESCO Committee,
which underlies the solemn obligation of the United Nations
to declare, not only to all governments, but also to their
peoples, the rights which have now become the vital ends of

human effort everywhere. These rights must no longer be confined to a few. They are claims which all men and women may legitimately make, in their search, not only to fulfil themselves at their best, but to be so placed in life that they are capable, at their best, of becoming in the highest sense citizens of the various communities to which they belong and of the world community, and in those communities of seeking to respect the rights of others, just as they are resolute to protect their own.

Despite the antiquity and the broad acceptance of the conception of the rights of man, and despite the long evolution of devices to protect some human rights by legal systems, the systematic proclamation of declarations of human rights is recent. The history of the philosophic discussion of human rights, of the dignity and brotherhood of man, and of his common citizenship in the great society is long: it extends beyond the narrow limits of the western tradition and its beginnings in the West as well as in the East coincide with the beginnings of philosophy. The history of declarations of human rights, on the other hand, is short and its beginnings are to be found in the West in the British Bill of Rights and the American and French Declarations of Rights formulated in the seventeenth and eighteenth centuries, although the right of the people to revolt against political oppression was very early recognised and established in China. The relation of philosophic considerations to the declarations of human rights is suggested by the differences of these two histories. The philosophic temper of the times was an indispensable background and preparation for each statement of human rights, but despite the broad agreements among the resulting statements there was no more agreement among philosophers in the eighteenth than in the twentieth century. Moreover, despite the faith in human dignity and the formula for human happiness prepared by philosophers, an implementation was needed in social and political institutions to secure human rights for men. An international declaration of human rights is involved in precisely the same problems. The philosophies of our times, notwithstanding their divergencies, have deepened the faith in the dignity of man and have vastly expanded the formula for his happiness; but the differences of philosophies have led to varied and even opposed interpretations of fundamental rights and the practical import of philosophies has become more marked.

The civil and political rights which were formulated in the eighteenth century have since that time been incorporated into the constitution or the laws of almost every nation in the world. During the same period, the developments of technology and industrial advances have led to the formation of a conception of economic and social rights. The older civil and political rights have sometimes been extended to embrace these new rights. In such applications and other context of the newer rights, the meanings have frequently undergone modification, and indeed the two have sometimes been thought to be in conflict. Finally, as science and technology have given men greater control over nature, rights which were in the past reserved for the few have gradually been extended to the many and are now potentially open to all. This addition of new rights and the changes in the significance of old rights in the context of developing knowledge and technology presents problems as well as opportunities. Perhaps the greatest problem involved in the basic ideas which underlie a declaration of human rights is found in the conflict of ideas which have been used to relate the social responsibilities entailed in the material and social developments of the nineteenth century to the civil and political rights earlier enunciated. This conflict has even shaken the simple form of the faith in the dignity of man which was based on the confidence in progress and the advance of knowledge, for it is the source of complexities in the interpretation of liberty and equality and of their interrelations, as well as of apparent contradictions among the fundamental human rights. In like fashion, the problem of the implementation of human rights, new and old, depends on the tacit or explicit resolution of basic philosophic problems, for the rights involve assumptions concerning the relations not only of men to governments, but also of the relations of groups of men to the State and of States to one another, and in the complex of these interrelations the inter-dependence of rights and duties has been redefined.

Notwithstanding these difficulties, the UNESCO Committee

on the Philosophic Principles of the Rights of Man is convinced that the perspectives open to men, both on the planes of history and of philosophy, are wider and richer than before. The deeper the re-examination of the bases of human rights that is made, the greater are the hopes that emerge as possible. The Committee has therefore circulated to a select list of the scholars of the world a series of questions concerning the changes of intellectual and historical circumstances between the classical declarations of human rights which stem from the eighteenth century and the bill of rights made possible by the state of ideas and the economic potentials of the present. On the basis of that inquiry, it has set down briefly, first, what seem to it some of the significant consequences of the evolution of human rights and, second, a schematic formulation of basic rights which in its opinion can and should be vindicated for all men. The history and the schematism grew out of the discussions of the Committee during its meetings in Paris from June 26th to July 2nd, but although they are based on a study of the replies received to the questionnaire, they do not represent the opinions of all the scholars who contributed to the symposium.

It is the conviction of the UNESCO Committee that these inquiries into the intellectual bases of human rights may contribute to the work of the Commission on Human Rights in two fashions: first, by a brief indication of the places at which the discovery of common principles might remove difficulties in the way of agreement and the places at which philosophic divergencies might anticipate difficulties in interpretation and, second, a more precise and detailed examination of the common principles that may be formulated and the philosophic differences that have divided men in the interpretation of those principles. The document which is here presented is an attempt to perform the first and preliminary task. The Committee is convinced that UNESCO will be able to muster the scholarly resources necessary for the accomplishment of the second task.

For the purposes of present inquiry, the Committee did not explore the subtleties of interpretations of right, liberty and democracy. The members of the Committee found it possible to agree on working definitions of these terms, reserving for later examination the fashion in which their differences of interpretation will diversify their further definition. By a right they mean a condition of living, without which, in any given historical stage of a society, men cannot give the best of themselves as active members of the community because they are deprived of the means to fulfil themselves as human beings. By liberty they mean more than only the absence of restraint. They mean also the positive organisation of the social and economic conditions within which men can participate to a maximum as active members of the community and contribute to the welfare of the community at the highest level permitted by the material development of the society. This liberty can have meaning only under democratic conditions, for only in democracy is liberty set in that context of equality which makes it an opportunity for all men and not for some men only. Democratic liberty is a liberty which does not distinguish by age or sex, by race or language or creed, between the rights of one man and the rights of another.

The Committee is fully aware that these working definitions are susceptible of highly diverse particularisations and that they contain, therefore, great ambiguity. But the Committee is convinced that the philosophic problem involved in a declaration of human rights is not to achieve doctrinal consensus but rather to achieve agreement concerning rights, and also concerning action in the realisation and defence of rights, which may be justified on highly divergent doctrinal grounds. The Committee's discussion, therefore, of both the evolution of human rights and of the theoretic differences concerning their nature and interrelations, was intended, not to set up an intellectual structure to reduce them to a single formulation, but rather to discover the intellectual means to secure agreement concerning fundamental rights and to remove difficulties in their implementation such as might stem from intellectual differences.

I

The fundamental human rights which were specified first and proclaimed widely at the beginnings of the modern period were rights which regulated man's relations to political and social groups and which are therefore usually referred to as *Civil and Political Rights*. They had as purpose to protect man in actions which do not derogate from the freedom or well-being of others and to assign to him the exercise of functions by which he might exert a proper influence on the institutions and laws of the State. As a result of religious movements and the development of national states, a series of freedoms were formulated more and more precisely and insistently from the Renaissance to the eighteenth century: to free man from unwarranted interference in his thought and expression, the freedom of conscience, worship, speech, assembly, association and the press. During the seventeenth century, each of these freedoms received eloquent defence on the grounds, not only that they may be granted without danger to the peace of the State, but also that they may not be withheld without danger. Legal implementation for their protection was step by step provided by the institution of courts or the extension of the jurisdiction of existing courts, and these rights may, therefore, be associated with respect to the means of securing them, with other personal rights and with the right to justice, by which it was recognised that all men have an equal right to seek justice by appeal to law and in that appeal to be protected from summary arrest, cruel treatment and unjust punishment. As civil rights, moreover, they are closely related to the right to political action by which the function of citizens in States is defined, and the growth of democratic institutions during this period is largely an expression of the conviction men can achieve justice and the defence of their rights only by participation direct or indirect in the governments by which they are ruled. Political rights were therefore written into instruments and institutions of government, whereas civil rights, protected from interference by governments by recourse to courts, were written into bills of rights. The right to political action within a State discussed during this period, moreover, in close conjunction with the right to rebellion or revolution by which men might set up a government in conformity with justice if the fundamental principles of justice and the basic human rights are violated in such fashion as to permit no redress by recourse to peaceful means, and also in conjunction with the right to citizenship by which men may abandon their existing citizenships and assume the citizenship of any country which is prepared to accept them as citizens. Finally, during the nineteenth century, the discussion of the right to political action made increasingly clear that it is a right which can be exercised wisely only in conjunction with the right to information by which the citizen may equip himself for the proper exercise of his political functions.

During the nineteenth century there were added to these rights another set of fundamental human rights which grew out of the recognition that to live well and freely man must have at least the means requisite for living and which was made increasingly practicable .by the advances in technology and industrialisation in making the means of livelihood potentially accessible to all men. These have come to be called *Economic and Social Rights*. They were first tedtrea as sub-divisions or extensions of civil and political rights, but in the course of the last hundred years it has become apparent that they are different in kind from the older rights and that they therefore require difference in implementation. In their earliest form they are associated with the right to property, which in the eighteenth century was conceived by many philosophers to be the basic human right from which the others are derived, in such a fashion that even liberty and the pursuit of happiness are often treated as property rights of man. The evolution of social and economic rights depended on the discussion of the relation of the ownership and the use of property, of private and common ownership, and of private rights and public responsibility. Similarly, the right to education was early conceived to belong to all men, and the institution of public systems of education was designed to effect the realisation of that right. Likewise, the right to work was treated first as a freedom consequent on the right to property and was only later implemented with legal provisions for bargaining and arbitration concerning the conditions and the rewards of work. The right to protection of health usually started in the various States from modest beginnings in pure food and drugs legislation under the provisions of police power, and slowly extended to the provision of minimum medical and dietetic services, while the end of the nineteenth century and the beginning of the twentieth century saw the growth of various forms of social security designed to embody the right to maintenance during infancy, old age, sickness and other forms of incapacity, and involuntary unemployment. Finally, there are few to deny, in the retrospect of technological advances, today, the right of all to share in the advancing gains of civilisation and to have full access to the enjoyment of cultural opportunities and material improvements.

Since the increased accessibility of economic and social rights was achieved as a consequence of the advances of science and since the ideals and accomplishments of an age find their expression in art and literature, a new emphasis has been placed on rights of the mind: on the right to inquiry, expression and communication. Whether the purpose of communication be the expression of an idea or an emotion, the furthering of an individual or social purpose, or the formulation of an objective and scientific truth, the right is grounded both in the purpose of developing to the full the potentialities of men and in the social consequences of such communications.

II

The evolution, extension and increase of human rights provide clear indication of their scope and of the problems which must be solved by a modern declaration of human rights. Rights which were first proclaimed effectively for only a privileged few have been extended until they may now be claimed by all. Rights which were imperfectly secured have been supplemented by rights which are essential to their realisation. But in that process of extension and growth, the significance of many basic rights has been changed. Their significance has sometimes been rendered more precise and that process has frequently led to the recognition of how far man is from the realisation of his rights. The change in their significance has frequently extended them to applications for which they were not originally intended, sometimes with good, and sometimes with evil, effect. It has sometimes rendered rights vague, and it has even perverted what had been conceived as rights to sources of abuse against the fundamental rights of other men.

The evolution of man's conception of his rights serves to make clear, moreover, not only the problems involved in a modern declaration of human rights, but also the means for the solution of those problems. Human rights have become, and must remain, universal. All the rights which we have come slowly and laboriously to recognise belong to all men everywhere without discrimination of race, sex, language or religion. They are universal, moreover, not only because there are no fundamental differences among men, but also because the great society and the community of all men has become a real and effective power, and the interdependent nature of that community is beginning at last to be recognised. This universality of the rights of man, finally, has led to the translation into political instrumentalities of that close interdependence of rights and duties which has long been apparent in moral analysis. But the enjoyment of rights involves, not only the acceptance by the individual of corresponding obligations to society but it is conditioned by the material resources of the society to which he belongs. Thus, the right to work implies the obligation to engage in work useful to the society; the right to maintenance, education, etc, can be enjoyed by each man only in so far as the society by productive work creates the resources out of which these rights can be assured. The problem, which the Commission of Human Rights must resolve, consequently turns on the relation of rights to political and economic institutions and the implementation of a bill of rights proclaimed for all men, as men and as members of the world community.

In the present world situation then, all of the rights which man has acquired through the centuries are important to the life of man and the development of the world community, but those which have been made possible by the most recent advances of knowledge and technology and by the institution of the agencies of the United Nations have assumed priority over, and have affected, the conception of the earlier rights; for the new rights have not only been added to the list of rights, but they have made also clear the full sense of older rights and have made them universally practicable. They make it possible to draw a list of fundamental rights on which, the UNESCO Committee on the Philosophic Principles of the Rights of Man is convinced, all men are agreed. They are rights which should inspire individual men, nations, and international agencies to work for their achievement and to use their full authority and power in support of them. They may be seen to be implicit in man's nature as an individual and as a member of society and to follow from the fundamental right to live.

1. The Right to Live

The right to live is the condition and, as it were, the foundation of all other rights. It is the condition of other rights since it is the minimum human right. It is inseparably involved in the very existence of man. But to live is more than barely to exist, and it is therefore the right which makes specific all other rights since they mark the degree of well-being which man may achieve. All rights derive, on the one hand, from the nature of man as such and, on the other, since man depends on man, from the stage of development achieved by the social and political groups in which he participates.

One group of rights is essentially connected with the provision of means for subsistence, through his own efforts or, where they are insufficient, through the resources of society.

2. The Right to the Protection of Health

3. The Right to Work

Every man has the right to work, at a wage which represents a fair reward for the quantity and quality of the work done, provided the wages be always at least sufficient to provide means of subsistence and provided the hours of work be reasonable and the leisure adequate.

The right to work implies the right of the workers to participate in the collective determination of the conditions of their work, as well as the right of the workers to understand the general significance of the work done. Work cannot be considered as a commodity, and the recognition of its moral and social value is, therefore, an essential right of the workers.

No discrimination will be set up to bar anyone from access to any form of work for which he is qualified.

4. The Right to Maintenance in involuntary unemployment, infancy, old age, sickness and all other forms of incapacity.

5. The Right to Property
Every man has the right to private property in so far as is necessary for his personal use and the use of his family; no other form of property is in itself a fundamental right.

Bare living, however, is not sufficient, and another group of rights supplements these, providing intellectual foundations for living well, training for the proper use of human as well as the opportunities for self-development and the advancement of the common good.

6. The Right to Education
Every man has the right to a certain minimum of elementary education. That elementary education should eventually be brought to a minimum level of fundamental education available to all men, which should in turn facilitate the mutual understanding of the peoples of the world. In addition, higher education should be accessible to all who have the capacity to benefit by it, and society should select such persons by appropriate means, with due respect to the principle of equal merit and the satisfaction of legitimate aspirations on the part of the individual.

7. The Right to Information
Every man, that he may play his part in human society, has the right to the fullest and most accurate information from all relevant sources.

8. Freedom of Thought and the Right to Free Inquiry
The right to live finds its most complete manifestation in the life of thought and in the various modes of artistic and scientific expression. Every man has the right to follow as he finds them compelling the consequences of his reasoning and to hold such doctrines as he judges to be true. He shall not be hindered in the pursuit of knowledge or in communicating the results of his inquiries to others in the effort to increase the sum of human knowledge.

9. The Right of Self-Expression

Even apart from direct calculation of social utility, however, every man has the right to express himself in art and science, not only as part of his own self-fulfilment, but also as a possible contribution to the culture of his nation and time, since the highest expression of culture and the greatest utility to society frequently derive from works little esteemed by their contemporaries for æsthetic value or immediate practical use.

Finally, there is a group of rights which bear on man's participation in society and his protection from social and political injustice.

10. The Right to Justice

Every man has an equal right to justice. He cannot be summoned for an act which was not a legal offence at the time when it was committed. He has the right to be protected by law from illegal arrest, brutality, torture, cruel and unjust punishment and double jeopardy. In the case of legal arrest, he has the right to a speedy and public trial by due process of law.

The inviolability of domicile and correspondence is limited only in accordance with due process of law and in so far as its enjoyment may endanger the existence of society or the principles on which it is founded.

11. The Right to Political Action

Every citizen is entitled, both by voting and by direct participation, to make his contribution to the conduct of public affairs. In pursuance of this aim, he has the right to express his ideas and to form associations for the promotion of his ideas, provided that such expressions and such associations are not incompatible with the principles of democracy or with the rights of man.

12. Freedom of Speech, Assembly, Association, Worship and the Press

As instruments, therefore, in the exercise of his right to political action, no less than as consequence of his right to self-expression, man has the right to set forth his ideas and to seek to persuade others to accept them. Society is entitled to limit the exercise of these rights only in exceptional circumstances and only in so far as their exercise might endanger the existence of the society or the principles on which it is founded.

13. The Right to Citizenship

In the event that a man is not satisfied with the institutions of the nation of which he is part, he has the right to abandon his existing citizenship and to assume the citizenship of any country which is prepared to accept him as a citizen.

14. The Right to Rebellion or Revolution

In the event that the government of his nation operates contrary to the fundamental principles of justice and the basic human rights in such fashion that no redress is permitted by peaceful means, man has the right to set up a government more nearly in conformity with justice and humanity.

15. The Right to Share in Progress

Every man has the right to full access to the enjoyment of the technical and cultural achievements of civilisation.

These rights, the UNESCO Committee on the Philosophic Principles of Human Rights is convinced, are of fundamental importance not only to the enrichment of the human spirit but to the development of all forms of human association, including the development of national cultures and international co-operation. The UNESCO Committee has attempted to indicate some of the intellectual ramifications and implications of the problem of human rights in the modern world and in the international framework of the United Nations by setting forth briefly the turns of the historical development of human rights and the broad lines of the interrelations of human rights which are consequent on that development. The Committee is particularly concerned to emphasise the dynamic character of the interrelations of human rights and the need, therefore, to explore and control the basic ideas which are in process of being fitted to new industrial and technological means for the achievement of human good. The Committee reaffirms its conviction that a further study of the oppositions of philosophic doctrines which lead to diversities of interpretations of human rights, or which conceal fundamental principles on which agreement is possible despite these diversities, might facilitate the discussion of human rights today. It reaffirms also its further conviction that UNESCO might properly take the study of these philosophic differences. Such a study should be undertaken, however, only if it is seen to contribute to the formulation and implementation of the Declaration of Human Rights which is in process of preparation by the Commission on Human Rights, for the UNESCO Committee is convinced that agreement is possible concerning such a declaration and that it will constitute a basic contribution to the fullness of man's life, and to the stability and to the effectiveness of the operation of the United Nations.

PARIS, July, 1947

The UNESCO Committee on the theoretical bases of Human Rights

EDWARD H. CARR, Chairman
RICHARD P. McKEON, Rapporteur
PIERRE AUGER
GEORGES FRIEDMANN
HAROLD J. LASKI
CHUNG-SHU LO
LUC SOMERHAUSEN

APPENDIX III

UNIVERSAL DECLARATION OF HUMAN RIGHTS

*COMPLETE TEXT ADOPTED ON DECEMBER 10th, 1948
BY GENERAL ASSEMBLY OF UNITED NATIONS AT THE
PALAIS DE CHAILLOT, PARIS*

*T*HE *reader will find on the following pages the complete official
text of the Declaration of Human Rights adopted by the General
Assembly of the United Nations. This document, which was finally
accepted on December 10th, 1948, at the Palais de Chaillot in Paris
will permit the reader to situate in their proper context the preceding
analyses of the problem of Human Rights written in their personal
capacity by those philosophers and writers who were consulted by*
UNESCO *during the summer of 1947.*

PREAMBLE

WHEREAS recognition of the inherent dignity and of the
equal and inalienable rights of all members of the human
family is the foundation of freedom, justice and peace in the
world,

WHEREAS disregard and contempt for human rights have
resulted in barbarous acts which have outraged the conscience of mankind, and the advent of a world in which
human beings shall enjoy freedom of speech and belief and
freedom from fear and want has been proclaimed as the
highest aspiration of the common people,

WHEREAS it is essential, if man is not to be compelled to
have recourse, as a last resort, to rebellion against tyranny
and oppression, that human rights should be protected by
the rule of law,

WHEREAS it is essential to promote the development of
friendly relations between nations,

WHEREAS the peoples of the United Nations have in the
Charter reaffirmed their faith in fundamental human rights,
in the dignity and worth of the human person and in the
equal rights of men and women and have determined to
promote social progress and better standards of life in
larger freedom,

WHEREAS Member States have pledged themselves to achieve, in co-operation with the United Nations, the promotion of universal respect for and observance of human rights and fundamental freedoms,

WHEREAS a common understanding of these rights and freedoms is of the greatest importance for the full realisation of this pledge,

NOW, THEREFORE,
THE GENERAL ASSEMBLY,
PROCLAIM this Universal Declaration of Human Rights as a common standard of achievement for all peoples and all nations, to the end that every individual and every organ of society, keeping this Declaration constantly in mind, shall strive by teaching and education to promote respect for these rights and freedoms and by progressive measures, national and international, to secure their universal and effective recognition and observance, both among the peoples of Member States themselves and among the peoples of territories under their jurisdiction.

Article 1

All human beings are born free and equal in dignity and rights. They are endowed with reason and conscience and should act towards one another in a spirit of brotherhood.

Article 2

1. Everyone is entitled to all the rights and freedoms set forth in this Declaration, without distinction of any kind, such as race, colour, sex, language, religion, political or other opinion, national or social origin, property, birth or other status.
2. Furthermore, no distinction shall be made on the basis of the political, jurisdictional or international status of the country or territory to which a person belongs, whether it be independent, trust, non-self-governing or under any other limitation of sovereignty.

Article 3

Everyone has the right to life, liberty and security of person.

Article 4

No one shall be held in slavery or servitude; slavery and the slave trade shall be prohibited in all their forms.

Article 5

No one shall be subjected to torture or to cruel, inhuman or degrading treatment or punishment.

Article 6

Everyone has the right to recognition everywhere as a person before the law.

Article 7

All are equal before the law and are entitled without any discrimination to equal protection of the law. All are entitled to equal protection against any discrimination in violation of this Declaration and against any incitement to such discrimination.

Article 8

Everyone has the right to an effective remedy by the competent national tribunals for acts violating the fundamental rights granted him by the constitution or by law.

Article 9

No one shall be subjected to arbitrary arrest, detention or exile.

Article 10

Everyone is entitled in full equality to a fair and public hearing by an independent and impartial tribunal, in the determination of his rights and obligations and of any criminal charge against him.

Article 11

1. Everyone charged with a penal offence has the right to be presumed innocent until proved guilty according to law in a public trial at which he has had all the guarantees necessary for his defence.
2. No one shall be held guilty of any penal offence on account of any act or omission which did not constitute a penal offence, under national or international law, at the time when it was committed. Nor shall a heavier penalty be imposed than the one that was applicable at the time the penal offence was committed.

Article 12

No one shall be subjected to arbitrary interference with his privacy, family, home or correspondence, nor to attacks upon his honour and reputation. Everyone has the right to the protection of the law against such interference or attacks.

Article 13

1. Everyone has the right to freedom of movement and residence within the borders of each State.
2. Everyone has the right to leave any country, including his own, and to return to his country.

Article 14

1. Everyone has the right to seek and to enjoy in other countries asylum from persecution.
2. This right may not be invoked in the case of prosecutions genuinely arising from non-political crimes or from acts contrary to the purposes and principles of the United Nations.

Article 15

1. Everyone has the right to a nationality.
2. No one shall be arbitrarily deprived of his nationality nor denied the right to change his nationality.

Article 16

1. Men and women of full age, without any limitation due to race, nationality or religion, have the right to

marry and to found a family. They are entitled to equal rights as to marriage, during marriage and at its dissolution.

2. Marriage shall be entered into only with the free and full consent of the intending spouses.

3. The family is the natural and fundamental group unit of society and is entitled to protection by society and the State.

Article 17

1. Everyone has the right to own property alone as well as in association with others.

2. No one shall be arbitrarily deprived of his property.

Article 18

Everyone has the right to freedom of thought, conscience and religion; this right includes freedom to change his religion or belief, and freedom, either alone or in community with others and in public or private, to manifest his religion or belief in teaching, practice, worship and observance.

Article 19

Everyone has the right to freedom of opinion and expression; this right includes freedom to hold opinions without interference and to seek, receive and impart information and ideas through any media and regardless of frontiers.

Article 20

1. Everyone has the right to freedom of peaceful assembly and association.

2. No one may be compelled to belong to an association.

Article 21

1. Everyone has the right to take part in the government of his country, directly or through freely chosen representatives.

2. Everyone has the right of equal access to public service in his country.

3. The will of the people shall be the basis of the authority of government; this will shall be expressed in periodic and genuine elections which shall be by universal and equal suffrage and shall be held by secret vote or by equivalent free voting procedures.

Article 22

Everyone, as a member of society, has the right to social security and is entitled to realisation, through national effort and international co-operation and in accordance with the organisation and resources of each State, of the economic, social and cultural rights indispensable for his dignity and the free development of his personality.

Article 23

1. Everyone has the right to work, to free choice of employment, to just and favourable conditions of work and to protection against unemployment.
2. Everyone, without any discrimination, has the right to equal pay for equal work.
3. Everyone who works has the right to just and favourable remuneration ensuring for himself and his family an existence worthy of human dignity, and supplemented, if necessary, by other means of social protection.
4. Everyone has the right to form and to join trade unions for the protection of his interests.

Article 24

Everyone has the right to rest and leisure, including reasonable limitation of working hours and periodic holidays with pay.

Article 25

1. Everyone has the right to a standard of living adequate for the health and well-being of himself and of his family, including food, clothing, housing and medical care and necessary social services, and the right to security in the event of unemployment, sickness, disability, widowhood, old age or other lack of livelihood in circumstances beyond his control.

2. Motherhood and childhood are entitled to special care and assistance. All children, whether born in or out of wedlock, shall enjoy the same social protection.

Article 26

1. Everyone has the right to education. Education shall be free, at least in the elementary and fundamental stages. Elementary education shall be compulsory. Technical and professional education shall be made generally available and higher education shall be equally accessible to all on the basis of merit.

1. Education shall be directed to the full development of the human personality and to the strengthening of respect for human rights and fundamental freedoms. It shall promote understanding, tolerance and friendship among all nations, racial or religious groups, and shall further the activities of the United Nations for the maintenance of peace.

3. Parents have a prior right to choose the kind of education that shall be given to their children.

Article 27

1. Everyone has the right freely to participate in the cultural life of the community, to enjoy the arts and to share in scientific advancement and its benefits.

2. Everyone has the right to the protection of the moral and material interests resulting from any scientific, literary or artistic production of which he is the author.

Article 28

Everyone is entitled to a social and international order in which the rights and freedoms set forth in this Declaration can be fully realised.

Article 29

1. Everyone has duties to the community in which alone the free and full development of his personality is possible.

2. In the exercise of his rights and freedoms, everyone shall be subject only to such limitations as are determined by law solely for the purpose of securing due

recognition and respect for the rights and freedoms of others and of meeting the just requirements of morality, public order and the general welfare in a democratic society.

3. These rights and freedoms may in no case be exercised contrary to the purposes and principles of the United Nations.

Article 30

Nothing in this Declaration may be interpreted as implying for any State, group or person any right to engage in any activity or to perform any act aimed at the destruction of any of the rights and freedoms set forth herein.

APPENDIX IV

Prussian Academy, of the American Academy of Letters and of the British Academy. Formerly Minister without portfolio.

Author of: *Filosofia dello Spirito (Esthetica, Logica, Filosofia della Pratica, Teoria della Storiografia—* all translated into English)
Materialismo storico ed economica marxistica (translated into English)
Etica e Politica
La Storia come Pensiero e come Azione
Storia d'Europa nel Secolo XX
and many other works.

A. P. ELKIN
Professor of Anthropology, University of Sydney, Australia. Chairman of the New South Wales Division of the Australian National Research Council. Vice-Chairman of the Aborigines' Welfare Board of New South Wales.

Author of: *Wanted: A Charter for the Native Peoples of the South West Pacific*
Citizenship for the Aborigines
The Australian Aborigines—How to Understand Them
Aboriginal Men of High Degree

GEORGES FRIEDMANN
Professor at the Conservatoire National des´ Arts et Métiers, Paris.

Author of: *La Crise du Progrés*
Problèmes humains du Machinisme industriel
Leibniz et Spinoza
(in collaboration) *L'Heure du Choix*
De la sainte Russie à l'U.R.S.S.
and other works.

MARGERY FRY, J.P., D.C.L., LL.D.
Formerly Secretary-General of the Howard League for Penal Reform. Author of many pamphlets on penal questions, including:
The Ancestral Child

MAHATMA GANDHI
The Father of Modern India.

R. W. GERARD
Professor, Department of Physiology, University of Chicago.
Author of: *Unresting Cells* (1940)
The Body Functions (1941), etc.

J. HAESAERT
Professor of Sociology and Political Science at the University of Ghent, Belgium.
Author of: *Introduction à la Philosophie Expérimentale* (1920)
Contingences et Régularités du Droit positif (1933)
La Forme et le Fond du Juridique (1934)
Défense et Aménagement des Libertés (1937)
La Portée politique du New Deal (1937)
Théorie générale du Droit (1948), etc.

SERGIUS HESSEN
Professor of History of Education at the University of Lodz, Poland.
Author of: *Individuelle Kausalität (in Kantstudien)*
Philosophical Foundations of Education (in Russian, translated into Latvian, Bulgarian, Serbian, Polish, Czech and Italian)
School and Democracy at the Cross-Roads (in Czech and Polish)
The Antinomies of Education and its Unity (id.)
The Structure and Contents of the Modern School (in Polish, translated into Italian)
and numerous contributions to Russian, German, French, Czech, Polish and Italian periodicals.

ALDOUS HUXLEY
English novelist and essayist.
Author of: *Chrome Yellow*
Jesting Pilate
Point Counter Point
Brave New World
Eyeless in Gaza
Ends and Means
Time must have a Stop

The Perennial Philosophy
and many other works.

HUMAYUN KABIR

Indian poet and philosopher. Professor at the Universities of Andhra and Calcutta. Formerly General-Secretary of the All-Bengal Peasants' Party and Leader of the Peasants' Party in the Bengal Legislative Council; Chairman, Ethics and Politics Section, Indian Philosophical Conference. Now Joint Educational Adviser to the Government of India. Deputy Leader of the Indian Delegation to the Third Session of the General Conference of UNESCO.

Author of many poetical works, including:
> *Monads and Society*
> *Our Heritage*
> *Men and Rivers*
> *Mahatma and Other Poems*

and of the first English translation of Kant's *Erste Einleitung zur Kritik der Urteilskraft* and of many works in Bengali: *Immanuel Kant, Marxvad*, etc.

I. L. KANDEL

Professor Emeritus of Education, Teachers' College, Columbia University. Editor of *School and Society*.

Author of: *History of Secondary Education*
> *Comparative Education*
> *Intellectual Cooperation, National and International*
> *The Cult of Uncertainty*
> *Impact of the War on American Education*
> *Education in an Era of Transition*

and other works.

HAROLD J. LASKI

Professor of Political Science in the University of London. Member of the Executive Committee of the Labour Party.

Author of: *Liberty in the Modern State*
> *An Introduction to Politics*
> *Democracy in Crisis*
> *The State in Theory and Practice*
> *The Rise of European Liberalism*
> *Parliamentary Government in England*

Reflections on the Revolution of our Time
Faith, Reason, Civilisation
American Democracy
and many other works.

LEVI CARNEIRO

Legal Adviser to the Brazilian Ministry of Foreign Affairs. Federal Deputy. Brazilian Delegate to the 8th Pan-American Conference and to the Peace Conference. Member of the Brazilian Academy of Letters. Member of the American Commission for the Codification of International Law. Chairman of the Brazilian National Commission for UNESCO. Member of the International Court of Justice.

Author of: *Federalismo e judiciarismo*
O Direito Internacional e a Democracia
and other works.

JOHN LEWIS

Editor of *Modern Quarterly*, London. Lecturer in Philosophy to the Extra-Mural Departments of the Universities of Oxford and London. Formerly a Presbyterian Minister (1916-36).

Author of: *The Old Testament in the Twentieth Century*
A Faith to Live By
Douglas Fallacies
An Introduction to Philosophy
Marxism and Modern Idealism
The Basis of Soviet Philosophy
Editor and Contributor:
Christianity and the Social Revolution
The Textbook of Marxist Philosophy

ARNOLD J. LIEN

Head of the Department of Political Science at Washington University, St Louis.

Author of: *The Privileges and Immunities of Citizens of the United States*
The Acquisition of Citizenship by the Native American Indians
The American People and their Government (with Merle Fainsod)

CHUNG-SHU LO

Professor of Philosphy in West-China University. Special consultant of UNESCO.

RICHARD McKEON
Formerly Dean of the Division of Humanities (1935-1947), now Distinguished Service Professor of Philosophy and Greek, University of Chicago. Fellow, Mediæval Academy of America, American Academy of Arts and Sciences. Member of the United States Delegation to the First, Second and Third Sessions of the General Conference of UNESCO, Paris, Mexico City and Beirut.
Author of: *The Philosophy of Spinoza*
Introduction to Aristotle

DON SALVADOR DE MADARIAGA
Formerly Head of the Disarmament Section, League of Nations; Ambassador of Spain in Washington and Paris. Now living in England. President of the International Commission for Folk Art and Folklore. Member of the Academy of Moral and Political Sciences of Madrid, of the Academy of Letters in Madrid, of the Belgian Academy and of many South American Academies.
Author of many works in literature, history and philosophy, including:
Englishmen, Frenchmen, Spaniards (in the three languages)
The World's Design
Anarchy or Hierarchy
Theory and Practice of International Relations
The Genius of Spain
Victors Beware
The Rise of the Spanish American Empire
The Fall of the Spanish American Empire

RENÉ MAHEU
Head of Division, Free Flow of Information, UNESCO. UNESCO representative at the U.N. Sub-Commission on Freedom of Information and at the U.N. Conference on Freedom of Information, Geneva, 1948.

JACQUES MARITAIN
Formerly French Ambassador to the Holy See. Head of the French Delegation to the Second Session of the General Conference of UNESCO, Mexico City. Now visiting Professor of Philosophy at Princeton University.

Author of: *Art et Scholastique* (translated into English)
Introduction à la Philosophie (translated into English)
Trois Réformateurs (translated into English)
Primauté du spirituel (translated into English)
Religion et Culture (translated into English)
Du régime temporel et de la Liberté (translated into English)
Humanisme intégral (translated into English)
The Rights of Man and Natural Law
Christianity and Democracy
and many other works.

F. S. C. NORTHROP
Sterling Professor of Philosophy and Law in the Law School and the Graduate School, Yale University.
Author of: *Science and First Principles*
The Meeting of East and West
The Logic of the Sciences and the Humanities

W. A. NOYES
Professor of Chemistry, University of Rochester. Member of the National Academy of Sciences of the U.S.A. Alternate delegate to the Third Session of the General Conference of UNESCO.

S. V. PUNTAMBEKAR
Head of the Department of Political Science, Nagpur University.
Author of: *Introduction to Civics and Politics*
Introduction to Indian Citizenship and Civilisation (2 vol.)
Foundations of Indian Civics
Constitutional History of England (2 vol.)
Paramountry in Indian Politics
Foreign Policy of the Indian Union
Historical Thought of European Historians

KURT RIEZLER
Professor of Philosophy at the Graduate Faculty of the New School for Social Research, New York. Visiting professor at the University of Chicago. Professor *honoris causa* at the University of Frankfurt-am-Main.
Author of: *Gestalt und Gesetz* (Munich, 1925)
Physics and Reality (Yale, 1940), etc.

LUC SOMERHAUSEN
Director of the Secretariat of the Senat, Bruxelles.
Author of: *L'Humanisme agissant de Karl Marx*

JOHN SOMERVILLE
Professor of Philosophy at Hunter College, N.Y.
Author of: *Methodology in Social Science*
Soviet Philosophy
The Philosophy of Peace, etc.

PIERRE TEILHARD DE CHARDIN
Of the Society of Jesus. Member-correspondent of the Institut de France; important discoveries in geology and paleoanthropology in the Far-East (discovery of the Sinanthropus); gradually specialised in the study of the structure and evolutive directions of man as a zoological group.

Cf. *Le phénomène humain* in 'Revue des Questions Scientifiques,' 1930.
La planétisation humaine, in 'Cahiers du Monde nouveau,' August, 1946.
La question de l'homme fossile, Ed. 'Psyché,' Paris, 1947.
Une interprétation biologique plausible de l' Histoire humaine: la formation de la Noösphère, in 'Revue des Questions Scientifiques,' January, 1947.
Le rebondissement humain de l'Evolution et ses consequences, in 'Revue des Questions Scientifiques,' April, 1948.

BORIS TCHECHKO
Professor of Law. Special Consultant of UNESCO.

QUINCY WRIGHT
Professor of International Law and Chairman of Committee on International Relations, University of Chicago.
Author of: *Enforcement of International Law through Municipal Law in the United States*
Control of American Foreign Relations
Mandates under the League of Nations
The Causes of War and the Conditions of Peace
Legal Problems in the Far Eastern Controversy
A Study of War